1295

D0765526

FEB 1 1 1981

APR 1 6 1981

MAY 2 2 1981

AUG 1

OCT 8 1981

DEC 7 - 1981 wS

JAN 2 8 1982

JAN 2 1984

SEP 1 8 1989

JAN 2 5 1995

JAN 2 7 1997

JUN 1 1997

JUN 2 0 2002

RPL
c-4/75

c.1
Mann, William Edward.
  The man who dreamed of tomorrow :
a conceptual biography of Wilhelm
Reich / W. Edward Mann and Edward
Hoffman ; foreword by Eva Reich. --
1st ed. -- Los Angeles, CA : J. P.
Tarcher ; Boston : distributed by
Houghton Mifflin, c1980.
  295 p., [4] leaves of plates :
ill. ; 24 cm.

  1. Orgonomy.   2. Psychoanalysts--
United States--Biography.   3.
Reich, Wilhelm, 1897-1957--
Biography.   I. Hoffman, Edward,
1951-   joint author.   II. Title.

The
Man Who
Dreamed of
Tomorrow

Published by J. P. Tarcher, Inc.
Los Angeles
Distributed by Houghton Mifflin Company
Boston

The Man Who Dreamed of Tomorrow

A Conceptual Biography of
Wilhelm Reich

W. Edward Mann
and Edward Hoffman

Foreword by Eva Reich

**Library of Congress Cataloging
in Publication Data**

Mann, William Edward.
The man who dreamed of tomorrow.

Bibliography: p. 279
Includes index.
1. Orgonomy.   2. Reich, Wilhelm, 1897-1957.
3. Psychoanalysts – United States – Biography.
I. Hoffman, Edward, 1951   Joint author.
II. Title.
RZ460.M36   150.19'5'0924 [B]   80-50405
ISBN 0-87477-143-9

The excerpt from *Me and the Orgone* by Orson Bean
on pages 125–127 is reprinted with the permission of
St. Martin's Press, Inc., New York, N.Y.

Design by John Brogna

Manufactured in the United States of America

Published by J. P. Tarcher, Inc.
9110 Sunset Blvd., Los Angeles, Calif. 90069

v 10 9 8 7 6 5 4 3 2 1
First Edition

To Dianne and Laurel

Contents

Acknowledgments

We want first of all to pay tribute to the two persons who helped in many different ways to assist us in finishing this work, namely Laurel Hoffman and Dianne Hughes. We are also greatly indebted to Janice Gallagher, who provided enormous counsel and advice on the perfecting of the manuscript and whose tirelessness was a constant support. Others who gave useful advice on the manuscript include Allan Listiak, Adam Schneid, and Arnold Rockman. Finally, many thanks to Donna Newman for fine typing support throughout as well as at critical junctures.

Foreword

Twenty-five years ago, Wilhelm Reich tried to tell the United States government, in a United States Federal District Court, that the Age of the Life Energy (orgone energy) had arrived. He had been ordered to stop publishing his works about the applications and healing properties of the orgone energy. His defense was the statement that research in basic natural science should not come under the jurisdiction of the legal branch of the United States government. Issued in 1954, the injunction still stands on the law books today. When Dr. Michael Silvert shipped one truckload of orgone energy accumulators across interstate lines from Maine to New York State, he was breaking the injunction. Consequently, the charge of contempt of court was made against Wilhelm Reich, Michael Silvert, and the Wilhelm Reich Foundation. For this "crime," Wilhelm Reich, M.D., was imprisoned for two years; Michael Silvert, M.D., for one year; and the Wilhelm Reich Foundation had to pay a stiff monetary fine. After having served six months of his sentence, shortly before a scheduled parole hearing, Dr. Wilhelm Reich was found dead in his cell on the morning of November 3, 1957. Death in prison was his reward for having made a discovery.

For those of us who lived through the period of the discovery of the life energy and the persecution and death of its discoverer, it is a healing experience to see a few signs that perhaps there is a beginning comprehension in the Western world of the importance and validity of Wilhelm Reich's pathbreaking discovery. Perhaps, now humanity begins to cherish the flow of feelings which result from allowing children from birth on to experience self-regulation and body pleasure. At last, one dares to be honest about private existence, which no longer has to be hidden so carefully from the public eye. Slowly, slowly, there appear signs of transformation. The family becomes a team, no longer a patriarchal dictatorship. One does not have to wear a mask to conceal the true interior anymore. Slowly, slowly, here and there, a new generation experiments with letting the baby, the child have a voice in running the institutions affecting their own lives. Here and there the "biological revolution," which Reich predicted would follow the sexual revolution, is happening. As the life instinct, the libido, is no longer repressed so constantly and severely, a new creative energy is emerging in a few countries on earth; and an unarmored, flexible, emotionally joyful Humanity looks back on the age of irrationalism with pity. A glimpse of a peaceful solution to the problem of human political confusion appears on the horizon. Life begins to know its own natural laws.

Commonsense sanity, our birthright, which allows for full growth to as-yet-undreamed-of human potential, becomes apparent to those with ears to hear and eyes to see. Joy of life will replace sadness and malaise, when at last neurosis becomes unnecessary, preventable.

Dr. Edward Mann and Dr. Edward Hoffman are to be congratulated on writing this timely volume correlating Wilhelm Reich's works with other diverse alternative-life-energy healing movements. They set forth the evidence that bears out the work of Wilhelm Reich in education, sexology, psychology, medicine, and religion. For Wilhelm Reich touched on many fields—he was a generalist, a synthesizer, the opposite of a specialist. The authors outline Reich's revolutionary impact and leavening influence.

This life work of Wilhelm Reich ran the gamut from protozoal neo-biogenesis to astrophysics, from the Reich blood test to the understanding of the cancer problem, from the mathematics of the Kreisel-welle to the construction and filming of the orgone energy motor. Reich, who always gave credit to his intellectual forerunners, felt related to the work of Leonardo da Vinci, Goethe, Kepler, Nikola Tesla, and Sigmund Freud. He admired all of them. He saw himself as a torchbearing messenger, lighting the way into the future—a theme he depicted in painting and sculpture. He said that "civilization has not been yet."

In this wide-ranging book, authors Mann and Hoffman give us their interpretation of the essential ideas of Reich, *The Man Who Dreamed of Tomorrow*.

Eva Reich
Hancock, Maine
July 3, 1980

Preface

Wilhelm Reich was a man years ahead of his time. His life was one of controversy, lived well outside the halls of the medical and scientific orthodoxy. Yet, in virtually every field of knowledge he touched, he excited innovative thinkers with his daring ideas. Then came his protracted legal battle, the burning of his books by the United States government, and, soon after, his death in federal prison in 1957. For almost a generation thereafter, his visionary work was relegated to near obscurity. Except for a handful of former co-workers and people who had known him personally, he was almost forgotten.

Then, around the beginning of the 1970s, an intense interest in Reich suddenly arose. In both the United States and Western Europe, the fervor of the preceding decade brought many persons to seek bold visions of cultural change. Reich's ideas now appeared highly relevant and worth considering closely; a new generation, restless under the status quo of the medical and scientific establishment, was eager for fresh explorations. New pro-Reichian journals appeared, his books were reprinted and widely distributed, and several accounts of his life came out. These included an interesting biography by his ex-wife and a novelistic effort by his son. In 1973, Dr. Mann published *Orgone, Reich and Eros,* which focused specifically on Reich's theory of a life energy and the evidence for it.

Since publication of this earlier work, we have helped organize and direct various workshops and conferences in the United States and Canada devoted to interpreting Reich's legacy for our time. Our goal has been to introduce Reich's work to both professionals and the general public previously unacquainted with it. To this end, we have sponsored various scientific speakers who had known Reich personally or who had acknowledged a growing admiration for his far-reaching discoveries. We have also sought to bring together in these conferences individuals from diverse disciplines in order to extend and develop Reich's own pursuits, from natural childbirth to holistic medicine.

In our respective fields of sociology (Dr. Mann received his doctorate from the University of Toronto in 1953 and is a full professor at York University in Toronto) and psychology (Dr. Hoffman received his doctorate from the University of Michigan in 1976, and is a clinical psychologist at South Florida State Hospital and an adjunct professor at Nova University in Fort Lauderdale), we have seen Reich's insights demonstrated again and again. Increasingly, we have become aware of a steadily growing body of scholars and lay persons avidly interested in learning more about this brilliant thinker and his daring theories and intuitive observations.

Along with a great deal of professional and personal interest, there has been an impressive burgeoning of scientific investigation—long overdue—into Reich's most intimate concerns, such as the mind-body relationship, healing, and the life energy concept. Many of these researchers are apparently unacquainted with Reich's original investigations, some of which have directly preceded—and predicted—theirs by as much as thirty or forty years. They would be startled to discover that, decades ago, Reich articulated and detailed so many of our purportedly "new" approaches in health and science. And, going beyond his clinical scientific and medical work, there are his sweeping social analyses of the necessity for and the inevitability of major changes in our society's most deeply rooted attitudes about love and sexuality, work and pleasure, which display an almost prophetic accuracy.

Still, we continue to find that, for some persons today, Reich's career is shrouded in the robes of distortion. Lurid press accounts depicting him as a kind of sex-obsessed archetypal mad scientist dogged him wherever he went, first in Europe and then in the United States. Occasionally such misguided descriptions crop up today, though far less often than in the past.

Consequently, we have gradually recognized the need for a book to help clear the record on Reich's own ideas and methods and to highlight his insights in areas of crucial interest for us as we move into the 1980s. This book is intended as a guide to the breadth and scope of his vision, which we are closer to realizing than ever before.

We have arranged the chapters to move through Reich's discoveries in rough chronological order. In this manner, his leaps of intuitive genius are somewhat easier to follow, for indeed there is a key thread running through all of his thinking. From his initial involvement with Freud in Vienna, he was led to early insights on sexuality in the industrial age, and from there, in a short time, to the uncovering of body language, body repressions, and the human "armor." After Reich realized that we live in a society that massively restricts our physical pleasure, he soon found himself on the trail of the mind-body connection and the nature of health and healing.

After he arrived in the United States, Reich focused on the phenomenon of the subtle body currents his patients kept reporting during therapy, and then he turned his full attention to the expression of a theory of a life force unknown to orthodox science. In his research, he seemed to find that this energy varied with the changing rhythms of the natural world and so, gradually, he embarked on a quest for the meaning of our place in the cosmos. Reich's spiritual transformation heralded his new outlook on social change and the future, the final aspect of his work to be explored here.

We believe that while Reich is without question a central figure for our age, he certainly was fallible and made errors in a number of areas. In *The Man Who Dreamed of Tomorrow*, we present a balanced view of this brilliant and uncompromising thinker. There have been many developments in science and society that he simply could not have foreseen at his death in 1957, a few weeks after the Sputnik satellite launched the Space Age, and yet his almost wholly lone-wolf and intuitive approach hit the mark again and again.

On the threshold of a decade that promises dramatic breakthroughs in our very understanding of ourselves and the universe, it is most stimulating to contemplate the vast territories of knowledge that Reich opened up during his tumultuous career.

CHAPTER 1

A Passionate and Persecuted Thinker

You want a *good* genius, one with moderation and decorum, one without folly; in brief, a *seemly, measured,* and *adjusted* genius, not an unruly, untamed [one].

—WILHELM REICH

G reat thinkers have seldom been honored in their own time. From medieval scholars who faced the torture of the Inquisition for challenging the dogmas of their day to modern-day innovators who have endured professional censure or scientific excommunication, history shows that it is a mixed blessing to be far ahead of one's time.

So it was with Wilhelm Reich. An assimilated Jew of Austrian birth and German tongue, he was born in 1897 into a well-to-do rural family and died in 1957 in a federal prison in the United States. He had written over twenty books and some 400 professional articles; his name had been advanced in the 1930s as a likely candidate for the Nobel peace prize. But in the 1950s he was subjected to vicious criticism, calumny, and persecution, and was finally imprisoned on a charge of fraud. His major published works had been ordered banned by the governments of three countries—Germany, Russia, and the United States—as an obvious threat to the welfare and security of humankind.

But history has caught up with Wilhelm Reich. Now, twenty-three years after his death, he is being recognized as an extraordinarily gifted innovator.

As a medical doctor in his early twenties, he quickly became one of Freud's closest disciples and in the course of three decades systematically developed a fascinating, and still controversial, theory of a fundamental life energy. His discoveries in such areas as sexuality, body language, and the mind-body relationship have influenced a variety of current trends in science and culture.

As far back as the 1930s, Reich prophesied dramatic changes in sexuality, marriage, and family relations. With an uncanny clairvoyance, he correctly predicted women's liberation, the sexual revolution, and the conservation movement. He suggested daring approaches to education, religion, and democratic control of industry that we are just now considering seriously. His uncompromising views on decentralization and bureaucracy are appearing under different guises in social and political manifestos. The dizzying economic changes around us bear out his vision of the collapse of the work ethic and the rise of alternative philosophies. Above all, as we move into the last decades of the twentieth century, we have become obsessed with the idea of the central importance of energy, for individual health as well as for the ultimate survival of civilization. It was Reich who concentrated on this theme forty years ago—and made some astounding breakthroughs.

To many, Reich is best known for his bodywork with patients and for his theories on sex. If only for this overriding emphasis on the body and bodily energies, he will take his place alongside Einstein, Freud, and Marx as a major influence on the consciousness of our century. While Einstein re-formed our conception of the physical universe, it now appears that Reich's discoveries on the centrality of the body have revealed to us a radically new universe that unites mind and body. We predict that in the 1980s his name will resonate with power and wide appeal.

BODYWORKER FROM THE BEGINNING

Early in his medical training, Reich became actively involved in a new seminar on sexology that had been organized by a small group of his fellow students. At the time, it was completely unheard of for either physicians or counselors to receive formal training in sexual matters. Within a few months of joining,

Reich was appointed by the group to serve as its chairperson. Soon he sought out his mentor, Freud, who seemed delighted by the new venture and supplied personal materials for the class. These included special editions of several of his own works, such as *The Interpretation of Dreams* and *The Psychopathology of Everyday Life*. Before long Reich became a favorite of Freud's and was a frequent visitor at his house in Vienna.

In 1920, at the age of twenty-three, Reich attained membership in the Vienna Psychoanalytic Society. Two years later, he was appointed clinical assistant to Freud's Psychoanalytic Clinic there. He was clearly marked as Freud's protégé.

Reich treated patients on a daily basis, seeking to understand and cure their emotional and physical ailments. Initially, he practiced the psychoanalytic techniques developed by Freud, and then gradually modified them to emphasize treatment of the individual's entire personality or character. As Reich soon discovered, sexuality played a pivotal role in his patients' lives. Specifically, he found that many experienced little feeling during sexual intercourse, despite their ability to physically complete the act. The way in which Reich reached this conclusion was brazen indeed by the standards of his colleagues: he elicited from his patients precise descriptions of their feelings while making love. From such descriptions, Reich quickly realized that his patients' bodies had become deadened.

The sexual problems of his adult patients, many of whom appeared to lead normal lives, seemed far more complicated and pervasive than Freud and his original disciples had thought. Reich was beginning to understand and articulate the way in which sexuality is intimately related to physical satisfaction in general.

In his first major book, *Die Funktion des Orgasmus,* published in 1927 (not to be confused with his later work, *The Function of the Orgasm,* which appeared in 1942), Reich declared that sexual prowess is of only secondary importance. What really matters, he wrote, is the extent to which we can fully let ourselves go during the sexual embrace, and this originates in our basic approach to life and pleasure. A radically different kind of therapy would be needed, Reich insisted, to restore the primacy of our sensual nature.

In contrast to traditional Freudian treatments, which had

relatively little to do with the body but focused on verbal associations, Reich argued for an entirely new way of understanding and healing emotional disorders. Moving from his first discovery, Reich found that beneath his patients' emotional-physical blockages, or *armoring* (as he poetically termed their chronic muscular rigidities), there was almost invariably a layer of violent and socially unacceptable emotions that had been suppressed since childhood. This notion is now basic to such contemporary psychotherapies as Gestalt, Primal therapy, and Bioenergetics, all of which were directly influenced by Reich's ideas. Freud had mistakenly believed this murderous layer to be instinctual. But below it, claimed Reich, lay decent, loving emotions, the human core.

Reich's radically new method of treatment involved an examination of each person's characteristic body and facial language. Repeatedly, he found a clear relationship between such cues and his patients' personalities and emotional problems. The way we speak, walk, even sit on a chair—all of our seemingly unimportant daily patterns—provide clues to our inner self. The analyst trained to read such signs can uncover a person's basic difficulties in life with relative ease. "When it becomes possible . . . to read emotional expressions, the patient does not have to talk," Reich commented years later in retracing his discovery. "If we know the patient well enough, we know what's going on without words being spoken."[1]

More than fifty years later, Reich's brilliant insights have been solidly confirmed by many scientific investigators. In fact, the study of *kinesics,* or how we communicate through body language, has gained importance in both anthropology and sociology. Researchers are learning that men and women express, nonverbally, an almost infinite range of hidden messages to one another. Moreover, such messages are much influenced by race, nationality, and station in life. This latter fact is interesting, for Reich always placed his patients' behavior and his recommendations for change in a wider sociopolitical context.

Based on this diagnostic analysis of body language, by the 1930s Reich had developed systematic techniques for making people aware of their body armor and then loosening and removing it.

During the late 1920s, he had begun to do character analysis of adult patients. For instance, he would often make use of the patient's typical nonverbal messages, such as tone of voice, degree of eye contact, or feigned politeness, as key indicators of the underlying emotional disturbance. In this way, the patient was encouraged to focus on the "here and now" and not take flight in intellectual analysis of the past. Reich found that exquisite sensitivity is needed in breaking down the emotional and physical rigidities, lest the sudden torrent of long-suppressed feelings prove overwhelming. Yet, using the proper care and skill, he saw that near-miraculous breakthroughs were possible with many persons who had benefited little from traditional Freudian verbal psychoanalysis. By learning to *feel* precisely how we make ourselves tense and deadened, we are able to recover the natural vitality we experienced as children, said Reich.

Such notions and techniques, however, were foreign to the orthodox psychoanalysts and physicians of his day. They were uncomfortable with Reich's bold interest in the language of the body and its relation to emotions. Rumors circulated that Reich was secretly masturbating attractive female clients or conducting group orgies. In a pattern that was to become characteristic for the rest of his life, Reich preferred simply to ignore such wild charges. In the years to come, the vehemence of the repeated attacks against his work and his integrity would leave him increasingly bitter, causing him to lash out against all critics. By this time, however, he had already become disenchanted with the narrow parochialism of Freud's supporters. And, true to his impatient nature, Reich had become restless with the day-to-day work of treating individual patients. He was ready for action on a wider stage.

THE SEXUAL REVOLUTIONARY

As a young man, Reich had been decidedly nationalistic. He fought eagerly in the Austrian army during World War I, seeing active duty on the Italian front. Later, during his medical training at the University of Vienna, he was politically inactive. He was a rather poor but hardworking student who devoted his spare time to such sports as skiing and mountain climbing. As a highly promising psychoanalyst under Freud's wing, for years he continued to stay clear of the political arena.

Then one day, in July of 1927, he witnessed a workers' demonstration in the streets of Vienna and a violent police retaliation that took more than sixty lives.

"That gave me the jolt," Reich was to recall decades later. "Shortly thereafter, I went to him [Freud] and I told him I wanted to work on a social basis. I wanted to get away from the clinics, from individual treatment, and get onto the social scene. Freud was very much for it."[2]

Reich soon became a socialist, joined the Austrian Social Democrat Party, and participated in its policymaking decisions. In contrast to Freud, he began to argue forcefully that the neurosis and unhappiness pervading all levels of society stemmed from specific, changeable economic conditions. He believed that unless Western society as a whole changed, little could be done to alter the massive psychological and social problems that existed. As a result, by the late 1920s relations between Reich and Freud had begun to cool considerably. Their notions of the basic human character were increasingly in opposition.

At this time the elderly Freud had stunned many of his disciples by suggesting that humanity had within it a "death wish." In such works as *Civilization and Its Discontents,* Freud argued that mass murder and violence, such as that manifested in World War I, could logically be explained by the existence of an innate human drive toward self-destruction. On an individual basis, Freud argued, violence, aggression, or suicide could be attributed to this same instinctual urge.

In Reich's view, in his old age Freud had weakened and become resigned to the large-scale insanities of the twentieth century. Freud was also suffering from cancer of the jaw, perhaps a more compelling explanation of this abandonment of his early fiery radicalism. Once determined to change the world with his radical theories of childhood sexuality and the unconscious, now he saw its wars and individual mental suffering as inevitable. As Reich later reminisced about his last meeting with Freud in 1930, "the Freud of the Victorian era contradicted the Freud who had discovered infantile sexuality. . . . He had had enough."[3]

Even before the final break with his mentor, Reich had become increasingly active politically. He organized the Socialist

Society for Sex Consultation and Sexological Research, a group that opened several "people's clinics" in Vienna. He gave public lectures on sexual topics and published articles linking sexual concerns, such as premarital sex or the availability of contraceptives, to economic and social issues of the day. "What I had to do," Reich recalled much later, "was to break through the barrier which separates the public from its own private life."[4] When he discovered that the Social Democrat Party was afraid to take aggressive action against the growing menace of Nazism and seemed to be delaying real social change, he joined the Communist Party.

The year 1930 marked a turning point of sorts in Reich's career. There was the schism with Freud, who was no longer pleased with Reich's radical political opinions. The same year, he and his wife and two daughters moved to Berlin, where the Communists were plotting revolution and seeking to outmaneuver Hitler. Reich belonged to a Communist cell that included various artists, musicians, and writers, including novelist Arthur Koestler. Also in this cell was the ballerina Elsa Lindenberg, who came to live with Reich after he separated from his wife several years later.

The antithesis of the armchair theoretician, Reich was arguing forcefully—in the early 1930s—for legalized birth control, abortion, and making contraceptives available to single teenagers, not just married couples. Decades ahead of his contemporaries, he opened his sex-counseling clinics to unwed teenagers, recognizing the legitimacy of their sexual needs and problems.

Reich brought his politically radical platform of sexual rights to the World League for Sexual Reform. The World League had been organized by leaders in the sexual-reform movement, including Havelock Ellis. Its social program pressed for such changes as sex education and the liberalization of divorce laws. Upon being rebuffed by the moderate World League, Reich found himself being warmly embraced by the Communist Party, where he quickly rose to prominence, drawing hundreds and even thousands of young people to mass meetings where he discussed the relation of sexual issues to politics. He had the Party publish several of his politically oriented pamphlets, articles, and booklets on sex education, while still engaging in the psychoanalytic treatment of patients and the training of psychiatrists. In public lectures and writings (some of them in collaboration with his wife, Annie Pink, also a psychiatrist), he took the cause of sexual freedom directly to the proletarian youth of Germany and nearby countries. Before long he was the head of a youth movement of more than twenty thousand members. Academic philosophizing was not for Reich; like Marx, he joined action to theory.

Then, almost as suddenly, Reich lost favor with German Communist Party bosses. In 1929, he had briefly toured Russia to investigate its day nurseries for children and its reportedly liberal sexual laws and practices. Although he was impressed with much of what he saw, he discovered that the new heaven on earth was something less than the Bolshevik leaders were claiming. It appeared to Reich that the new Russian officials had failed to actualize some basic ideals of the 1917 revolution. In fact, once Stalin had consolidated his power, he had systematically begun to undermine many of the genuine social reforms of the early 1920s: legal cohabitation without marriage, equal rights for homosexuals, easy divorce, and communal living for men and women. Under Stalin's directives, the Party was repealing even mildly liberal legislation and reintroducing repressive laws, such as making homosexuality a criminal offense.

Reich's criticisms did not sit well with German Communist leaders. Even worse, Reich flatly rejected their new dictum that sexual rights and freedoms would, after all, have to wait until *after* the revolution was won in Western Europe. The Party stopped distributing his writings by late 1932, and in 1933 he was expelled. Because of this experience Reich later came to favor a social anarchist philosophy, and, as early as 1934, he did not hesitate to characterize Soviet Russia as a case of "red fascism." After arriving in the United States in 1939, Reich developed the novel concept of a "work democracy," in which he advocated cooperative rather than bureaucratic styles of work relationships.

Reich's fiery iconoclasm had been too much for the organization-minded Communists to accept. And for quite some time, his concepts and techniques of therapy had become distasteful to orthodox psychoanalysts. More important, he had become too politically radical for the conservative Psycho-analytic Congress, which feared losing popular acceptance. To cast out an open leftist like Reich, they reasoned, might appease the Nazis into sparing the psychiatrists from the first wave of purges, and it would certainly rid them of a perennial trouble-maker. And so in 1934, much to his outrage, Reich was expelled from the organization.

By the mid-1930s, then, Reich had been cast out by both the psychoanalytic and leftist movements with which he had been so closely associated. He had already published several major books: *Die Funktion des Orgasmus* (1927), *Character Analysis* (1933), and *The Mass Psychology of Fascism* (1933). By now the Nazis had come to power in Germany and fascism was on the rise in many European and Asian countries. Utilizing both Freudian and Marxist theories, Reich began to investigate the psychological attraction that fascism held for so many millions.

The fascist individual had a definite personality type, Reich observed, and even a characteristic body language—a way of looking, standing, and speaking. This commonality was no acci-dent. An individual who adopted the characteristic military or fascist bearing—tight, expanded chest; rigid pelvis; hard, tough jaw—was, in effect, announcing to the world the suppression of all loving emotions. Furthermore, children who grew up in the absence of tenderness, vulnerability, and warmth—in short, in the type of family Reich associated with the German lower middle class—would be drawn to an ideology that stressed disci-pline, obedience, and the venting of repressed anger. Far from a loving preparation for adult life, such a family was the backbone of authoritarianism, Reich claimed.

Fascism was succeeding precisely because it tapped the hidden emotional and nonrational needs of the masses. "Fascism is not a political party but," Reich declared, "a specific attitude toward people, toward love and work."[5] He warned, therefore, that fascism could *not* be effectively countered with rational or liberal-sounding arguments or appeals to "moderation" and "reason." Only immediate and direct reforms aimed at meeting the repressed emotional needs of Europe's millions might be effective. Otherwise, he predicted, the European liberal democ-racies would soon be crushed.

At the same time, Reich explored the reasons behind the need of European masses for an all-powerful, all-wise "leader," be it Hitler, Mussolini, or Stalin. He believed that the authoritarian structure of organized religion created in the masses an emotional longing for a parentlike god to solve their problems from on high. Reich related this emotional longing to the appeal of organized religion, with its emphasis on a distant heavenly "God the Father." As we shall see in Chapter 7, Reich's experience with the Nazis and their twisted mystical system left him with an almost lifelong unease with all religious or spiritual systems, an unease that he assuaged by working out a concept of "natural religion" for himself. In recent years, several books have clearly documented the important role that mysticism played in the Nazi ideology.

Reich's warnings proved all too prophetic. Fascism triumphed in a Germany under the sway of Hitler's charismatic leadership. The Nazis authorized the Gestapo to find and shoot Reich, and his books were burned by the Nazi government. Under an assumed name, disguised as a tourist, Reich managed to escape across the border. He eventually made his way to Denmark, then to Sweden, and finally found haven in Norway. In 1934, Elsa Lindenberg moved with him to Oslo. The two lived together until shortly before Reich's emigration to the United States, though they were never legally married. Reich's children, Eva and Lore, remained in Vienna, boarded out with a family friend. Their mother, Annie, continued to practice as a psychoanalyst in Prague during most of the next few years. Reich was now thirty-seven; he already had major discoveries behind him, but was eager to get on with his work.

NORWEGIAN INTERLUDE

At this time, Reich was invited to join the faculty of the Psychological Institute of the University of Oslo. He was to lecture on his work in character analysis and the relationship between the body and emotions. The Institute's facilities were placed at his disposal, thus finally allowing him to embark on experiments concerning the biological nature of sexuality, anxiety, and emotional expression. Using many of his colleagues and students in his experiments, Reich attempted to measure fluctuations in the electrical charge given off in various parts of the human body during differing emotional states, such as sexual arousal, pain, or fright. No one had ever directly examined the relation between emotions and the electrical skin potential in this way before.

In groundbreaking experiments, several significant findings emerged. First, specific parts of the body, particularly the erogenous zones (tongue, inner surfaces of the lips, genitals, nipples, earlobes, etc.), apparently showed more striking variations in charge than the skin nearby. Second, persons differed widely in the way such measures fluctuated, though the nonerogenous zones showed little variation from individual to individual. And, most important, the electrical potential of these zones varied considerably with the individual's emotional state. For instance, pleasurable stroking of the skin resulted in an increase in electrical charge; uncomfortable pressure produced a decrease. Preceding contemporary biofeedback research by almost forty years, Reich found that the research participants could subjectively tell whether a particular effect, such as mild shock or enjoyable stroking, would cause an increase or decrease in the electrogram tracing before they even saw it. Feelings of pleasurable excitation produced a sharp rise in voltage, whereas anxiety, annoyance, or fright produced sharp drops.

During this Scandinavian period, Reich trained a number of psychiatrists and psychotherapists. He wrote innumerable articles on political psychology and the relationship between sexuality and social issues. But compared with his Vienna and Berlin days, he was much less politically active. He continued to refine his method of therapy, a form of manual manipulation he now termed *vegetotherapy*. Reich insisted that this approach, which emphasized the release of vegetative (life energy) currents, did not replace character-analytic work, but rather extended its focus to the body. Briefly, this technique involved relaxing areas of chronic tightness and bodily rigidity (armoring) by pressing or prodding them and thereby changing the patient's typical patterns of breathing. Reich strongly believed that neurotic persons breathed in a shallow manner due to their emotional repressions. He therefore sought to deepen the respiratory function and make it more even, both by encouraging his patients to express long-suppressed feelings and by directly manipulating tense areas of the breathing musculature.

During these years, a number of psychiatrists, psychologists, educators, artists, and others came to Oslo from Europe and the United States to visit his Institute for Sex-Economic Bio-Research, which he established in 1936. Among these visitors was A. S. Neill, the founder of Summerhill, the alternative school for children in England. Neill first received therapy under Reich and then became a staff member of the Institute. He was to become one of Reich's closest friends. Another visitor was Dr. Theodore Wolfe, an associate in psychiatry at Columbia University, the foremost American researcher in psychosomatic medicine. He was to become another lifelong friend.

In 1937 and 1938, Reich began to examine the movement and energetic aspects of the tiny bits of living matter called protozoa. In studying them, he sought to understand the energetic functions of all living forms. He made several films of protozoan movement, using advanced methods of time-lapse photography. These experiments led him to claim discovery of the smallest units of living matter—which he called *bions*—and to theorize about how they arose spontaneously from disintegrating matter.

The Norwegian press became aware of Reich and began to criticize his scientific work almost daily. He was branded a "sex fiend" and, more viciously, a "Jewish pornographer." Some articles even denounced him as a madman, an enemy of the nation. This was not the first time his work had aroused enmity. Nor, unfortunately, was it to be the last. He publicly ignored the attacks and made virtually no attempt to refute them. This policy dismayed many of his supporters.

In the spring of 1939, with the assistance of anthropologist Bronislaw Malinowski and Theodore Wolfe, Reich secured a teaching contract from the New School for Social Research in New York City. The two researchers had persuaded officials of the school to appoint Reich as an associate professor of medical psychology. Reluctantly, he decided to leave Norway, feeling that the social climate in the United States would be more amenable to his work. His library and laboratory were dismantled and shipped to the United States, and he left Oslo in August 1939, just a few days before the outbreak of war. His second wife, Elsa, did not accompany him, as relations between them had begun to deteriorate.

HARBINGER OF HOLISTIC HEALTH

Beginning in Norway in the late 1930s and continuing throughout the 1940s and 1950s, Reich articulated an extremely broad and interpretive notion of a universal life energy, akin to and yet different from electricity and magnetism. In a series of pioneering, though not always replicated, experiments, Reich became firmly convinced of the power of this cosmic energy. In Chapter 6, we will closely examine contemporary theory and research, from realms as diverse as physics and cellular biology, that tend to suggest that Reich's orgone theory is at least partly on the right track.

Reich's findings indicated that this energy varies in intensity in every living form, that it exists in the atmosphere, and that many diseases could ultimately be conceptualized as imbalances in its flow. Beginning with mice and then moving on to human cancer patients, Reich experimented with a device he had built called the *orgone accumulator*. It resembled a large box and was constructed out of alternating layers of organic and inorganic material. In repeated studies, Reich found that the orgone accumulator apparently displayed a higher temperature within its confines than outside its walls. After systematically ruling out alternative explanations, Reich concluded that the apparatus was somehow trapping or accumulating an energy heretofore unknown to modern science. (Instructions for the construction of this device are provided in Appendix E.)

In 1941, he contacted Albert Einstein and was invited to Einstein's home to discuss his findings. Reich spent five hours in excited discussion with the great mathematician. Einstein was at first quite interested and requested a small accumulator for experimenting. Soon after, though, Einstein stopped corresponding with Reich, as the mathematician believed the accumulator's heat effects could be explained by convection. It was not clear to Reich why Einstein had suddenly terminated their budding relationship. Ilse Ollendorff has speculated that Einstein simply was not willing to devote the time to pursuing an unconventional line of inquiry when he was deeply engrossed with the issue of atomic energy. This interesting historical episode, and the letters between the two thinkers, is recorded in a now out-of-print monograph entitled *History of the Discovery of the Life Energy—The Einstein Affair*, written by Reich and published by his press in 1953.

For Reich the 1940s were characterized by a tremendous intellectual momentum. He continued his study of the life energy, which he decided to name *orgone*, based on the fact that its discovery had resulted from his original focus on the sexual orgasm and on the fact that the energy had organic effects. At the same time, Reich gradually developed a theory on the relation of emotional expression to health and illness. In particular, his attention was drawn to cancer, even then among the most menacing of diseases.

Through clinical practice in Forest Hills, New York, and later laboratory experiments on an estate in Maine, Reich came to the conclusion that virtually *all* diseases are, in essence, products of some type of mental-physical imbalance in the human organism. Thus, by the mid-1940s he had specifically identified such illnesses as asthma, allergies, colitis, heart disease, high and low blood pressure, and even cancer as being related to the patient's emotional state and personality type. Later he came to view all noninfectious (degenerative) illnesses, which he termed *biopathies*, as resulting from energy blockages in the body.

While Reich did not claim to understand what caused the cancer cell to go haywire, he believed that cancer, like other diseases, could best be understood holistically—that is, by a perspective that encompassed the individual's lifestyle, emotional makeup, and health history. This, he believed, meant examining the various muscular tensions that constituted the body armor. One had to treat the whole person and not the disease. In *The Cancer Biopathy* he singled out cancer as a symptom of some deeper imbalance in the body, and said that the disease was preceded by specific body changes. "Long before the development of the first cancer cell in the organism," Reich declared in this book, "there are a series of pathological processes in the respective tissue and its immediate surroundings."[6] Specifically, he argued, there was a systematic depletion in the intensity of the life energy force within the body, brought on by a chronic emotional deadening in the individual's personality. Today, increasing numbers of medical practitioners recognize the inextricable link between mind and body. Reich always insisted, of course, that mind and body constitute a complex unity.

During that same period, Reich argued that modern medicine and biology had come to ignore our emotional and spiritual processes. He decried medicine's reliance on pills and chemicals and, decades before Ralph Nader's research, he pointed out the economic and political collusion among the major drug companies, the medical establishment, and federal regulatory agencies. He insisted, too, that to safeguard our own mental and physical well-being in an industrial society, we must heed the body's inner voice. "Only you yourself can be your liberator," he declared.[7]

During the mid-1940s, Reich's personal and professional life was marked by the gradual transfer of his activities from Forest Hills to an estate in rural Maine. Within months of his arrival in the United States, he had fallen in love with Ilse Ollendorff, a friend of a mutual acquaintance. He and Ilse soon married and spent their first summer together camping in the beauty of rural Maine. They bought a cabin there the following summer, and then they purchased 280 acres of farmland near the small town of Rangeley. He called his property Orgonon. A son, Peter, was born to them in 1944.

In New York City Reich had a lucrative private practice as well as a flourishing training program for psychiatrists and psychotherapists, but he decided that the calm and beauty of the lake-dotted Maine countryside would be a better atmosphere in which to write and experiment than the frenzy of New York.

In 1945, following several years of the Institute's gradual expansion, Reich constructed additional research facilities at Orgonon. It now housed a large main hall for his microscopic work, an animal room, and a special chamber designed to study orgone energy effects. In retrospect, while this move gave Reich the solitude and tranquility he had always sought, it also served to insulate him from the realities of the scientific mainstream.

During these years, he and Theodore Wolfe collaborated extensively. Wolfe translated a number of Reich's earlier works into English, and they were published by the Orgone Institute Press, a firm the two men had founded together in New York City. Over the years, Reich sponsored seminars and workshops at the growing Institute at Orgonon. The topics included childbirth and infancy, body language and personality type, and the mind-body relationship. He was also busy conducting new experiments with orgone energy.

In 1945, at his headquarters in Maine, Reich sponsored a summer symposium on the child. Decades before the surge of interest in natural childbirth and childrearing, Reich advanced the notion that healthy child development begins with the birth process. The newborn infant, he insisted, is capable of emotions and reacts to his emotional environment. He attacked the childcare practices of modern hospitals, which separate the infant from the mother right after birth. That attending physicians and nurses fail to feel the anguish of such infants was, for Reich, a perfect example of how the emotionally armored re-create this armoring in infants.

During the late 1940s, Reich began to study schizophrenia from a life energy vantage point. Well ahead of others, he contended that the incongruous sensations and electriclike currents that schizophrenics typically feel in their bodies were real, not hallucinatory. Though Reich's view at the time had little impact on the field, today such iconoclastic thinkers as psychiatrist R. D. Laing, as well as more conventional researchers, are coming to similar conclusions. Recent evidence is bearing out Reich's notion that schizophrenia is a perceptual disturbance involving visual, auditory, or kinesthetic anomalies.

Reich had thus begun to develop a new paradigm for Western science. This model was to encompass his many inquiries, including orgasm and sexuality, bodywork therapies, and the energy relation between humans and our universe. In *Ether, God and Devil*, published in 1948, he called for a new scientific approach, one that would reject both what he labeled "mechanistic thinking" and mysticism. It would seek to understand the natural world rather than try to control it, and it would view the universe in holistic terms. Reich argued that modern science had become much too fragmented, with its countless disciplines and subdisciplines. He urged an interdisciplinary approach and also demonstrated it himself. "Nature is imprecise," Reich wrote. "Nature does not operate mechanically, but functionally."[8] He argued that, in nature, all living forms are in constant interrelationship. Just as the human brain and heart, for instance, cannot really be studied in isolation from one another, neither can living things be understood apart from the larger energy forces in the universe.

REICH VERSUS THE ESTABLISHMENT

By the late 1940s, as Jerome Greenfield reports in *Wilhelm Reich vs. the U.S.A.*, the authoritative account of Reich's legal battle, the United States Food and Drug Administration (FDA) had become concerned about Reich's work with cancer patients and his use of orgone accumulators. A series of lurid articles in the yellow press pictured his institute as the scene of wild sex orgies, presumably financed by profits from orgone accumulator distribution, which they dubbed the "orgasm box." The accumulator was misinterpreted as a device intended to "improve one's orgasms." Actually, the accumulators were rented out at $10 a month for experimental use by physicians. Whatever their ultimate therapeutic value, they were clearly not part of any get-rich-quick scheme. Reich devoted nearly all his income to his scientific and clinical experiments.

Reich initially refused to respond to these attacks, just as he had ignored earlier charges that his bodywork therapy involved sexual misuse of female clients and that his sex-education pamphlets would incite sex orgies among youth. He continued his work, no doubt hoping and believing that the attacks would eventually die down and disappear.

As always, Reich prided himself on his independence from scientific or political establishments. Despite the slanderous accusations, he refused to solicit official support among professional organizations. In fact, he almost took pride in being rejected by the medical and scientific establishment. His move to

Maine was consistent with this spirit. He would not condescend to argue his theories in academic journals or other conventional forums. His pride may have been his undoing.

Upon emigrating to the United States, Reich had even refused to fulfill the necessary bureaucratic requirements of obtaining a license to practice medicine in New York State. Dismissing the warnings of friends, he insisted that his close personal association with Freud, his international reputation as a psychotherapist, and his prestigious teaching position at the New School in New York were sufficient proof of his medical competence. At his trial years later, this decision would come back to haunt him with a vengeance.

Despite his apparent aloofness from the mainstream of science and politics, Reich was deeply concerned about the continuing lack of recognition for his work. *Listen, Little Man!*, a book written in 1946 for the archives of the Orgone Institute and not intended for public distribution, reveals the depth of these frustrations. "You don't know what a genius is," he wrote. "Genius is the trademark you put on your products when you put them on sale. You are afraid of genuine love, afraid of your responsibility for your own work, afraid of knowledge. You yell because you are afraid."[9]

Though he took his work with deadly seriousness, Reich also enjoyed leisure activities. His hobbies included painting and playing the piano and organ. An observer at the Reich Museum at the Orgonon estate noted in 1975 that Reich's paintings are "the work of an inspired amateur, done with the impressionist passion of D. H. Lawrence. The colours are bright and primary, the brushstroke explosive."[10] Without question, Reich's sensitivity to color, nature, and emotions were extraordinarily developed.

Reich also had a quick and furious temper. He put into daily practice his conviction that emotions ought not be held back, and this dictum applied to anger as well as love. There was nothing of the detached scholar in Reich's methods. Throughout his life, he pointed to the wider social, political, and economic implications of his work and never played the aloof academician.

Like many, Reich was a difficult person to work or live with. His capacity for intellectual analysis was great, but he was fundamentally an intuitive thinker. He saw connections between ideas or events that few others perceived. Friends describe incidents from his clinical work that suggest a "sixth sense." He was a man of great emotion, sexuality, energy, and confidence. Those of his friends who expected more scientific "proof" for his bold, sweeping views unwittingly invoked his wrath instead.

Unfortunately, Reich tended to vent his anger and frustrations on those close to him. His third wife, Ilse Ollendorff, emphasized this in her generally sympathetic biography, published in 1969. Colleagues also felt his anger, including Theodore Wolfe, his closest associate during the 1940s. Over the years, Reich's insistence on the complete correctness of his ideas, combined with his furious temper, lost him considerable sympathy and many followers, including Wolfe. While quite tender and accepting with patients or students, Reich tended to expect too much of his friends and colleagues.

By the early 1950s, McCarthyism was gaining momentum. Though Reich was not the only physician pursuing radical approaches to cancer, he *was* a former German Communist. Jerome Greenfield makes clear in his book that Reich's background played a large part in his persecution. Moreover, Reich was a caustic critic of American society, and particularly of its power structure, pointing to collusion among drug companies, the medical profession, and regulatory agencies such as the FDA. He was also foreign-born and of Jewish background. And finally, his books advocated controversial changes in sexual mores such as premarital sex, legalized abortion, and contraceptives for adolescents.

The FDA spent years gathering evidence against Reich. In 1954, an FDA-initiated federal court injunction ordered his hardcover books banned from circulation and his softcover books, including all his English-language scientific periodicals, burned. It also ordered him to stop manufacturing and distributing his orgone-energy accumulators. His close assistant, Dr. Michael Silvert, disobeyed the directive, however, and shipped out several of the accumulators to physicians. A criminal contempt-of-court order was issued against Reich and his colleagues. A lengthy appeals procedure began, culminating in his sentencing in May 1956.

His last few years put a great strain on Reich. He insisted on carrying out his own legal defense, which involved protracted work. By the mid-1950s, he and Ilse had separated, another severe blow. Then Theodore Wolfe died after a lingering illness, adding another hammer blow. Reich began to drink heavily and, from reports of his wife and others close to him, he was no longer quite himself. His legal briefs were a bizarre mixture of visionary, almost Blakean rhetoric and naive bravado.

His writings during this period included a number of allusions to UFOs. From 1954 through 1956, he published several articles on UFO sightings in his journals and speculated as to their nature. He also wrote a book, *Contact with Space*, about his growing involvement with the UFO phenomenon, which was not published until after his death. Until quite recently, even those most sympathetic to Reich viewed his claims of repeated UFO sightings in the remote Maine woods as another indicator of his fragile stability. Yet, as recently declassified documents have shown, the U.S. government—and the military—has taken UFO reports quite seriously since the first rash of sightings in the late 1940s.

In the spring of 1956, Reich's legal appeals came to an end. On May 25, in a tiny Maine courthouse, the sentence was handed down. The Wilhelm Reich Foundation was ordered to pay a fine of $10,000, a substantial sum in those days; Michael Silvert was sentenced to a year and a day in prison; and Reich himself was sentenced to two years. He and his colleagues were stunned. The sentence was harsher than anyone had expected.

Shortly thereafter, in what is clearly one of the most ignoble acts in the history of American civil liberties, all of Reich's softcover books that even mentioned the orgone theory were burned on the orders of the United States government. (His hardcover books were "merely banned.") All of the orgone energy accumulators and related devices in his laboratory were destroyed. Appeals by the American Civil Liberties Union proved fruitless. It is hard to imagine how a man who had witnessed the banning of his books by Hitler and Stalin two decades earlier could have withstood much more.

He entered Danbury federal prison on March 12, 1957, and was transferred to Lewisburg federal prison ten days later, where he was examined and pronounced mentally competent by prison psychiatrists. While in prison, his heart condition worsened (he had had a severe heart attack several years earlier), but Reich tried to ignore it. He still planned on resuming his work when he was released from prison. He corresponded with his children and friends, worked in the prison library, and wrote a book concerning gravity and energy entitled *Creation*. And, revealing another turn of thought, this confirmed religious skeptic now put together a book called *Prayers and Poems* for his thirteen-year-old son, Peter.

On November 3, 1957, two days before his parole hearing and two weeks after the Russians had launched the Space Age with Sputnik, Reich was found dead in his cell. An autopsy performed at his family's request indicated that heart failure was the apparent cause of death. A test for poison was also requested by Reich's friends. It proved negative.

THE TIME TRAP: TOO FAR, TOO SOON

After making a number of key innovations, many brilliant thinkers have apparently gone astray. For instance, after discovering the laws of gravity and motion and contributing much to mathematical thought, Sir Isaac Newton puzzled and dismayed his scientific admirers by devoting his later years to theology and mysticism.

Closer to our own time, Sigmund Freud attempted in his later years to apply psychoanalytic insights to politics and religion. After his impressive insights into personality formation, the unconscious, and childhood sexuality, Freud's later works on Woodrow Wilson and Moses failed to win wide respect. Carl Jung is another modern thinker who delved deeply into esoteric fields in his later years, studying alchemy, parapsychology, and such Eastern esoterica as the *I Ching*. While these pursuits lost him the respect of many conventional scientists at the time, today this work is being re-examined by scholars. Even Albert Einstein dismayed his colleagues in his later years. For decades he searched for a unified field theory to integrate all known concepts of space, time, and energy. He refused to believe that the universe operated solely on laws of probability, as suggested by quantum mechanics theory, and died a disappointment to himself and his public.

Thus it seems that many influential thinkers are compelled to delve into ever more complex fields. As a result, they may push too far ahead of their contemporaries, either extending their insights into dubious realms or tackling problems beyond their grasp. This may be what happened with Wilhelm Reich; it is too early to say.

Reich himself, never one for false modesty, explicitly viewed himself as a latter-day Christopher Columbus who had inadvertently come upon a vast, only vaguely defined continent of knowledge involving biological energy, the body, health, and the natural environment. He acknowledged that other explorers would eventually come along to map out in detail the uncharted terrain he had opened up, but insisted that the momentum of these discoveries forbade him the luxury of a leisurely concentration upon one or two problems for a lifetime. Indeed, even his friendliest critics have suggested that his writings were too elliptical and that he leaped from one discipline to another too abruptly. Late in his career, Reich acknowledged that such criticism was legitimate.

Perhaps the best way of understanding Wilhelm Reich is through his own eyes. Today's visitors to the Orgonon Museum at Rangeley, Maine, will see in the library, "set on a table—a thin, tense bronze statue cast from a clay model made by Reich himself, of Mercury-Hermes, the messenger, running with an erect penis into the future. The same Mercury is found above the bed, on the wall of Reich's bedroom. Here Mercury is painted by Reich with a calligraphic intensity of line." This observer notes, "It looks as if he had been painted in one stroke at three o'clock in the morning!"[11]

Some feel that in his book *The Murder of Christ* Reich portrayed himself as a Christ figure. Clearly, there were self-references implicit in his interpretation of Christ's life, and, since Reich's death, some followers have cast him in a messianic role. But we prefer to see Reich as a modern-day Mercury, the messenger, seized with the concept of life energy, rushing to alert the planet to the dangers and opportunities ahead.

CHAPTER 2

The Quest for Full Sexual Union

People get into this or that frenzy, or remain stuck in this or that lamentation, because their minds and bodies have become rigid and because they can neither give love nor enjoy it.

It's not . . . the embrace in itself, not the intercourse. It is the real, emotional experience of the loss of your ego, of your whole spiritual self.

—WILHELM REICH

*T*hroughout his life, Wilhelm Reich remained a dedicated critic of repressed sexual behavior and attitudes. As the result of his radical ideas, some critics have charged him with impracticality, even utopianism; others have linked his ideas to those of D. H. Lawrence, the literary prophet of freer sexuality. Nonetheless, it was through his revolutionary views on sex that Reich was led to later discoveries: the mind-body relationship, bioenergy, holistic health and healing, and finally an entirely new model for understanding our relation to the universe.

From his earliest days, sexuality occupied an important part of Reich's life and thinking. During his childhood, his mother had an affair in their home with Reich's private tutor. One day young Willy was pressured into relaying incriminating information to his father. His mother subsequently committed suicide, and his father never recovered from the grief. He purposely stood for hours in cold ponds on the farm, ostensibly fishing, and died shortly afterward of pneumonia, also an apparent suicide.

Starting at about age fourteen, Reich is said to have led an active sex life, so it is hardly surprising that as a medical student in his early twenties he became involved in organizing a seminar on sexology for himself and his classmates. At the time, sex apart from its procreative aspects was a taboo subject in most medical and other professional training programs. Only in the last decade, in fact, have courses in human sexuality become part of the curriculum in American medical and social service training.

Nor is it surprising that, as a perceptive young physician and psychoanalyst, Reich—like Freud a generation earlier—found that his patients were plagued by a host of sexual disorders, from impotence and frigidity to anxiety about masturbation or about any contact whatever with the opposite sex. While many of these problems had been identified and analyzed by Freud years earlier, the issues ran far deeper for young Reich.

Despite his emphasis on childhood eroticism, Freud had actually gone into little detail about sexual intercourse in *adult* life. He was still inhibited himself. In fact, anecdotes from his own life suggest that he was embarrassed that at the "ripe old age" of forty he could still become sexually aroused by attractive women. In the late 1920s, as Reich recalled in *Reich Speaks of Freud,* almost anything could and was encompassed by phrases like "So-and-So and I slept together last night." Psychoanalysts did not dream of inquiring explicitly into their patients' sexual experiences. In Europe and America there was virtually no scientific study of adult sexual needs, variations in sexual preference, or even individual differences in sexual drives.

The physicians of the day believed that if a man could maintain an erection and ejaculate during intercourse, his sexual functioning was adequate. And if a woman could muster any excitement or interest at all, she was doing well. Meanwhile, through psychoanalytic treatment of hundreds of patients,

Reich found that many men who were able to maintain erections and ejaculate nevertheless felt very little *pleasure* during the act. In fact, they often felt anxiety about the act itself and experienced little satisfaction, to say nothing of joy, afterward. For many women, sexual arousal was seldom spontaneous, and in many instances they unconsciously stiffened their bodies, thus minimizing pleasurable sensations. In fact, many women viewed the sex act as no more than a marital duty.

Reich discovered that men and women in modern society were afraid of *losing control*. As he stated, "You are afraid of falling and of losing your 'individuality' when you should let yourself go."[1] Both during and preceding lovemaking, this anxiety was manifested in the body as well as in the mind. Though many men professed a good deal of sexual experience or prowess, beneath the bravado there was a rigidity that permitted little spontaneity and feeling during the sex act. Gradually, Reich came to the conclusion that patients seeking therapy exhibited characteristics that were common to the majority of adults in Western society.

As early as his first book, *The Function of the Orgasm*, Reich argued that men and women in modern industrial society have internalized alienating stereotypes of their roles both as sexual and social beings. Men and women, said Reich, are conditioned not only to think about sexuality and love in specific ways, but also to restrict their behavior to socially approved patterns of interacting.

Thus, many men are concerned with "how well they are doing" or how potent they are. Throughout his life, Reich emphasized that such concern about arousal, achievement, and conquest of the woman is evidence of a crippled and joyless sexuality. As he stated, in sex "nothing is there to 'prove' or to 'achieve' or to 'get.'"[2] This concern with performance is still a common source of anxiety among men in our culture.

For many women, Reich observed, sexual intercourse was only mildly pleasurable, and at worst it produced disgust and loathing. He also noted that because women were widely viewed as sexual creatures, society made it very difficult for them to be assertive about specific needs and wants during the act. Reich criticized the double standard that dampened the natural sexual drive of women, adding that even those who experienced a vigorous and healthy sexuality often suffered from debilitating guilt feelings, sometimes believing they were immoral or even perverted for enjoying sex, their partner, and themselves. For its participants, the experience of intercourse could range from near-ecstasy to boredom, or even to mere discomfort at the discharge of organic fluids. Work with his patients convinced Reich that few of them—and few nonpatients, either—enjoyed sex very much or experienced a full release at orgasm. He concluded finally that the notion of potency should not be confined to the ability to have an erection and an ejaculation but should include the capacity to have a full orgastic release.

COMING TO OUR SENSES: FULL ORGASM

In a full orgasm both partners enjoy the experience of spontaneity and surrender. The natural buildup of sexual excitement gives way to a graceful release, like the breaking of an ocean wave. The entire body, not just the narrow pelvic area, becomes physically aroused and charged. The mind is aware only of the physical sensations of the moment. In defining this experience, Reich developed the concept of *orgiastic potency*, "the capacity to surrender to the flow of biological energy, without any inhibition, the capacity for complete discharge of all dammed-up sexual excitation through involuntary, pleasurable contractions of the body."[3]

Reich's approach meant giving significance to erotic foreplay. Rather than rushing toward a climax, partners should allow the excitement to build gradually. Nor should one partner concentrate on trying to arouse the other, for this goal might negate the spontaneous, wavelike buildup of arousal, what Reich called "calm excitement."

At the point of discharge, each person should experience a qualitative change in the feelings of pleasure. Whereas during foreplay these are concentrated on the skin surface and in the genitals, at climax they flood the deep bodily tissue. The flow of energy into the other person is reversed, and the energy flows back into the individual bodies, often producing deep melting sensations. As Boadella, the leading English interpreter of Reich, notes, "the re-charging and nourishing effects of a good orgasm ascend the body in an upward wave, which produces the clouding of consciousness, incompatible with a cool head in sex. This ascending flow brings with it a feeling of rooted spirituality."[4]

According to Reich, however, full orgasm can only happen if the two partners love each other and can express this love to each other. Reich was talking here of mature love based on a strong sense of identity. People who cannot love themselves—including their bodies—are unable to give such a love. Their feelings and desires for their partners are vivid but infantile, determined by the need to be loved, held, and cared for.

A second requirement for full orgasm is that both partners be sufficiently free of "armor" for their bodies to function as clear channels for the unimpeded flow of energy and excitement. When this occurs, involuntary muscle contractions and movements occur just before climax.

In the full orgasm, breathing is of central importance. During therapy, Reich had observed that virtually all his patients characteristically breathed in a shallow, jerky, or tense manner. Shallow breathing, he believed, functions physiologically to cut off deep feeling of any kind. In the sex act, breathing should become deeper, more rhythmic than normal, and pleasurable in itself. Body movements become increasingly more vigorous, the skin becomes flushed and radiant, and the eyes glow.

Furthermore, shortly before orgasm, both sexes should experience deep, delicious, currentlike sensations running up and down their bodies. Reich termed these *streamings* and identified them as the peaks of physical pleasure during sex. To a lesser degree they may be experienced by the relatively unarmored person during full, deep breathing.

If these conditions are not met and the energy flow is blocked, several consequences follow. The climax will be localized in the loins. Pleasure from foreplay and climax will quickly evaporate, and instead of deep satisfaction a sense of emptiness or fatigue will take over. Its residue may be a feeling of having missed out. If one attempts restimulation through "novel" techniques, or erotic fantasizing, it will prove to be of little avail.

Reich saw that the ability to lose ourselves wholly in the sexual embrace is the fundamental sign of emotional, physical, and sexual well-being. As he observed, "The ability to concentrate oneself with one's personality upon the orgastic experience, in spite of possible conflicts, is a further criterion of orgastic potency."[5] Thus, for Reich, the power of sex is not to be found in the orgasm per se, but in completely entering into the enjoyment of the *present*.

The Hite Report (1976), based on the answers to thousands of detailed questionnaires about women's sexual experiences, contains numerous statements that support Reich's description of full orgasm. For instance:

> First, all feeling seems centered in the genital area and it spreads through my entire body in great waves of sensation and sensitivity.

> It is difficult to describe—my body is electric all over, and I desire physical and spiritual union with the other.

> My vision dissolves into brilliance behind my eyes, blinding me; my body dissolves into pure light. I see nothing but light, hear nothing at all, feel nothing that can be named—but every blood cell is dancing and every pore outpouring radiance.[6]

Another book, *The Power of Sexual Surrender*, by Dr. Marie Robinson, also confirms some of Reich's observations on the orgasm. She points out, "One of the most amazing aspects of sexual intercourse is . . . that all five senses become extremely dulled as the act increases in intensity. . . . The eyes take on a characteristic trancelike stare. . . . The entire mind and body are concentrated fully on the mounting sexual feeling and exclude all else. In orgasm itself, the anesthesia of the senses is almost total. Indeed, many people experience a temporary loss of consciousness for a matter of seconds."[7] Reich called this the *clouding of consciousness* and saw it as an essential part of the full orgasm.

Robinson goes on, speaking of the woman in orgasm: "And now [at climax] her whole body suddenly plunges into a series of muscular spasms. These spasms take place within the vagina itself. . . . They are felt simultaneously throughout the body: in the torso, face, arms, legs—down to the very soles of the feet."[8]

These are the convulsive movements that Reich speaks of. Then: "If the woman is satisfied by her orgasmic experience she will discharge the neurological and muscular tension developed in the sexual buildup. . . . Full sexual satisfaction is followed by a state of utter calm. . . . Psychologically the person feels completely satisfied, at peace with the world."[9]

As to its implications, Robinson observes: "There is no physiological or psychological experience that parallels its sweeping intensity or its excruciating pleasure. . . . There are many who take a mystical view of this ecstatic coupling of man and woman in love. Others see it as a foretaste of heaven, the carnal representation of endless spiritual delights for mankind."[10] Here again she echoes Reich.

Finally we find Robinson, a psychiatrist and psychoanalyst, emphasizing, as did Reich twenty-five years earlier, the necessity of surrender as essential to true orgasm. "The excitement comes from the act of surrender. . . . Concentrating on one's sensations . . . wondering if one is feeling the 'right' feelings can destroy real sexual passion."[11] One must pursue self-surrender to succeed, she repeatedly emphasizes.

Reich called those people for whom the complete orgasm was a frequent or regular occurrence—as opposed to a once-or-twice-in-a-lifetime experience—*genital characters*. They possess true emotional and physical health. He noted that anyone who is tense and immersed in fantasies or fretful thoughts during intercourse cannot be fully alive to the experience. So he maintained that the ability to enjoy a complete orgasm is a sure indicator of one's capacity to be truly spontaneous in life, to love in general, and to be emotionally and physically sensitive to the world at large. It is important to see that Reich was *not* advocating sexual intercourse for its own sake or claiming that orgasm was the summum bonum of existence. Rather, orgastic potency was conceived of as an important criterion of full emotional health.

In *The Function of the Orgasm*, Reich advanced the highly original notion that orgasm has the biological task of discharging pent-up energies in the organism—energies that, if not discharged, can have harmful effects. In this "sex-economic" approach, the natural function of orgasm is therefore to regulate the energy economy and flow of the organism by releasing energy that, unexpressed, can easily produce anxiety and, eventually, psychosomatic complaints.

The notion of *sex economy* was one of the most original of Reich's theories. In economics, the focus is on supply meeting demand, or consumption keeping up with production of goods for the stability of the economy. Reich took up this concept and applied it to people. He claimed that the biological organism inevitably creates or produces a certain amount of sexual energy that is creative and dynamic (Freud called it libido). This energy builds up in many adolescents and adults every two to four days and needs to be released (or consumed). The natural way is during the orgasm. If "consumption" fails to equal "production," psychic disturbances will ensue in the form of free-floating anxiety, compulsive behavior, or psychosomatic symptoms. The key point is that the human body, like other organisms, produces energy—that is, gets charged up—and this stage is normally followed by a discharging experience. In the neurotic, the sexual discharge is limited and partial, leaving him or her feeling empty or unsatisfied, not fully at peace.

Reich argued that the use of sex techniques interferes with full orgasm, which requires total surrender to the flow of the moment. While not condemning the use of sexual techniques, he repeatedly emphasized their extreme limitations, and fifty years ago he warned that a reliance on technique represents a serious distortion of natural sexual enjoyment. And in 1978, Stella Resnick, a Gestalt therapist in California, repeated his warning: "Sexual technique, no matter how polished, is the kiss of death to satisfying sexual contact, connoting as it does fixed behaviors and preconceived notions of what feels good."[12] Reich insisted that no amount of technical expertise would enable a neurotic person to love someone; by the same token, a person secure in his or her own sexuality and lovingly receptive to his or her partner would need no technical manuals.

Reich's close scrutiny of the sexual experience led him to several brilliant insights that others are just beginning to appreciate. He deplored the fact that women had been brought up to be passive in general and that in sex they often unconsciously shut off receptivity by tightening their breathing and pelvic areas. As Stella Resnick says, "We are a people whose pelvises have been bound 'psychologically' like the feet of the prerevolutionary Chinese women."[13] Statements from typical American women quoted in *The Hite Report* are also illustrative: "During the orgasm, every muscle (that I'm aware of) tenses completely." "My body is usually tense, with legs straight out, pelvis thrusting erratically."[14]

According to Reich, the rigidly held-in pelvis clamps down on the flow of sensual feelings in that area, cuts off the pleasurable streamings, and greatly reduces the ecstatic potential of sexual union. Sociologically, it makes men agreeable to the orders of authority figures (the boss, the policeman, etc.), and it keeps women in line with middle-class notions of propriety and authority and binds up their sexual desire so that they will accept a generally subordinate role to men. In short, sexual repression functions to make people submissive and inclined to irrational behavior, and it thus paralyzes the rebellious potential of both men and women. The fact that women have experienced more sexual suppression has made them more passive and politically inactive than men.

Reich maintained that people's sexual satisfaction "is not simply satisfaction of a need like hunger or defecation, but their spiritual development, their freshness of life, their capacity for work, and their enthusiasm for struggle"[15] are affected as much by their sexual life as by their material existence. Once women experience deep pleasure in their sexual relationships, they are liable to feel more powerful and increasingly resentful of being kept down by the male sex.

Both men and women typically hold back other strong emotions, such as anger or aggression, as well. The unconscious intent behind this physical *armoring* is to ward off the ripples of ecstasy (streamings) that course through the body during sex. (The concept of armoring will be fully elaborated in Chapter 3.)

Reich insisted that women are as sexual as men. At a time when people had just begun to accept Freud's notions of masculine sexuality, Reich stood up for women's rights in love and sex as well as in the economic sphere. He argued that changes in this direction were inevitable. In the 1930s he foresaw a time when more and more women would become attuned to their bodies and their sexual needs.

Similarly, Reich noted that in Western society men are brought up to keep vulnerable and tender emotions tightly repressed. In the professional realm they must avoid all extreme emotions. Even within the confines of the family circle, men, especially Anglo-Saxons, are expected to hold back gentle or demonstrative feelings. So, many men have tremendous difficulty in being really open with women and in letting themselves go in the sex act. Their social conditioning has led them to fear being vulnerable and fully open to tenderness and other deep feelings. Quite recently, encounter groups and other therapies of humanistic and transpersonal psychology have emphasized the value of touching and hugging; by providing new opportunities for physical closeness and giving, they have begun to make such men aware of the warm pleasures of giving and receiving.

Reich's analysis of sexuality and the orgasm failed to win him many friends among orthodox psychoanalysts. His writings were criticized as pornographic, much as Freud's books had been condemned a generation earlier. Many of Reich's critics, loyal to Freud, reiterated that sexual intercourse was nothing but a simple biological act. If people couldn't consummate it, then that was a matter for therapy, but Reich's ideal of the full orgasm was dismissed as irrelevant.

Such criticism, however, failed to deter Reich. As we will explore in the next chapter, he came to realize that sexual anxiety is directly related to anxiety about bodily pleasure in general, an anxiety that permeates life in our industrial society. Those who experience little physical pleasure in intercourse are alienated from their entire bodies, not simply inhibited genitally.

On the other hand, those who typically experience full orgasm are already highly sensitive, sensual persons. They enjoy life in an immediate, physical way, and their sexuality is a manifestation of this sensual capacity. These people were Reich's "genital characters." Decades later, Abraham Maslow, one of the founders of humanistic psychology, came to somewhat similar conclusions through his studies of what he called "self-actualizing" individuals.

SEXPOLITICS

As soon as Reich turned his attention to bodily pleasure and how it is expressed or deadened in modern society, his ever-questing mind led him into the area of social criticism and then political action.

Quite early in his psychoanalytic practice, he had found that experiences of the full orgasm, or orgastic potency, were extremely rare. He observed that not only his patients but most adults in industrial society found sex a very troubling issue and were often subtly blocked in expressing these basic needs. He came to realize that sexuality cannot be divorced from other aspects of our social existence, and he sought scientific explanations by examining our social and political institutions.

By the late 1920s, Reich began to argue that distorted sexual attitudes and behavior stemmed from the major emphases and characteristics of capitalistic society itself: its methods of child-rearing and education, its patriarchal patterns of family life, its work and social institutions. Eventually he came to view modern capitalism, with its rigid moral structure and alienating modes of work, its social inequalities and authoritarian system of relationships, as antilife. And he went on to argue that capitalism inevitably engenders certain kinds of character structures in adults that directly affect success and pleasure in the sex act. In short, sexuality is not restricted to performance in bed but, in its many expressions, is an outgrowth of the entire personality, including that part of us which reacts to the social, political, and economic climate of our times.

All this led Reich to construct a platform of sexual rights and freedoms. As mentioned in Chapter 1, he first took this platform to the World League for Sexual Reform. When they rebuffed his ideas as too politically radical, Reich turned in the very early 1930s to the German Communists for backing. It is worthwhile to cite this platform in some detail, to show how far ahead of its time it was. He called for:

1. An end to the housing shortage, then widespread in Europe, which meant young lovers often could not find space for privacy.

2. Abolition of all laws against abortion, birth control, and homosexuality.

3. Reform of marriage laws to make divorce more liberal.

4. Free availability and distribution of contraceptives to all, including teenagers.

5. Sex-education programs in the mass media, such as radio and newspapers.

6. Sex counseling to be made available at each business concern of a specified size.

7. Abolition of all laws prohibiting sex education.

8. Full conjugal rights for people in prison.

Deeply concerned with the need to transform the apparently crumbling capitalistic system of the early 1930s, Reich grappled with a way to unite the best insights of Freud and Marx. He expanded the concept of sex economy to refer to the husbanding and use of human biological energies, of which the sexual was seen as the most powerful. One implication of the term "sex economy" is that the successful discharge of the libidinal energies of the masses is essential to a harmonious society. In short, such energies are realities that require understanding and effective expression in order to guarantee a free society.

Leveling a critique at capitalism as a fundamentally authoritarian, patriarchal, and sex-repressive system in the early 1930s, Reich called for free sexuality within an egalitarian socialist society. The political structures of this system, Reich noted, are patriarchal and uphold property rights (which divide people from each other), and include the patriarchal family, authoritarian work relationships, and religion. He called the family "the factory of submissive beings."[16] At the core of the family is a fixation on the mother, leading to guilt and a sticky sentimentality, which makes any rational understanding of the family very difficult. In short, Reich linked the repressive characteristics of the capitalist economy with similarly repressive power structures in politics, work, family, and religion.

His "Sex-Pol" writings, collected by Lee Baxandall (Sex-Pol Essays), are an attack on laissez-faire capitalism. These and related writings actually inspired the 1968 student uprisings that swept Germany and France. The leaders of both the German and French student movements that produced these insurgent actions publicly acknowledged their intellectual indebtedness to

Reich as an inspired update of Marx's ideas. In February 1967, Boris Frankel spoke on Reich and the social function of sexual repression to several hundred students at a branch of the University of Paris in Nanterre. The response was enthusiastic. During the next week, Reich's booklet, "The Sexual Strength of Youth," was sold door to door in residence halls. This led to a widespread sex-education campaign based on Reich's ideas, which resulted in "the occupation by men and women students of the women's dorms to protest against their restrictive rules. The consciousness which culminated in the events of May 1968 was first awakened in a great number of Nanterre students in the struggle against their sexual repression."[17] And the French journal *Sex-Pol,* which devoted its entire December 1977 issue to Reich, carries on this sexual-political tradition of Reich's thinking.

It must be clearly noted that after living several years in the United States, which he grew to admire, and observing the failure of socialism in Russia and elsewhere, Reich turned away from a Marxist socialism and its form of revolutionary politics.

He felt the repressive regimes in Russia and the Iron Curtain countries showed that violent means of changing society, with their accompanying slogans of freedom to the masses, were sadly misconceived. To be effective, major social change must be introduced slowly and only after appropriate education and the cultivation of democratic support. Long critical of liberalism, in the 1950s Reich turned away from left-wing and collectivist ideologies and contended that the U.S. Republican Party, with its open conservatism and its belief in basic human freedoms, was preferable to "freedom peddlers."

Better, in the long run, the avowed conservative who may introduce some changes under pressure than liberals or leftists who rush into change that tears down or disrupts rather than heals or builds constructively. Reich became enormously critical of communism, felt that Russia was *the* enemy of humanity, and toward the end saw himself as the victim of a sinister Communist plot to ruin his work. This does not mean that Reich abandoned his analysis of capitalism's and industrial society's involvement in sex repression, but that he lost confidence in left-wing political attempts to change the system. He no longer believed in the efficacy of sudden, violent changes in the political system.

In order to make possible healthier sexual attitudes in adults, Reich emphasized the importance of a proper sexual upbringing for children. He took an accepting attitude toward masturbation years before most educators and physicians would view it as natural in youth, and before statistics on its prevalence became available through Kinsey. Reich viewed masturbation as a normal release of sexual tensions, a function of sex economy. In fact, for some especially repressed patients, Reich counseled that they should first be able to masturbate freely and without guilt before attempting intercourse. This approach, it is worth noting, is now being adopted by many sex counselors, including Masters and Johnson. Thus, Reich allowed that masturbation in children is a natural and life-affirming activity.

Reich also regarded it as a healthy outlet for adults, particularly for those who lacked sex partners. However, he noted that, for the healthy adult, "Masturbation never provides the same gratification as sexual intercourse."[18] He added that if one chose this solitary behavior over the joys and unknowns of a real relationship, it could lead to serious psychological problems. Nor did he see all masturbatory fantasies as equally healthy. Some, such as those picturing rape, were evidence of an emotional sickness. Later, Reich came to believe that intercourse involves a highly significant exchange of energies between the partners, and thus he felt that no other sexual act could be seen as totally satisfying and complete.

Reich insisted that if children and adolescents fail to learn positive attitudes about sex, they will undoubtedly pick up negative attitudes. He did not outline in detail a specific sex-education curriculum, but he emphasized that *how* sex is taught by the schools or by the family is at least as important as *what* is taught. The teachers must themselves be relatively free of sexual conflicts and anxieties; otherwise, they will be unable to nourish healthy attitudes in the children.

Sex education in the home, in Reich's view, was more a matter of example than of explicit instruction. First came breast-feeding and an easy acceptance of nudity. Within the home, the children would see each other and their parents naked, and the door of the bathroom would not normally be closed during use. Young children would bathe together naked; would see their parents expressing physical affection; and would be free to ask any sexual question, to explore their bodies, to indulge in normal sexual play, and to masturbate. Masturbation, in fact, would be regarded as totally natural. A new pregnancy would provide an occasion for natural learning about childbirth. An interesting book detailing how all this worked out in one British family is *The Free Family* by architect Paul Ritter.

Teachers must be willing and able to discuss quite frankly such topics as premarital sex, the experience of orgasm, sexual attraction, infatuation, and love. Reich declared that to properly handle our children's sexuality, we must ourselves have experienced what love is. Clearly, to restrict sex education to lectures on the anatomy of reproduction or to hygiene is to dodge key issues. Except in free schools modeled after A. S. Neill's Summerhill, it would seem that Americans are still far from even approaching Reich's views on sex education.

By puberty, Reich argued, adolescents should have access to contraceptives. Once given an adequate grounding in intelligent sex education, adolescents physically capable of sex should be allowed to experience it, as they are in certain primitive tribes. To make them wait until the magic age of eighteen or later only serves to poison sexual urges with guilt, resentment, and frustration. Reich also claimed that if young persons experienced coitus before making emotional commitments, they would be far more realistic and objective about an eventual love relationship. On the other hand, Reich argued, children and adolescents who come to regard sex in an obsessive or furtive manner will be unable to experience full sexual satisfaction as adults.

Throughout childhood and adolescence, Reich believed, the emphasis ought to be on self-regulation (a concept discussed more fully in Chapter 8) and responsibility in sexual matters. Children who receive intelligent sex education and who regularly witness their parents expressing healthy physical affection are likely to be able to handle the complexities of sexual relationships. He attributed the widespread lack of maturity and sexual responsibility in contemporary society to the absence of such an upbringing.

During his years as a sex-political activist, Reich directed most of his efforts toward working-class youth. In talks, all articles, and some personal consultation, he sought to clarify their sexual confusion. Rather than "promote sex," as he was often accused of doing, he concentrated on correcting the false notions that underlie most sexual prohibitions and on linking youth's sexual plight to capitalism. Intercourse, masturbation, sexual desire, orgasm, venereal disease, and abortion, were all discussed in connection with existing repression and the social prerequisites for a healthy sexual life. Reich scorned a false neutrality and placed himself four-square on the side of young people and their physical needs.

In other words, Reich believed that what works within such tribes as the Trobrianders, Samoans, or Nagas could also work in a large, complex civilization. While many authorities today still support Freud's view that civilization requires sexual repression—and that sublimation leads to creative achievements—no thoroughgoing sociological examination of Reich's claims has emerged. The question remains open.

VIOLENCE, SEX, AND MARRIAGE

Above all, Reich felt that modern industrial society must change its fundamental approach to sex and the body. He was concerned about the degree to which sexual relations involve sadism and/or emotional or physical violence, from slapping and hitting to a subtle put-down—in other words, a power play—and contended that such unhealthy actions were usually connected to early experiences that associated a mixture of frustration, guilt, and self-hate with sexual feelings. For example, people who are drawn to films featuring violent or sadistic actions, including rape, have been brought up from childhood to associate feelings of disgust or fear with physical love and affection. They are simply incapable of expressing tender, loving emotions in a natural and spontaneous way, and yet at the same time they cannot control their deep sexual cravings. Thus, ultimately, the amount of physically violent sex depicted in the mass media reflects the extent of guilt, resentment, and contempt that its members feel toward physical love and self-vulnerability. One consequence, according to Reich, is that "what I call the loving embrace becomes . . . a pornographic act."[19]

Similarly, obsession with sex is an unhealthy sign, indicative of sexual anxieties. For the ideal individual—the genital character—sex is not a consuming passion. It is the neurotic, said Reich, who goes "around in a perpetual state of sexual starvation" or who constantly talks "about love in terms of dirty jokes."[20] Later in his career, Reich pointed out that our general preoccupation with sex indicates the widespread presence of unhealthy frustrations.

On other sexual issues, Reich was far ahead of his time. He emphasized that homosexuals had the right to their sexual preference, though he personally regarded homosexuality as an aberration originating in conflicted childhood experiences. Until a society was ready to support truly healthy, loving sexual relations, he felt that it exhibited the greatest hypocrisy in condemning homosexuality.

Early on, Reich was a passionate defender of women's rights in all areas. The general lack of equality between the sexes in society and in marriage, he stated, helps prevent satisfying sexual relations. "Furthermore," he observed, "the education for the supremacy of the man makes companionship with the woman impossible."[21]

Reich identified six factors as essential in his conception of an enduring, loving sexual relationship:

1. Full orgastic potency of the partners—that is, no disparity between tenderness and sensuality.

2. The overcoming of incestuous ties and infantile fears of sexuality.

3. No repression of any unsublimated sexual impulses, be they homosexual or nongenital.

4. The absolute affirmation of sexuality and joy in living.

5. Overcoming the basic elements of patriarchal moralism.

6. The capacity for intellectual companionship with the partner.[22]

With respect to love and marriage, Reich went further. On the basis of trends taking shape in the 1930s, he argued that the nuclear family and the monogamous marriage bond were out-moded. With the coming changes in women's rights and sexual values, he predicted, the nuclear family (based on male domi-nance and widespread emotional inhibition) would be irrepara-bly undermined. A new system was needed, one that would include serial marriage.

Based on what he had learned from his medical practice and from anthropological studies (among which he was strongly influenced by Malinowski's *The Sexual Life of Savages*), he advo-cated an arrangement in which partners would remain faithful to each other while the relationship lasted, but that either partner would be free to terminate the liaison at any point. In short, there would be minimal social pressure to continue a relationship that was viewed as unsatisfying, even if neuroti-cally so. While viewing lifelong monogamy as one viable alterna-tive, he argued that it should not be the only socially and legally sanctioned sexual partnership. What might prove eminently workable for one couple might be totally confining for another.

But he emphasized that he was *not* advocating an uninhibited, "swinging" lifestyle. It is doubtful if he would have thought highly, either, of group-marriage arrangements. He stated flatly that "those people who are incapable of establishing a lasting relationship are dominated by an infantile fixation of their love life." On the other hand, he was quick to say that he would place no time limits on how long partners ought to have known each other before engaging in intercourse.

What Reich did endorse was a marriage contract in which the rights and equality of women are fully protected. In this he accorded with the views of Judge Ben Lindsey of Denver, the pioneer who in the 1920s proposed a legalized form of trial or contract marriage for adolescents. Reich deeply respected Judge Lindsey's courageous and prophetic work. Several years after Ilse Ollendorff left him, he entered into a relationship with a young woman named Aurora Karrer. (Later, when he attempt-ed to marry her legally while he was in prison, his request was turned down.) Reich endorsed contract matrimony, including arrangements by which the couple agree to stay together for a certain number of years, whereupon the contract, like a lease, may be renewed or terminated. In view of the vast uncertainties of modern life, such contracts appear to be one practical option, especially if couples are not planning to have children.

Reich did not believe in lifelong monogamy as the rule for most persons. He regarded it as both unnatural in the animal species and uncommon in nontechnological cultures. In many tribal societies unspoiled by Western civilization, he contended, sexuality was untrammeled by confining laws or norms governing premarital sex, marriage, and divorce.

We are aware today that Reich oversimplified the complexities of tribal sexual and marital customs. He was arguing from anthropological evidence available during the 1930s, when much less was known concerning the norms of tribal societies. From more recent evidence, we know that while many of these societies allow children and adolescents greater sexual freedom than does ours, it is hardly accurate to characterize them as shining examples of sexual freedom. Many, in fact, have stricter norms governing whom one may marry than our own.

REICH'S SEXUAL LEGACY

Reich's rejection of the traditional patriarchal family, combined with his early Marxist views, has been taken up by a number of left-wing groups, one of the most interesting of which is Actions Analysis Organization (AAO). Launched in 1973, the AAO began as a rural commune in Austria that practiced a unique type of self-presentation psychotherapy and what it called free sexuality. Besides following Reich in encouraging childhood masturbation and easy acceptance of nudity within the group, AAO believed in common property, direct democracy, collective work, and norms against pairing off sexually.

The way the organization, which originated as a counterculture commune, developed into its present form is recounted by one of its leaders in the magazine *AA News:*

> We were a typical commune of this period, we all had long hair, took part in the stereo fashion . . . it was creative and chaotic, we lived like children. We enjoyed being superficial, we danced constantly. But we soon noticed that we couldn't keep going like this. As I began with so-called "consultations" in the summer of 1972, inspired by Wilhelm Reich, because I saw that many people

needed it, the climate in the group changed very rapidly. We began discussing sexuality and the couple relationship, and also ... some kind of work that we could all do together. The "consultation" also changed rapidly and became actions analysis: breathing, shouting, physical touching soon became more important than speaking. . . . I felt the emotional possibility of free sexuality in the group. At that time I said that I was not going to get involved in another relationship. Several individuals and also several pairs joined me. It went without much difficulty. After the first tears were dry, we were amazed how simple everything in the group had become. The only people who had difficulties were those who were unable to claim this new freedom for themselves. [By "this new freedom" he means having free access to any woman in the group.]

Some of them stayed for a while and blamed the group for their lack of communication. Some began to demand free sexuality like a welfare check. But unfortunately free sexuality cannot be prescribed, it must be earned every day with the ability to communicate . . . cannot be extorted or blackmailed. Free sexuality is not possible without communication, without positive emotion, without love. Free sexuality is free of obligations, pity and compulsions. Free sexuality is collective sexuality within the group, it is not private property, it is social, it corresponds to collective property on the economic level. The unification of the individual group members in free sexuality led to economic unification in common property.[23]

Couples who enter the commune are urged to begin sexual liaisons with others, but prolonged sexual pairing-off is discouraged. Each adult woman in the group is given a double bed, and in the afternoon, or a day earlier, an interested man may approach her, suggesting that they sleep together. Property is held in common, and income from various work projects is shared; this same sharing is carried over to sexual relationships. In the group's literature, however, which outlines rather rapid expansion of the commune to Germany, Switzerland, and Norway, it is noted that in spite of group norms there is a tendency for some degree of pairing-off to occur.

While the AAO pays tribute to Reich as the source of many of its ideas and is devoted to a form of group-therapy session in order to break down armoring, it obviously goes beyond Reich's expectations in its sexual nonpairing norm. Since the authors have not visited the commune and must rely only on its literature, they are unable to honestly evaluate it. We mention it here because the group does practice certain of Reich's sexual beliefs (nudity, masturbation for children) within a noncompetitive type of economic setting.

The mid-nineteenth century had seen the establishment in the United States of somewhat similar, sexually free rural communes, although only one—the Oneida—lasted more than a few years. It was founded and led by a charismatic clergyman, John Humphrey Noyes, who

> decried monogamy on the grounds of its exclusiveness and offered in its place the practice of couple marriage [with] all females ... potentially available to all males, although in practice it worked out that older males gained greater access to young females. In spite of some such inequities, women probably derived much greater sexual satisfaction than was the case for the average housewife in Victorian America.
>
> The formula for the success of the Oneida Community rested largely on the practical genius and charismatic leadership exerted by Noyes. Unlike the grand Utopian designers of Enlightenment philosophy, Noyes possessed a unique capacity to develop and sustain the economic means by which Oneida could survive.[24]

Oneida collapsed after Noyes's death. Time will tell whether AAO will follow the fate of Oneida and other sexually open experimental communities. Much will depend on its leadership, its economic viability, and its continuation as a small, rural-based group, as well as on ideological developments in the surrounding society.

Masses of our youth have recently received a taste of the sexual freedom that Reich espoused. Equal rights for women are nearer to realization in law and sexuality. Recreational sex is gaining ground. Nude bathing is winning more acceptance. New styles of pairing are emerging, supplanting the former dominance of conventional marriage: homosexual couples, common-law partnerships, contract marriages, and group marriages. Clearly, differentiation is replacing uniformity in sexual matters.

The emerging new structure involves some trade-offs. On the one hand, the new sexual freedom makes possible greater variety and satisfaction. Contraceptives and abortions help prevent the birth of unwanted children. Some middle-class women are gradually assuming fuller rights as sexual beings. These are valuable gains. On the other hand, the new developments have encouraged an explosion in promiscuity, which is fueled by dozens of exploitative magazines with a total circulation in the millions (*Penthouse, Playboy, Chic, Hustler,* etc.) and a flood of sensationalizing paperbacks and films. Reich foresaw this trend and labeled it "free-for-all four-lettering," meaning that everyone feels free to use four-letter words. He considered it an unfortunate but unavoidable phase in history's slow march toward an authentic sexual revolution.

The process by which sexual pleasure is promoted as a product has been described by the neo-Freudian philosopher Herbert Marcuse as "repressive desublimation." Simply put, this means that although our society does not require us to sublimate sexual desire to the same degree as in the past, by turning sex into a purely casual, mechanical pastime we are experiencing a subtle form of repression—the repression of true passion. Marcuse saw the shift away from early laissez-faire capitalism to monopoly-finance capitalism as an underlying cause, since capitalism in its present form requires people to consume more and more commodities in order to keep the productive system functioning. He believed that this emphasis on consumption renders sex a commodity and is the force behind the "four-lettering" explosion and preoccupation with casual sex.

Some radical feminists agree, claiming that today's eroticism is the new opiate of the people, a large-scale distraction of the masses from the business of feeling and living deeply. Absorption in the chase for even newer sexual thrills, they maintain, vainly promises to alleviate the boring drudgery common to the white-collar work world. A group in Toronto is writing a parody titled *The Bore of Sex.* "The premise," explains Professor Mary O'Brien, "is that sex is time-consuming and not very rewarding. But when one structures a whole social life around the pursuit of sex, as we seem to being doing, whether one really enjoys it or not, sexual activity becomes the standard of a life well lived. The pressure to show oneself off as a sexually liberated person becomes immense. So, as feminists we are considering whether we should withdraw from the whole thing."[25]

At the same time, many newly orgasmic women are uncertain about what to do with their new freedom. Some are fearful that they will be regarded as promiscuous. Some seem driven to seek advice from self-styled media experts, asking: What goals and techniques are valid? How can guilt be avoided? In short, the new freedom may lead to increasing confusion. As a reaction to all of this, some radical feminists are talking about a return to a kind of neo-puritanism.

Indeed, the shift in mores may not last. Our deepening energy and economic crises, along with the continuing depletion of global resources (and especially of oil and other petroleum products), may usher in a period of resource scarcity and produce a scarcity economy. The consequences could be a tightening of moral standards in both pre- and postmarital sex. Already the signs of a swing away from pornography and a turn toward right-wing politics is evident; this may herald a gradual return to some variant of traditional morality.

In family life, separation and divorce have become extremely common. While, in many cases, such breakups may have healthy emotional outcomes, their prevalence may also lead to a vast increase in neurosis, sadism, and stress diseases as armies of children are raised without consistent or loving parenting. Serial marriage, which Reich both practiced and recommended, may bring in its wake enormous personal and social costs. These changes, too, may help precipitate a swing of the pendulum toward traditional moral standards of behavior.

It seems likely that opinion will polarize between the traditionalists and those seeking personal freedom and sexual pleasure. In all this it is important to see that Reich stood for responsible action, commitment, and healthy functioning, and that he believed the culture must pass through an unhappy transitional period of uncertainty and excess to signal its rejection of the previous era of repression. As Boadella has so admirably pointed out, "The real distinction is not between nondeviant sexuality and deviant sexuality, or between 'moral' sexuality and 'immoral' sexuality; it is between surface-pleasure and depth-pleasure, and between the voluntary head-driven process, and the involuntary process of organismic surrender."[26]

Thus, in the short run, two trends are apparent. On the one hand, the mass media and sex merchandisers will continue to exploit the mechanistic, cool-headed approach to sex. Casual sex will be easily available to those who are unable or unwilling to sustain a responsible emotional commitment. More sex therapists will emerge to "treat" sexual disorders by rather superficial, technique-oriented methods. In various ways, our "four-lettering" epidemic will continue for a time. Nonetheless, increasing numbers of thoughtful adults will seriously try to raise their children in a sex-positive fashion and will themselves experience the potential joys of the loving sexual embrace.

So, while we are still far from the sexual revolution Reich envisioned, sexual expression and physical love will gradually come to be more widely accepted as legitimate human needs. And for Reich, the ability to love fully is intimately related to overall bodily sensitivity and emotional health. It is to this theme that we will turn next.

CHAPTER 3

The Surrender of the Body

You tell me what you are by way of your expression.

Full living means full surrender to any kind of functioning. No matter whether working, or talking to friends, or rearing a child, or listening to a talk, or painting, or anything else.

—WILHELM REICH

Whereas Freud opened our eyes to the reality of the unconscious mind—and its power to shape our lives—Reich rediscovered the primacy of our physical bodies. Basically, he argued, we *are* our bodies, and every part of the body can be a potent source of pleasurable sensations. Modern industrial society, however, limits us to the pleasures of the body inherent in eating, exercise, occasional touching, and sexual relations.

Reich deplored the fact that, aside from these isolated experiences, we are encouraged to live in our minds, not our bodies. "Think, plan, scheme, decide, analyze, follow this or that mental strategy," society urges. "Drag the body after you. Attend to it only when it complains through sensations of exhaustion, tension, or distress. Otherwise, follow the head. To succeed, concentrate on your goals. Use your brain and discipline your feelings. Don't expect much real pleasure in life; it is just not meant to be."

Unlike Freud, who remained wedded to the Victorian tradition of denial of the body, Reich argued convincingly that bodily sensitivity and sensual awareness are not only a deep source of happiness but bear directly on virtually every aspect of personal existence. Already, Reich's insights concerning the denigration of the body by technological society, as well as the therapies he developed to restore it to its place, have begun to exert a powerful transformation on the West.

Reich's focus on the body distinguishes him from nearly all the leading psychological and sociological innovators of the twentieth century. None of the others—such as Alfred Adler, Carl Jung, or Otto Rank in Freud's day, or Erik Erikson, Abraham Maslow, or R. D. Laing in our own time—has so cogently articulated how the denial of the body in modern industrial society alienates us from ourselves. At best, in the theories of these other thinkers, the body is viewed as a hindrance, a reflection of our animalistic origins. These theorists, to be sure, saw that our biological makeup contributed to our enjoyment during sex, but otherwise, they felt, we could and should minimize bodily awareness as much as possible. Reich insisted, however, that in the very way we speak to one another, walk, play, or even breathe we reveal our displacement from our innermost selves.

Reich, of course, did not formulate a single, unified theory in one year or through a single leap of analysis. But in the mid-1920s his insights began coming in quick succession. Some of his views startled and outraged his contemporaries. And yet, vindicating the accuracy of his clinical and intuitive findings, most of his earliest discoveries relating to body language and personality were later subsumed under orthodox psychoanalysis or psychotherapy, though Reich himself was rarely acknowledged as the original innovator. For example, Reich's emphasis that the therapist must treat the entire personality or character of the patient, and not simply his or her neurotic symptom or complaint, has become almost a truism. Similarly, Reich's focus on the nonverbal messages relayed during therapy to the practitioner by the patient is by now a well-accepted element of psychoanalytic treatment.

Reich was essentially an intuitive thinker, and while he maintained an active intellectual exchange with Freud and Freud's inner circle for a number of years, his theories were, for the most part, independently generated. Indeed, as with other great thinkers, he was in many ways isolated from routine activities in his field, particularly during his time in the United States. Reich's insights came primarily through observation and analysis of patients within a clinical setting. This fact makes his dis coveries in such areas as body language, emotional spontaneity, and the sensual deadening of our society all the more striking. Furthermore, many of his insights have now been confirmed by hundreds of carefully constructed research investigations.

Reich acknowledged that his discoveries concerning the body and emotions left room for clarification and additions. He declared that his main task was to bring forward only the broad outlines of a theory and let these generate their own momentum. In this vein, late in his career, he observed that he frequently had to defend himself against the criticism that he had overextended himself scientifically by exploring too many fields of science at the same time. Yet, he insisted, the facts kept flowing toward him. He freely admitted that he had indeed left many gaps in his work, but asked to be excused by his colleagues because of the pioneering nature of his many discoveries.

Because we cannot explore in detail the whole edifice, we will enter Reich's mind through several of the windows and doors he has provided. Three of these are most important: (1) that through physical expression, or body language, we constantly reveal a great deal of our emotional makeup, particularly our unresolved tensions of suppressed feelings; (2) that certain bodily rigidities, such as a tight jaw, raised shoulders, rigid pelvis, or stiff neck, relate to specific personality types; and (3) that in our technological society, most persons typically remain unaware of these chronic tensions, which Reich termed *armor;* this armor, he found, is greatly resistant to change.

Reich discovered that long drawn-out conversations with patients about their childhoods or personal difficulties were really not necessary for an accurate diagnosis. The patient's own body loudly and clearly disclosed basic difficulties, such as the inability to make full emotional contact with others or to completely release longings and pent-up feelings. Reich emphasized to the patient precisely what his or her body language revealed, using such information as the basis for his psychotherapy. Far more than the intellectual material the patient might wish to discuss, often out of unconscious desires to avoid real inner growth, Reich relied upon the patient's nonverbal messages to guide the direction of his therapy.

Looking back on this initial discovery, Reich later observed:

> Analytic psychology paid attention only to *what* the children suppressed and to the reasons for the suppression. However, no attention was paid to the *manner* in which they fight against their emotions. It is, nevertheless, just this *physiological* side of the process of repression which merits our closest attention.[1]

Reich found that this emotional suppression, typically involving various physiological functions such as respiration or digestion, is almost always rooted in childhood. It eventually becomes a chronic and pervasive aspect of personality and body language.

A DYNAMIC LANGUAGE

Reich noted that in countless minute and subtle ways, the body sends a loud, urgent message to those able to read it. "Words can lie. The mode of expression never lies," he declared. "It is the immediate, unconscious manifestation of the character."[2] Usually we are aware, of course, when a friend is angry simply by the way he or she is sitting. Or, by the way he or she steps into a room, we can often tell that an acquaintance is elated about something. Poets, novelists, and artists have always called our attention to such details. What Reich did was to make the language of the body a legitimate field of scientific inquiry. Many social scientists have clarified and extended Reich's insights, a great many of which remain relevant today.

Reich specifically focused on our way of breathing. He observed that persons with emotional problems invariably breathed in a shallow, superficial manner. Their breathing was often far from regular, with numerous spurts and sudden shifts in rhythm. It was very rare for a neurotic to breathe regularly in a deep, full manner. Why, Reich asked, was this pattern so prevalent? How did it originate? He observed:

> Let one imagine that one is frightened, or in anticipation of great danger. Instinctively, one will draw in one's breath and remain in this attitude. As one cannot continue to do this, one will soon breathe out again. However, expiration will be incomplete and shallow; one does not breathe out completely in one breath, but in fractions, in steps as it were.[3]

Reich insisted that breathing is the primary regulator of energy and emotional aliveness. When we breathe more freely, in fact, we feel more fully alive, more able to cope with life. Moreover, different emotional expressions are characterized by different ways of breathing: "Pleasurable breathing is long and easy, grieving breathing is labored while angry breathing is short, sharp, and expulsive. We breathe deeply and fully in a sauna, and hard and fast after a long run, and fully and warmly during sex."[4]

General body posture is also a key element in revealing the inner person. If the head is thrust forward or the pelvis pulled back (retracted) or the legs locked tight at the knees, it tells us a lot about inner repression. As Reich himself observed in the 1940s, "In a state of anxious anticipation, one instinctively draws the shoulders forward and remains in a rigid attitude; sometimes the shoulders are pulled upward."[5] Another indicator of emotional state is gait or style of walking. If the shoulders are hunched up, it signifies that the person is frightened and ready to ward off an expected attack. The extent to which an individual moves in a relaxed, straightforward manner or keeps the shoulders erect and balanced with the ground is a measure of a healthy self. As we shall see in Chapter 5, contemporary forms of psychotherapy such as Bioenergetics have emphasized Reich's view that physical gracefulness is an important clue to the person's emotional well-being.

Still another significant indicator of inner state is vocal quality. All of us respond spontaneously to the sound of others' voices, independent of the specific meaning of their words. Reich found that the quality or emotional tone of the voice is often far more important to diagnosis than what is being said and is a basic indicator of emotional and physical well-being. He commented, "In the region of the head and face, the expressive peculiarities of speech are of particular significance. They are mostly the result of spasms in the musculature of the jaw and the throat. In two patients I found a violent defensive reaction which promptly appeared as soon as one, ever so gently, touched the region of the larynx. Both patients had fantasies of having their throats injured by being choked or cut."[6]

Confirming Reich's insight here on the relation of voice to personality, several studies (M. Friedman and R. H. Rosenman, 1959; R. H. Rosenman and M. Friedman, 1961; D. Glass, 1977) have suggested that we can determine the likelihood of an individual's susceptibility to heart disease simply by listening closely to his or her vocal quality. Tendencies to interrupt or complete the words of others or to speak too quickly are considered prominent indicators of the heart-attack-prone personality.

For decades, acting studios have relied on such insights in their training of aspiring thespians. A common method is to require the student to convey a variety of emotional meanings and nuances by saying a simple phrase, such as "It's raining," in different ways. Just as any competent actor can evoke emotions ranging from desperate passion to boredom to utter despair from such a phrase, each of us similarly and unthinkingly expresses emotional states by tones and inflections.

It was Reich's conclusion that the body has its own language, with its own vocabulary, syntax, and grammar, and that the astute observer can use these as a map of another's emotional makeup. But there is no quick and simple way to master this method. Popular accounts of body language are at best stimulating guides for real preparation; at worst, they are misleading and guilty of gross oversimplification. Reich wrote, "It is difficult to say what enables us to have such an immediate feeling of a person's body expression and to give adequate words to this feeling."[7]

Reich also pointed out that body language is highly personal in nature. He focused on the person's *overall* bodily expression or demeanor before concentrating on particular gestures. In other words, each individual's nonverbal messages are ultimately a reflection of his or her innermost thoughts and feelings. It is incorrect to simply label a specific gesture as representing one or another emotion without first coming to know that person. Many recent books on body language ignore this holistic view.

In recent years, anthropological and sociological research has pointed out something that Reich was apparently unaware of: body language is also cultural in nature. Some of the most well-known researchers include Drs. Ray Birdwhistell (*Kinesics and Context*, 1970), Seymour Fisher (*Body Experience in Fantasy and Behavior*, 1970), and Edward T. Hall (*The Hidden Dimension*, 1969; *Beyond Culture*, 1977). Studies carried out by these and other investigators indicate, for instance, that individuals in Mediterranean climates tolerate and accept more physical touching in daily life than those in Northern Europe. By the age of three or four, children are sensitive to the culture's unspoken rules for bodily contact and behavior. Children from different cultures exhibit significant differences in the amount of physical touching and bodily closeness expressed in their play. Most scientists researching this field believe that these findings reflect *learning* and are not intuitive or inborn. As Birdwhistell has commented, "This does not deny the biological base in the behavior but places the emphasis on the *interpersonal* rather than the *expressional* aspects of kinesic behavior."[8] That is, our bodily messages are constantly changing according to our activities and relationships with others. Although Reich did not deal with this particular cause of body language, he certainly recognized its reality.

THE "MUSCULAR" PERSONALITY

Another basic Reichian insight is that specific chronic muscular tensions relate to certain personality types. In various ways, many of us have gradually learned to keep strong emotions, such as anger, tightly locked within us. We chronically, and unconsciously, tense the appropriate muscles when upset by something we don't feel we should express.

Facial expressions are often the most revealing. The look in the eyes—beady, bulging, withdrawn, or vacant—is meaning-ful. Chronic tensions or lines around the eyes often suggest long-suppressed crying.

Reich's comments here are quite relevant and interesting.

> The facial expression *as a whole*—independently of the individual parts—has to be observed carefully. We know the depressed face of the melancholic patients. It is peculiar how the expression of flaccidity can be associated with a severe chronic tension of the musculature. There are people with an always artificially beam-ing face; there are stiff and sagging cheeks. Usually, the patients are able to find the corresponding expression themselves, if the attitude is repeatedly pointed out and described to them, or shown to them by imitating it.[9]

Some individuals display almost constant surprise by the lines of their foreheads and eyebrows. According to Reich, such an expression is a form of defensive reaction to inner psychic strain. The pencil-thin mouth, with lips tightly drawn, typically indicates someone who has learned since childhood to lock in-side many strong feelings. The voice of such persons, Reich found, was usually low, monotonous, or thin, another sign of suppressed emotionality, particularly the impulse to cry. "Chil-dren acquire such conditions often at a very early age," he commented, "when they are forced to suppress violent impulses to cry."[10] Another common facial expression indicative of emo-tional blocking is the "frozen smile," in which the mouth ap-pears to express happiness but the eyes reveal a joyless or cold interior.

Reich observed that chronic muscular tension or armoring in the abdominal region is often directly related to suppression of anger. "If one inquires about such behavior," he pointed out, "the patients will remember that, as children, they practiced this anger toward parents, siblings, or teachers. To be able to hold one's breath for a long time means a heroic feat of self-control."[11] Reich found that many patients unconsciously took in small, quick bursts of air to cut off the eruption of a deep feeling. This automatic "device" serves to abort strong feelings.

A common emotion suppressed by the abdominal muscles is that of longing, popularly expressed by the term "heartache."

When feeling loneliness or the loss of a loved one, many will experience a physical sensation of gnawing in the upper abdominal region. Those who have never felt this sensation, observed Reich, were usually "hard, cold, and ill-natured persons."[12]

Another example of how muscles are related to personality is the familiar military bearing or posture. Reich observed that in virtually all Western cultures, soldiers carried themselves "chest up, eyes front"—a supposed sign of emotional and physical toughness. Analyzing the personality type of such an individual, Reich commented:

> The military attitude is the complete opposite of the natural mobile attitude. The eyes must stare and appear empty. The neck must be kept stiff, the head stuck forward, chin and mouth must have a hard masculine appearance, the chest must be pushed out, the arms must be tensely beside the body, the hands must be stretched along the edge of the trousers, the stomach must be pulled in, and the pelvis must be pulled back. The legs are straight and hard.[13]

As part of body language, chronic muscular tensions are broad and interrelated. It is inappropriate to focus separately upon an individual body segment. "It is never a matter of individual muscles that become spastic but of muscle groups forming a functional unit," Reich noted.[14] When, for instance, we suppress an impulse to cry, not only does the lower lip become tense, but also the entire muscular system of the mouth and jaw, as well as the related musculature of the throat. In short, Reich argued, chronic repression of anger, sadness, anxiety, and other emotions typically involves an integrated, coherent system of muscles, not just one or two of them. These systems make up the character armor.

It should be noted that several of Reich's students, especially Drs. Elsworth Baker and Alexander Lowen, extended his analysis of the relationship of the armor to the individual's personality makeup. In his book, *Man in the Trap*, for instance, Baker provides a typology, or classification system, for understanding the nature of various kinds of emotional disturbance. One of the indicators of schizophrenia, for example, is seen as the presence of intense armoring around the eyes. Lowen, the founder of Bioenergetics, comments:

> The first feature which strikes the observor as odd about the appearance of the schizophrenic or schizoid individual is the look of his eyes. His eyes have been described as "off," "blank," "vacant," "out of touch," etc. This expression is so characteristic that it alone can be used to diagnose the presence of schizophrenia. . . . Wilhelm Reich, for instance, says that both the schizoid and schizophrenic personalities "have a typical *faraway* look of remoteness."[15]

In Chapter 5, we will discuss in some detail Reich's view of the segmental characteristic of the body armor and the most appropriate method of its dissolution. We will also examine the psychotherapies of both Baker and Lowen.

CHARACTER ARMORING AND LIFE'S BATTLES

In Reich's third major insight on the body's armoring, what surprised him was that his patients had little or no awareness of how their physical movements or "expressions" were actually communicating deep emotions. When so informed, some patients became extremely defensive, reacting with heated denial. Worse, others accepted the realization intellectually but responded with little feeling. Reich argued that intellectual comprehension has little therapeutic value in breaking down physical armoring.

Armor, explained Reich, is built up gradually. The armoring that develops in the early years next to the core of the organism is termed "primary" and is most difficult to get at. "Secondary" armoring develops as a result of the primary and is closer to the body surface. The knot of tension that leads to muscular armoring does not arise directly from a single traumatic experience but through repeated trauma, though certain intensely painful experiences such as the loss of a loved one may be extremely armoring if the attendant emotions are not fully discharged.

We store every significant conflict within ourselves. Reich likened these unresolved conflicts to "frozen history." If grief, anger, rage, fear, or apprehension is repeatedly blocked off or only minimally expressed, such chronic repressions affect the musculature of the shoulders, chest, neck, and other body parts, and so we begin to put on our suit of armor. It functions partly to hold in the unexpressed emotion and partly to help ward off the pain of similar experiences in the future. Armor then acts like a trap, preventing us from expressing spontaneous feelings, thwarting and then enraging us. It cuts us off from feeling inner sensations and reduces empathetic responses to other beings.

"This armor may be superficial or deep-lying, soft as a sponge or hard as nails. In each case its function was to protect against unpleasure," Reich declared. "However," he added, "the organism paid for this protection by losing a great deal of its capacity for pleasure."[16] He added, "The energy which held the armor together consisted mostly in destructiveness which had become bound."[17]

When, during therapy, the armor is experienced and slowly dissolved (Reich's methods are discussed in Chapter 5), intense emotions, long pent-up and forgotten, are invariably released. "Whenever I dissolved a muscular inhibition or tension," related Reich, "one of the three basic biological excitations made its appearance: anxiety, anger, or sexual excitation."[18] Many contemporary therapists report the same finding: when muscular armor is touched in a deep way, old memories, typically of a highly charged nature, break loose. It is important that a trained therapist be on hand, for the sudden appearance of such long-buried memories can be highly disturbing. Indeed, their emergence, if quite sudden, may cause more harm than if they were left dormant. Imagine someone who never really mourned the death of a beloved parent during childhood; suddenly, twenty or thirty years later, the original intense feelings of loss and abandonment erupt, seemingly out of nowhere: extreme panic ensues.

So, throughout his life, Reich emphasized the necessity for *gradual* dissolution of the armor. To point out to someone that her rigid neck and shoulder muscles or tight pelvis reveal armoring and intense emotional suppression is intellectually enlightening but unhelpful. To press and poke around such armored spots just to arouse a dramatic discharge can be downright dangerous. There are no easy shortcuts to remove emotional-

physical armoring; the repressed emotions have to be emotionally and physically re-experienced and discharged effectively in
a slow, step-by-step fashion if great harm is not to occur. One
vivid description of this kind of patient reaction was provided by
Reich himself, in his presentation of a case history.

> During one of the following sessions, the patient had a severe
> anxiety attack. He suddenly sat up with a painfully distorted
> mouth; his forehead was covered with perspiration; his whole
> musculature was tense . . . he emitted sounds which seemed to
> come out of his chest, "as if without vocal chords," he said later.
> He had the feeling that somebody was coming dangerously close
> to him and was threatening him. . . . After this, he calmed down,
> and in the following hours we worked it through.[19]

As an individual's armor is slowly and painstakingly dissolved,
profound changes begin to occur. The senses are gradually
sharpened, sensitized to new dimensions or vitality, pleasure,
and excitement. As armor is loosened, music, scents, and colors
seem more intense, because hearing, smelling, and seeing are all
diminished by armoring. Simple physical acts, like breathing or
walking, become pleasurable. And, most curiously and strikingly, Reich observed that his patients began to gradually perceive our society's dominant attitudes toward such things as
sexuality and love, social relations, and even work as often
hypocritical or stifling. Social relationships or jobs that had been
accepted as routine and mechanical were no longer bearable.
Patients with no social awareness or interest in politics quite
spontaneously began to question assumptions of the society
that they had previously taken for granted.

Soon after this discovery, Reich began to shift his focus from
strictly clinical, psychoanalytical concerns. He increasingly realized that his patients were not alone in being grossly out of
touch with their bodily needs and impulses. Armed with his
method of character analysis for observing and interpreting
body language, he began to observe that multitudes of men and
women throughout Europe bore the same types of armoring as
seen in his clinic.

He thus began to argue that pervasive deadening of the body
is sociological rather than individual. The pressing question was

why so many people experience so little physical pleasure. Beginning in the 1930s, Reich argued that individual armoring isn't restricted to one social class or to the members of one culture. Rather, he concluded that chronic bodily tensions and character armoring are virtually universal.

In other words, modern industrial society as a whole cripples our sense of aliveness. Social dictates devalue the body and suppress its needs. During the early 1930s, Reich saw capitalist society as the primary cause of mass armoring, but later in his career he viewed its origins as predating the capitalist era. He insisted, though, that the existing social structure has a strong interest in maintaining the anxieties, tensions, and repressions of its members. The basic concerns of modern technological society are achieving efficient production and maintaining the stability of its institutions. To keep this vast social machinery functioning, Reich contended, people are programed to accept living in a half-dead state. If they were truly alive they would refuse to go along with most of the routine activities of the system. Reich saw modern civilization as the symptom and cause of human armoring. He proclaimed that the only real solution to its deadening effects is its total transformation.

But, Reich stressed, the change has to come from within the structure, for were it to be imposed by an elite, the repercussions would be destructive. He pointed to the Russian Revolution as a prime example of how changes imposed externally fail to work. The early days of freedom soon gave way to "red fascism." "Our freedom peddlers soon and easily become freedom robbers," Reich noted.[20] Until the masses are psychologically prepared to take responsibility for their own armoring, legislated social changes will have little benefit. Shortcuts can be traps. Group or individual therapy, despite its achievements, is not the answer. In fact, our culture imposes so many restrictions and taboos on vital living and experience that even those who have undergone prolonged Reichian therapy often find themselves redeveloping their armor.

Reich eventually argued that only over a long historical period, certainly spanning decades at the very least, could mass society be expected to surrender much of its armoring. The real hope lay in protecting infants and children from the pervasive effects of the larger society, he believed. In this manner, we would not need to develop the armor that we encase around us to minimize the countless indignities of twentieth-century urban life.

PLEASURE AVOIDANCE

Reich declared that many of us possess an actual fear of pleasure because of inhibitions formed in childhood and adolescence. He observed: "When its course is inhibited, pleasure has the characteristic of turning into unpleasure. When in spite of continual very high sexual excitation, a person is not capable of experiencing final gratification, a fear eventually develops not only of the final gratification but also of the excitation which precedes it."[21]

In another form we see this in armored adults who are unable to tolerate the natural exuberance of unarmored children. The children's open, spontaneous, noisy outbursts of emotionality and happiness make such adults nervous and edgy, and their typical reaction is to stifle the children's pleasurable excitement or get away from the scene.

Similarly, heavily armored persons cannot tolerate intense excitement in their own bodies and unconsciously seek to release or abort such mounting sensations before they reach a natural peak. Here the armoring acts to keep strong emotional and sexual needs fundamentally unfulfilled.

In many people, fear of pleasure is associated with feelings of discomfort or even hatred toward certain parts of their bodies. Clinical studies show that men often feel inadequate about the size of their penis; women typically believe that their breasts and hips are either too large or too small. As Reich observed, dissatisfaction with our body images is not surprising, given the false values endemic in our society. Advertisers and the mass media exploit these notions, preying upon our insecurity about our physical appearance. From products to personalities, they convince us that our supposed inadequacies can somehow be overcome by the right mixture of colorings and scents, or that we cannot be happy or sexually successful without possessing the physical attributes of certain celebrities.

In fact, studies (Kleck, Richardson, and Ronald, 1974; Richardson and Friedman, 1973; Staffieri, 1967, 1972) indicate that by the age of eight or nine most children have already begun to acquire a predominantly negative view of their bodies while accepting stereotypes of idealized body images. Patently, perfectionist and fantasy-laden images of what our bodies should look like inhibit us from enjoying ourselves fully. It seems reasonable to suppose that as children sense their failure to live up to cultural ideals of physical beauty, they subtly withdraw awareness from their bodies and thus develop the first stages of armoring.

THE CHILDHOOD FORGE

A good deal of Reich's study of armoring in infancy and childhood took place in the 1940s, when his son Peter was growing up. At that time, he began seminars at his farm in Maine for professionals concerned with the care and education of young children. He also established a small child-care program through which he hoped to expand his theoretical research. At one point, he invited A. S. Neill to direct the proposed children's center, but Neill declined, on the grounds that it would make him into a disciple rather than a friend.

Reich traces the beginning of armoring as far back as the prenatal period. He felt that the fetus was inevitably affected by the shifting moods, suppressed conflicts, and more permanent emotional characteristics of the mother. The more tense she is, the more likely her baby will be born fretful and illness-prone. Through the hormonal system, emotional upsets in the mother may be passed along to the fetus; in addition, tense or troubled mothers may resort to excessive use of tobacco, alcohol, or other drugs to alleviate emotional strain. These chemicals may harm the unborn, since they pass through the placenta into the fetal bloodstream.

Reich was also a caustic critic of modern hospital delivery practices. He condemned the traditional separation of mother and infant immediately after birth—with the mother often sedated into unconsciousness—as a heavily armoring experience for the newborn. No other mammal would tolerate such separation. In his later years, he came to view the birth process as a most critical period of early development, and insisted, "This world will not change as long as the adults cannot cease to let their own deadness take effect on the still unspoiled plasma system of the infant."[22]

As early as the 1940s, Reich analyzed in detail the destructiveness of hospital delivery-room practices. In tones of outrage, he described at length—in *Ether, God and Devil*—the baby's screams and the unfeeling reaction of hospital personnel to the "massacre of the newborn." He claimed that both mother and infant are armored by the cold sterility of an experience that forces the mother into the helpless, sick-patient role, when instead she could be undergoing one of the most intensely gratifying and spiritual experiences of her life. As anthropologist Ashley Montagu and others later emphasized, separating the newborn from its mother, just when it most needs her close, reassuring embrace, is a very armoring experience. Reich insisted that the newborn is very much adversely affected by such treatment:

> The concept of the "autism of the infant," of his "being withdrawn into himself," is widespread. Nevertheless it is *erroneous:* the autism of the infant is an *artifact* resulting from the behavior of the adults; it is *artificially produced* by the strict isolation of the infant and by the character armoring of the persons who take care of the child. . . . It is understandable that the infant will not reach out toward the world if the environment does not meet him with alive warmth but only with rigid rules and spurious behavior.[23]

Besides viewing the dominant hospital delivery-room practices as contributors to early armoring, Reich also believed that armoring occurs even at the prenatal stage. Specifically, he emphasized that the more emotionally alive the pregnant mother, the healthier the environment that is provided for the fetus. As he stated in *The Cancer Biopathy*, "Not only is the circulation of blood and body fluids more complete, the energy metabolism [is] more rapid in a strongly orgonotic uterus. . . . Thus it becomes understandable why the children of orgastically potent women are so much more vital than those of frigid and armored women."[24] In other words, women who experience deep sensual pleasure during pregnancy, Reich suggested, are likely to have a more vital flow of the life energy, which, in turn, would contribute to greater fetal well-being. In Chapter 6, we will explore Reich's orgone energy theory in some detail.

In recent years, the theme of natural childbirth has been expounded upon most persuasively by the French obstetrician Frederic LeBoyer, author of the widely selling *Birth Without Violence*. His own special method involves total silence during the birth, a minimum of light, close physical contact between mother and child, a warm bath, and the gradual, slow-paced introduction of the child to the world around it.

Another major source of early armoring results from a lack of breast-feeding. Back in the 1940s, Reich boldly argued that we would one day recognize the profound emotional *and* physical benefits of breast-feeding. The healthy mother finds the experience to be extremely gratifying, almost erotic in nature; the infant's urgent, intense sucking at the breast is deeply pleasurable and contributes to its development of a sense of trust and love. Reich also believed that breast-feeding can lead to a vibrancy and glow in the infant's face, especially around the mouth. In fact, infants who enjoy the breast may experience an oral orgasm, indicated by involuntary quivering of the lips. However, the mother must also enjoy the experience. If she engages in it out of obligation, her lack of pleasure is communicated to the infant, who will gradually withdraw.

Alice Gerard highlights the physical benefits of breast-feeding in *Please Breastfeed Your Baby*, noting the nutritional superiority of breast milk to cow's milk and formulas, the presence of immunizing antibodies in mother's milk, and the way in which vigorous sucking on the breast aids proper development of the child's teeth and jaw. Ashley Montagu, synthesizing the latest research on breast-feeding and its advantages, emphasizes the great emotional importance of bonding between mother and child, the advantages to the mother of immediately taking the infant to the breast, and the superiority of home to hospital deliveries. Other research has recently shown rather conclusively that children who are breast-fed are less susceptible to allergies and certain other health problems.

Though it is more difficult to determine scientifically the emotional effects of the breast-feeding experience for the infant, there is a growing literature, vividly discussed by Margaret Mead, Montagu, and others, that suggests the benefits are powerful and long-lasting. Thus, support of Reich's insights is growing.

Another cause of sensual deadening is the institution of the classroom. From the age of five or six each child is required to sit at a desk for hours at a time. Physical movements are restricted to a minimum. There is little opportunity for children to engage in exercise and release pent-up tensions in a healthy manner. It is no wonder, then, that today's schools are marked by so much wild and unmanageable behavior among children.

The school curriculum itself provides little opportunity for children to learn how to channel their emotions. Nor are children taught how to pay attention to the subtle messages of their bodies. In fact, from the first grade on, many children are taught to ignore their physical impulses and to sit as quietly as possible.

Moreover, the curriculum traditionally bypasses intensely emotional subjects. Sex education remains an unwanted addition, at best, to daily academic training. Even then, it is reduced to anatomical lectures about "what goes where." The emotional aspects of sexuality and love are almost totally avoided, despite the fact that this is what youngsters really want and need to learn.

The competitiveness of the typical classroom, in some ways a miniature version of the adult society, further armors children against their feelings of caring and affection. As Reich has stated, "Education serves the purposes of the social order at any given time. If this social order contradicts the interests of the child, then education must leave the child out of consideration."[25]

Perhaps one vivid example of the way in which schools help develop childhood armoring is in the traditional physical-education curriculum. Differing radically from the Greek ideal of mind and body complementing one another, physical education in our schools has been relegated to occasional monotonous calisthenics and competitive team sports, often conducted in a quasimilitary atmosphere. Children are frequently required to march in unison, rather than being given free rein to express the rhythms of their own bodies. Some adults shun all types of physical exercise partly because of their forced participation in its unpleasurable form as children. Similarly, many adults who do exercise regularly cannot conceive of vigorous physical activity unless it is competitive in nature. When Reich insisted that modern men and women are grossly out of touch with their bodies, he did not view competitive team sports as the antidote.

Above all, Reich identified the family as the most significant source of childhood and adolescent armoring. He noted that not only do most parents provide their children with too little physical affection, like hugging and caressing, but that many adults, probably unconsciously, suppress their children's desires for emotional and physical intimacy because they are unable to tolerate it in themselves. So their armoring prevents them from satisfying their children's innate need for affection. The tragedy is that after a certain period of time, an infant no longer expects that his or her longing to be held or caressed will be noticed and fulfilled. As Reich observed:

> The contact of the mother with the infant is governed not by language but by the motor expression; the adult perceives the infant's motor expression. ... If the adult's own motor expression functions well, he will also comprehend the infant's expression. If, on the other hand, he is armored, hard in his character, pleasure-shy, or otherwise inhibited, then his understanding of the infant is severely limited, which will inevitably impair the emotional development of the child in various ways.[26]

The key here is the adult's ability to *feel* and react spontaneously to the infant's unspoken emotional needs. Reich maintained that adult suppression of children's interest in sex games or masturbation is an early contributor to armoring; it is equally damaging when children are taught or obliged to stifle natural impulses to cry or get angry.

With the birth of his son Peter in 1944, Reich sought to carry his ideas into practice. From Peter's first days of life, his father was convinced that the baby exhibited very real signs of desires for communication and novelty. The key issue in responsiveness to the boy, Reich came to believe, was the ability to "read" the nonverbal messages constantly displayed by the infant. This was no easy matter, Reich initially discovered, but he soon gained confidence in his capacity to do so.

After childhood, we are loosed upon the workplace. Reich singled out the world of work as an important source of armoring. Most individuals in our society are raised to value competition as the means to achievement and self-satisfaction, an emphasis that has been viewed by various critics, such as Montagu, as especially damaging to men in our society (and recently to career women). It takes its toll in different ways. It may help explain the fact that men's life span in the West is nearly seven years less than women's. In Chapter 8 we shall examine in some detail Reich's concept of work democracy, which he advocated as an alternative to the extreme competitiveness and lack of cooperation in the business world.

Yet, despite the influence of the workplace, Reich emphasized the importance of childhood and adolescence as the stages of life in which our aliveness is most critically affected. Regardless of the tensions in adulthood, Reich believed, those who have had a truly healthy, emotionally satisfying, and physically gratifying childhood can remain closely in touch with their feelings and their awareness of others. Conversely, as Reich never ceased to stress, therapy for adults requires imagination and hard work to overcome the chronic armoring begun in childhood or adolescence. While not totally discounting the usefulness of such therapy, a disillusioned Reich believed that "once a tree is bent, it cannot be made straight again." In a word, therapeutic success is bound to depend on the patient's age and degree of armoring.

For Reich, the family provides the best "therapy." The ideal family is one in which all natural emotions are expressed and communicated directly. Anger and hostility are as legitimate as caring, excitement, or laughter. In such a free family, Reich felt, children would learn a respect for their own feelings and bodily impulses as well as for those of others. In turn, they would mature and come to tolerate, perhaps even cherish, such qualities in their own children. A fascinating book by architect Paul Ritter, *The Free Family*, discusses how this works in practice. As few of us are blessed with even relatively unarmored parents, we reach adulthood with emotional and physical blocks. We often acquire the negative attitudes toward physical pleasure that our parents were taught by *their* parents. We have obviously not yet reached the day when, in Reich's vision, "human faces on the street will express freedom, animation, and joy, and no longer sadness and misery."[27]

TOWARD THE SURRENDER TO PLEASURE

Still, we may be approaching that day. There is a lively trend toward greater respect for and acceptance of the body. More men and women are able to hug their friends, and some churches are instituting the practice of a physical embrace as part of worship. Increasing numbers of us are participating in vigorous exercise. Health clubs are now widespread in the cities, making exercise respectable and providing the physical pleasures of saunas, steam baths, Jacuzzis, and massage.

Though Reich himself died before much of the evidence became known, we are now aware that physical hazards in the work environment threaten the health of both body and mind. These hazards include the unhealthy effects of air conditioning, fluorescent lighting, and overheated offices as well as more subtle and less understood forces, such as microwaves and an overabundance of positive ions. A great deal of evidence, too, has been accumulated on the hazardous effects of prolonged noise and monotony, as well as a bewildering array of carcinogenic and toxic chemicals, ingested through both touch and breathing in factories or mines. The battle for adequate protection from carcinogenic and other health-destroying substances accords more importance to the body than previously. Unions, in fact, are placing as much importance on physical safety and long-term health as they traditionally attached to salary and job security. Not only the factory but the office will be affected as well. Perhaps one day we will see detailed labor contracts specifying adequate negative ion concentration, lighting, and fresh air.

We already see a great awakening in our awareness of diet and its effects upon our health and vigor. Reich failed to stress the role of nutrition in bodily aliveness; in fact, A. S. Neill often argued with him on this issue. People now discriminate more between nutritious and "junk" foods, and there is an emerging trend within public schools to ensure that fresh fruits and vegetables are available. The rise in consumption of noncaffeinated beverages, such as herbal teas, suggests that we are slowly learning to avoid the traditional abuse-the-body syndrome.

Jogging represents another positive trend. It is teaching many of us the value of strenuous exercise and the pleasure of a strong body. It may also help alleviate some chest armoring. In fact, some observers suggest that it can produce an almost "peak" experience, as the intense deep breathing promotes a brief transcendence of the conscious ego. On the other hand, jogging can be simply another way of driving the body to perform beyond its limits. Clearly, Reich would prescribe a gradual jogging program, one that is an enjoyment rather than a "pursuit."

Another positive trend is the growing interest in natural childbirth among many thoughtful couples. In a major shift away from old-style hospital deliveries, pregnant women are taking courses to prepare themselves for childbirth with little or no anesthetic. Husbands are being allowed into the delivery room to assist and support their wives during childbirth and to share directly in its joyous moments. The LeBoyer or Lamaze method, emphasizing close physical contact between mother and infant after delivery, is gaining in popularity. Increasingly, health professionals themselves argue that a maximum of physical closeness and a minimum of chemical influences on the delivery are the best means of assuring a healthy, vibrant child.

In American education today, there are some hopeful signs of a greater respect among professionals for the bodily pleasure of children and adolescents. One trend has been in the field of physical education, where there is a greater emphasis than ever before on sports that develop grace and physical sensitivity, such as acrobatics. Rather than intensely competitive and media-oriented games, students in many school systems now have the opportunity to participate in "New Games," a rapidly expanding collection of activities designed to promote cooperation. No doubt the continued impact of the women's movement in the schools has helped to generate much of this new involvement. Under the prod, too, of recent federal legislation (Public Law 94-142) to protect the educational rights of handicapped children, more and more physical educators are embracing forms of noncompetitive and body-enhancing exercise. The kind of classes that many of us were subjected to, in which gymnastics were taught in a military-drill atmosphere, may soon be a relic of the past.

Within increasing numbers of families today, children experience a good deal more bodily freedom than in earlier generations. To be sure, the collapse of the nuclear family, accurately predicted by Reich more than forty years ago, has imposed many emotional strains on children, and has unquestionably induced armoring on a wide scale. However, Reich believed that a social transition from the old patriarchal family system to a more egalitarian system was inevitable. He would no doubt be gratified to witness the growing recognition of the legitimacy of children's desires for physical pleasure. Having been exposed to countercultural values during their own youth in the 1960s, many of today's parents are also eager to savor such enjoyment. We know personally of many parents who regularly participate in such activities as hatha yoga and tai chi with their children.

We believe that Reich would also be encouraged to see these forms of exercise, as well as such others as aikido and modern dance, gaining popularity throughout the society. All of these are noncompetitive, enhance physical grace, and are physically pleasurable. The active meditation program of Indian guru Shree Bhagwan Rajneesh, who now has numerous centers in North America, is especially liberating; its shaking and dancing contribute to the loosening of the armor.

In his later years Reich realized the necessity of slow, gradual change. He insisted that rapid social changes are dangerous, as they may precipitate a sudden breakdown of armoring during which long pent-up inner impulses can too easily rush out. He called this tendency "freedom giddiness" and argued that it occurs "in children as well as in adults who are too suddenly transplanted from an environment that functions entirely in accordance with principles of armoring into an environment relying on natural principles of self-regulation."[28] He emphasized that "if today or tomorrow the authoritarian state organization were suddenly abolished . . . chaos, not freedom, would result."[29] Reich believed that as our children are raised in a more free, body-accepting family and culture, they will grow up with more healthy attitudes and behavior that will in turn be passed on to their children. This is the basis of our hope for a better future.

CHAPTER 4

Pioneer in Holistic Health

All that brain surgery, all that stuff, the chemistry racket business—no good. That's medicine of the past.

There is a unity between body and mind. I followed this track and I found that you reach out with your life energy when you feel well and loving, and that you retract it to the center of your body when you are afraid.

—WILHELM REICH

I t has become almost a truism to say that mainstream medicine is under fire today. Both the methods and the underlying philosophy of conventional health care are being challenged, even by physicians themselves. The medical profession, in the past accorded the highest respect, admiration, and at times awe, is now seen in a very different light.

Several social barometers reflect this tremendous change in attitude. One indicator is the phenomenal rise in malpractice litigation. Another is the steady stream of books, magazine articles, and news programs analyzing the "crisis in medicine" and its alternative, holistic health care. Such accounts describe how the rise in medical costs far exceeds the rate of inflation. Others criticize basic concepts and techniques of modern medicine and argue that it is grossly expensive, not very effective, and often detrimental.

Defenders of the system argue that good professional care is not cheap, that no ethical physician knowingly prescribes unnecessary or potentially hazardous treatment, and that by no stretch of the imagination do health professionals regard themselves as infallible. They charge that many of the alternatives to dominant practices are dangerous or fraudulent. They further argue that the apparent increase in many diseases, such as cancer or high blood pressure, is largely the result of better diagnostic tools, not wider prevalence.

In the midst of this controversy, the life and work of Wilhelm Reich shine as a clear beacon for the medicine and healing of a future that is almost upon us now. Decades ago, he engaged in extensive groundbreaking research on psychosomatic medicine. He related individual health to emotional makeup and lifestyle and urged the adoption of a natural medicine emphasizing the body's ability to heal itself. As far back as the early 1940s, he condemned medicine's overriding emphasis on needle-and-pill methods of treatment. "We must give up the air germ theory and recognize *endogenous* [originating from within] *infection*," he declared.[1] Reich flatly predicted that one day this system would be laid to rest as obsolete. Now, more than twenty years after his imprisonment on charges that included medical quackery, Reich emerges in many ways as a prophetic figure in medical care. Indeed, Reich claimed that his theory and research would help slay our medical behemoth.

Reich's brilliant insights into the nature of health and illness followed soon after his earlier discoveries relating to body language and its analysis, gathering momentum in the 1930s and 1940s. While still in Scandinavia, he began his first research into the nature of cancer, which was to occupy much of his thinking in the ensuing years. Reich's productivity in this field is remarkable in that he was almost literally "on the run" during the 1930s, fleeing the growing menace of fascism in Germany, Austria, and Scandinavia, before arriving in the United States as a political refugee. In 1939 he landed in New York to start his most stable, productive period, but within a decade he again found himself under surveillance, this time from the Food and Drug Administration of the United States government.

During those decades, he formed innovative hypotheses on the causes of modern noninfectious diseases, delivering his pronouncements in his characteristically fiery, impatient style. His theories on the link between illness and emotional factors had little scientific evidence to back them up at the time, and while Reich occasionally conceded this, he insisted that the alarming increase in illnesses such as heart disease and cancer necessitated a new approach. For decades a solid body of information has been accumulating on the subject of emotions and health, and, along with many other medical and scientific researchers, Reich has made his contribution.

THE MIND OF THE BODY

Reich gave voice to a basic tenet of holistic health when he declared, "Every living organism is a functional unit. It is not simply a mechanical sum total of organs."[2] Mind and body are not separate or parallel to one another, but constitute a unity. Every moment of our lives, both waking and sleeping, our emotions affect our organs, musculature, and hormonal processes, and vice versa. Every experience we undergo leaves some residue in our bodies, and every unexpressed feeling continue to exist within us. In sum, character and body are fully interdependent. We are neither "all spirit" nor "all mind," Reich declared.

He criticized mainstream medicine for its dualist philosophy, which views mind and body as wholly separate entities and relegates the treatment of emotions to the narrow purview of orthodox psychiatry. While physicians are aware that patients have emotions, their standard medical-school training generally discounts the role of emotions in health or illness. The medical eye has applied itself to the minute labeling and detailing of bodily structures, and yet the field as a whole is myopic to the individual's mind-body unity.

The reason for this, Reich maintained, is that modern medicine is entranced with technology and what he termed the "mechanistic" model of health. "The mechanistic and purely materialistic concepts of medicine of today have to be partly replaced and partly overcome by a functional concept," Reich declared.[3]

What Reich termed "functional" illnesses are those in which emotions play a major role. To understand and cure such illnesses as heart disease, asthma, arthritis, or even cancer, Reich believed, it is absolutely essential for physicians to be familiar with emotions and how they are suppressed or distorted. Studies of organic structures, no matter how thorough, can only provide a partial picture of the dimensions of health or disease. Reich argued that dominant medicine and health education, as they were officially taught, did not really understand the living organism. The emphasis on quantification and statistics was detrimental, he argued. "I speak of life processes, and not of the number of red blood corpuscles."[4]

Reich became convinced that medicine's emphasis upon "air germs" as the cause of most diseases was no longer valid. In *The Cancer Biopathy* he insisted, "The air germ theory is not only experimentally shown to be erroneous. It is not only incapable of explaining central phenomena of biology and pathology; more than that, it obfuscates a true comprehension of disease mechanisms. It is a dogma which, like all dogmata, saves one thinking and searching."[5] Reich noted that modern medicine was based almost soley on the early discoveries of the so-called microbe hunters of the latter part of the nineteenth century, like Louis Pasteur and Robert Koch. They had brilliantly pinpointed the causes of such serious illnesses as smallpox, typhoid, malaria, and tuberculosis. The identification of certain microorganisms as the primary cause of such diseases quickly made possible appropriate vaccinations. Once understood, these diseases could be overcome through the eradication of breeding grounds such as swamps or heaps of decaying garbage. As a result of this approach, which Reich readily applauded, once-dread diseases were either eliminated or greatly reduced in scale.

However, in the twentieth century, a new set of diseases began to ravage humankind, particularly in the most technologically advanced nations. High blood pressure, arthritis, hypertension, heart disease, and cancer have now become virtually epidemic. Pointing to statistics that showed that while infectious diseases had sharply decreased, new, noninfectious illnesses like heart disease and cancer were on the rise, Reich stated:

> These figures show not only that the biopathies are *fundamentally* different from the nonbiopathic diseases, but also that they are *not* understood. Mechanistic medicine, lacking a sex-economic orientation, has no access to the biopathies. . . . They have essentially a social causation and are, basically, diseases resulting from . . . [a] disturbed economy of the biological energy.[6]

By *biopathies,* Reich referred to degenerative diseases, whose basic cause, he felt, was chronic malfunctioning of the body's biological energies. Such diseases, Reich argued, could not be understood in the same light as infectious, bacterially caused illnesses. In fact, he claimed, their development is largely attributable to the patient's emotional makeup and lifestyle, not to outside "germ agents." As we shall see in Chapter 6, Reich believed that both physical and emotional well-being stem from a steady, even pulsation of this energy in all body organs. When this energy flow is blocked in some way, illness results.

Reich also emphasized that the etiology of infectious diseases such as typhoid or tuberculosis was not as simple as it had appeared in the days of Pasteur or Koch; susceptibility to such illnesses was intimately related to the overall emotional-physical health of the individual. It was well known even in Reich's time, for example, that many people could be exposed and never develop the disease, some persons would succumb very quickly to bacterial infections, and others would become ill more slowly.

Reich argued that our basic "constitution" is really the critical determinant of whether we develop a cold, influenza, or worse. This susceptibility encompasses both emotional and physical factors. Thus, the individual's characteristic emotional state is one determinant of whether foreign microorganisms will multiply or be repelled by the body's natural defenses. Reich stated:

> Fortunately, the view begins to prevail in medicine that specific "microorganisms" and specific "causes" can become effective

only if the organism permits it. Tubercle bacilli, for example, can affect the organism only if it affects certain conditions of bioenergy. . . . *Disposition to disease is determined by the nature and the extent of the emotional—or orgonotic—motility of the organism.*[7]

The medical field has slowly acknowledged that illnesses are not just statistical accidents or "something going around." As most of us know intuitively, we are more likely to develop a chill or fever after a particularly stressful week or during a personal crisis of some sort. No matter how widespread an influenza epidemic is, some people will remain in perfect health; conversely, in the mildest winter, when nearly everyone feels energetic and alive, some will develop protracted head colds or respiratory infections. As Reich himself said in explaining this theory: "It is a great relief to be able to give the medical term 'disposition' a concrete content, to learn to understand why one individual suffers from frequent colds while another does not; why only certain individuals fall victim to an epidemic and others not; why one individual dies of cancer or hypertension and others not."[8]

Indeed, as we shall see later in this chapter, there is now a body of extremely convincing research clarifying the impact of stressful life events upon health. In recent decades, some of the chief investigators have included Dr. Hans Selye of the University of Montreal and Dr. Thomas Holmes and his associates at the University of Washington. Reich emphasized that, in general, the more emotionally integrated and satisfying our lives, the less likely we will be to develop persistent or chronic ailments.

Reich believed that anyone who typically suppresses his or her emotions runs the risk of serious health consequences. Most modern degenerative diseases, he argued, originate in these longstanding patterns of emotional deadening, which begin to create subtle bodily tensions. And the insomnia, tension, or depression that results is perhaps eased, but not erased, by tranquilizers. The only means of relieving such tensions, Reich believed, is their full emotional-physical expression. "We must fully accept the role of emotions in organic diseases,"[9] he declared, emphasizing that the impact of chronic emotional deadening is gradual, paralleling the slow onset of many modern diseases.

A heart attack or stroke does not "suddenly happen." Until the emergence of holistic medicine, Reich's insight that such illnesses have antecedents dating far back into one's life was seldom recognized. Reich argued that our dispositions are established during the first few years of life. In infancy and childhood, we form particular ways of reacting to tension-producing situations, and these patterns remain deeply embedded in both our character and our body armor. It is really only through intensive therapy, Reich believed, that such behavioral patterns can be effectively altered. For instance, Reich suggested that both schizophrenia and cancer have their roots in the first weeks of infancy, the critical factor in each instance being the quality of the mother-child relationship.

Reich pinpointed the physiological mediator between environment and the appearance of disease as the nature of the individual's breathing. "To an increasing extent, the chronic disturbances of biological functioning undermine respiration and pulsation in the tissues."[10] Respiration, which ensures an adequate supply of oxygen to the blood and tissues, and pulsation, which Reich noted constitutes the fundamental process of life itself, are basic to our overall health. Disrupt their normal operation and the person's overall vitality will eventually suffer. In other words, the more emotionally tense or unfulfilled the individual, Reich believed, the worse the integrity of his or her breathing. This would inevitably lead to a decrease in the health of body tissues. Reich stated, "Organs with poor respiration . . . are biologically weakened."[11]

Reich also stressed that accumulated emotional suppression contributes in another important way to illness. "The body armor makes inaccessible the basic organ sensations, and with them a genuine feeling of well-being," he aptly observed.[12] The heavily armored person is likely to develop a serious disease later in life, through both self-destructive means of coping with chronic pent-up feelings and insensitivity to the body's messages: when to rest, sleep or engage in vigorous exercise.

Reich warned that unless we have vividly experienced a sense of physical well-being, we will not be aware that certain chronic tensions or emotional strains can be triggers to disease. And the less able we are to "hear" our body's inner voice, the greater the likelihood of pushing the body beyond its optimal limits, creating the potential for illness.

IN SICKNESS AND IN HEALTH

Another of Reich's valuable insights was that modern medicine has lost sight of what *health* is in its obsession with treating *disease*. Health, for Reich, always comprised both emotional and physical aspects. He maintained that medical professionals need to be aware of general indicators of health and that blood tests, X-rays, and other technological diagnostic devices are often of limited use. "Before trying to treat disease, we must first comprehend health," he declared.[13]

For Reich, the visible signs of health are a relaxed, relatively armor-free musculature, with good posture and muscles capable of alternating tension and relaxation; a warm skin with good turgor, capable of producing warm perspiration; a lively and variable facial expression; and a regular, quiet, strong pulse. Healthy individuals are able to breathe fully and deeply. Their eyes are bright and alert, with lively pupillary reactions, and the eyeballs are neither protruding nor sunken. Their blood will show taut, pulsating erythrocytes (red blood cells). Above all, these persons will feel emotionally and physically strong and able to experience sensual pleasure emotionally, without guilt.

There are other emotional indicators of good health. These include the capacity for regular sexual orgasm, free of anxieties; the ability to perform work in a satisfying, productive way; and, particularly, the capacity for close, loving relationships with others—spouse, parent, children, friends. Reich insisted, for example, that those who for one reason or another are incapable of achieving intimacy with others run a higher probability of eventually developing some form of serious illness.

In terms of sex, Reich is often misunderstood and misinterpreted. He did not wish to imply that sexual potency by itself is the single, absolute measure of an individual's mental and physical health. Rather, he emphasized, what is essential is the ability to give and receive love in all its forms. During the sexual act itself, Reich indicated, the presence of the *orgasm reflex* was an important sign that the individual was free from significant armoring and able to surrender completely to natural body movements. But in his later writings, such as *The Murder of Christ*, published in 1953, he made it clear that the capacity to love fully had little to do with popular concerns about achieving potency through the right techniques or displaying one's prowess through sexual athletics.

Reich was quick to caution that the indicators listed above were not hard-and-fast rules for evaluating health; one must always take into account the individual's particular makeup and life history. In his tart, analytic style, he predicted that if his ideas were latched onto simplistically and implemented without serious thought,

> The constant, patient struggle for improvement of *health*, based on carefully drawn experiences, will be replaced by the idea of a "perfect," ready-made "Health" as an absolute ideal with a new social stratification into "healthy" and "neurotic" people. Physicians and philosophers, to judge from past distortions, will probably establish a new virtue, the perfect ideal of *"freedom of emotion"* which will then harass human interrelations. Rage will have no reason nor rational direction.[14]

Another of Reich's conclusions, basic to the holistic-health movement, is that each of us must assume direct responsibility for our own health. Too many persons, Reich believed, are raised in anxiety-ridden, authoritarian families in which they never learn to take much responsibility for anything. First as children and then as adults, they indulge themselves by overeating, consuming harmful substances, and otherwise disregarding their bodies. Then they suddenly "fall ill."

The "disease" identified by the physician is only the most visible physical aspect of these individuals' chronic neglect of their emotional and physical needs. They then expect their physicians to somehow "make them well" with a few pills. Some doctors, of course, help to perpetuate this dependency by denying their patients specific, detailed information about the nature of their illnesses and by minimizing the role the patients must play in overcoming self-destructive life habits. Reich always told his patients that they were responsible for regaining health and wholeness by altering their lifestyle. During the 1940s, Reich wrote, "You come running to me and ask me: 'My good, dear, great Doctor! What should I do? . . . My child and my wife are sick, and so am I. What should I do?' . . . The answer is . . . listen to what is in you."[15]

Personal responsibility entails a healthy skepticism toward all artificial means of "cure." Reich was never very much impressed with the needle-and-pill emphasis of modern medicine. Decades before Western society would reach the point where almost 225 tablets of aspirin are consumed by the average American per year, or when 19 percent of American women swallow a prescribed tranquilizer daily, Reich bitterly attacked our enormous reliance on drugs. He contended that this dependency is not historically accidental, but stems from the influence of powerful pharmaceutical companies upon national health practice and policy. He pointed out that "a drug, which, though it kills bacilli, damages at the same time the blood cells and plasma system instead of invigorating them, should not be tolerated, powerful interests notwithstanding."[16] Similarly, he noted that the radium industry has much to gain by its role in cancer treatment and much to lose by the rise of alternatives to it. It is probable that such criticism helped to launch the FDA's persecution of his work. Although that response may have shocked us in the past, today we are more quick to recognize and criticize the close links between large pharmaceutical companies, medical schools, and the governmental agencies supposedly designed to regulate them.

Reich advocated a natural approach to understanding and treating modern degenerative diseases (the biopathies), and he especially underlined the body's ability to heal itself, once given the opportunity. He thus states:

> Personally, I have always had a strong aversion to the injection of foreign substances, be they drugs or sera, into a living organism. It was only too apparent that so many sedative drugs, while efficacious in alleviating pain, at the same time damaged the autonomic apparatus. . . . Are there any drugs which will kill microbes, or pain, without injuring the life system? Thus far, chemical research has not been able to produce them.[17]

Later in his life, Reich envisioned a medicine of the future that would rely on the body's natural healing processes. He believed that, like other living organisms, we possess an innate ability to heal ourselves. Just as animals instinctively know how to care for themselves when they are ill and know when to eat and when to sleep or rest, so humans possess a similar inner wisdom. But modern industrial society conditions us to ignore many subtle messages from the body and to rely on pills and injections. "You listen on the radio to the announcements of laxatives, dental creams, and deodorants," Reich wrote, "but you fail to hear the music of propaganda."[18] He was certain that the best way of ensuring personal health is to rely upon the body's inner knowledge as completely as possible.

Of course, Reich was aware that in a society with so many artificialities it is necessary to distinguish carefully our inner messages from those foisted upon us by the advertising industry. For example, so many prepared foods have sugar and salt added to them that it is easy to develop an unnatural craving for them. So while there *is* an internal regulator of our health rhythms, we often distort or misread its signals. Had Reich lived longer, he might have been able to develop techniques for more easily differentiating natural needs from artificial ones. He might also have investigated the healing techniques of naturopathy—spas, natural diet, vitamins, sunlight, and exercise—and incorporated them into a preventive-medicine program.

THE PERSONALITY OF DISEASE

Reich foreshadowed holistic thought not only in his belief that modern diseases are often related to the emotional state and lifestyle of the individual, but also in his assertion that the particular disease a person develops relates very much to his or her personality traits. He also claimed that the site of that disease represented the body's storehouse of chronic tensions. He argued for this approach as early as the mid-1940s, when only the slightest evidence existed to support the idea. Here, as in many other aspects of his work, Reich was primarily an intuitive thinker. He formed his bold hypotheses based largely on his personal work with patients.

During the 1940s, Reich singled out and described several major chronic illnesses as representing particular syndromes involving emotional suppression. These include heart disease and related cardiovascular illnesses, rheumatoid arthritis, peptic ulcer, spasms of annular muscles, and cancer. For instance, persons with cardiovascular problems such as tachycardia, high blood pressure, and hypertension react to chronic stress in a unique way, Reich believed. As far back as 1926, he later reminisced, he had discussed this theory with Freud, who categorically "rejected the connection between anxiety and the vasovegetative [pertaining to the life energy] system."[19] Reich commented that he had never understood why Freud had not been impressed by the evidence he presented. "It became increasingly clear that the overburdening of the vasovegetative system with undischarged sexual energy is the fundamental mechanism of anxiety. . . . Anxiety always develops . . . when the vegetative system is overstimulated in a specific way," he observed.[20]

By "sexual excitation," Reich was referring broadly to the general energy system of the body. He felt that individuals who are prone to cardiovascular disturbances suffer from an overabundance of emotional energy and exhibit a kind of "explosive" quality in their emotionality. They are unable to express feelings in a complete and cleansing manner. When tensions build up, they are dissipated in incomplete staccato bursts so that residues of unexpressed emotion accumulate. Ultimately, this chronic stress on the heart and the cardiovascular system results in a serious illness. Anticipating contemporary theory and research on the heart-attack-prone individual by more than thirty years, Reich argued in *The Cancer Biopathy* (1948), "Hypertensives . . . , people who suffer from chronic vascular constriction, are 'emotionally labile,' more or less explosive, characters. This is expressed in their acute anxiety attacks. . . . The organism, in its state of contraction, . . . reacts with outbreaks of anxiety or anger."[21]

Muscular rheumatism is another disease that Reich related to psychosomatic or emotional influences. He viewed it as a manifestation of the body armor and suggested that "if hypertension of the muscles exists over a period of years and decades, it leads to chronic contracture and the formation of rheumatic nodules as a result of the deposit of solid substances in the muscle bundles. . . . It affects, in a typical manner, those muscle groups which play a dominant role in the suppression of affects and bodily sensations."[22] That is, the specific muscles or bodily areas affected possess a functional or emotional meaning. In other words, those segments of the body in which armoring is especially heavy are most likely to become rheumatoid. These include the neck muscles, important in suppression of anger; the pelvic muscles, crucial to suppression of sexual excitation, and lower back muscles, which relate to chronic tensions in the anal area.

Another illness that Reich identified as psychogenic in nature is peptic ulcer. "Peptic ulcer has been recognized so thoroughly as an accompaniment of chronic affective disturbance that its psychosomatic nature can no longer be doubted."[23] In other words, Reich was convinced that this common gastrointestinal disorder was strongly related to a particular character or personality type. Prolonged emotional stress, he observed, causes an overstimulation of the digestive glands, which in turn produces overacidity in the digestive system. As a result, the mucous membrane of the stomach is exposed to the effect of gastric acid, leading to the formation of an ulcer. A number of studies have now demonstrated the link that Reich hypothesized between emotional states and the development of this condition.

Spasms of annular muscles are linked to another set of diseases that Reich viewed as essentially psychosomatic in nature. These, he felt, included spastic attacks at the entrance and exit of the stomach, leading to chronic indigestion; chronic constipation; and hemorrhoids. All of these forms of distress are related to emotional disturbances, particularly the withholding of strong emotions such as anger or rage.

Among Reich's most startling claims was that cancer, the most dreaded of all modern diseases, is at least partly caused by emotional factors. In the early 1940s, when he advanced this notion, there was virtually no systematic evidence in medical literature to back it up. On the basis of some laboratory experiments and personal observation of patients, Reich nonetheless affirmed that just as with asthma or peptic ulcer, a specific type of individual seems predisposed to cancer. Though he acknowledged that the dynamics of the disease were far from clear, he believed that his own explanation was the most compelling theory yet to be advanced.

In *The Cancer Biopathy*, Reich hypothesized that the person most likely to develop cancer is markedly identifiable as *resigned*, having "given up on life," particularly life's physical, sensual, and emotional pleasures. Cancer-prone persons, he declared, tend to be ones who from childhood have experienced little physical satisfaction in life and who have grown up in physically unaffectionate and loveless families. Their childhoods are marked by little warmth and a minimal display of emotionality. As they mature into adulthood, they naturally find it difficult to express strong feelings in a direct, open way or, indeed, to intensely experience very much *to* express. Thus, cancer patients are essentially subdued, well mannered, and quiet, unable to give vivid emotional expression to anger, rage, or grief. "Cancer characters show predominantly mild emotions and characterological resignation," he concluded. "I have never seen cancer patients with violent emotions, explosions of anger, etc."[24]

Reich felt that before the physically identifiable symptoms of cancer existed—that is, the tumors or metastases—nearly every such patient had built up a rather solid history of biophysical weakness, indicating a gradual lessening of what Reich viewed as life energy. "In cancer ... the biological core reduces its energy production," he stated. "Chronic emotional calm ... must correspond to a depletion of energy in the cell and plasma system."[25] The most significant indicator of the *potential* for cancer cannot, therefore, be observed in a laboratory serum or under X-ray examination. Reich believed that the tumors associated with cancer are triggered by this deep emotional resignation. "Long before the plasma is directly disturbed," he argued, "the peripheral physiology and character functions are disturbed: first the ability to establish social contact, to enjoy life and pleasure, the ability to work, and then plasmatic excitation and pulsation."[26] Somehow, and he did not claim to understand fully the specific processes involved, anyone who is chronically deadened in basic emotional expression sows within his or her body the seeds of a later cancer growth.

Reich acknowledged, of course, that environmental substances—that is, carcinogenic agents—play a role in the final appearance of the disease. But he pointed out that not everyone exposed to such substances develops cancer and that autopsies routinely show the presence of cancerous cells in people who have lived into their eighties or nineties. Carcinogenic agents provoke extremely dangerous cellular conditions in some individuals; in others, the same environmental substances have little effect. An immunizing process is clearly at work. In other words, the internal conditions that *precede* exposure and cellular aberration are most important. "The fully developed cancer cell is only the final phase of a long series of pathological tissue changes which hitherto have remained unexplored," he insisted.[27]

To sum up, Reich believed that cancer is essentially rooted in longstanding life-negative emotional patterns. Persons who are deeply repressed, meek, and go through life with neither many complaints nor much exuberance appear particularly susceptible. The underlying process involves a gradual and not easily detectable lessening of the bioenergetic vigor of the tissues and especially of the blood. Over many years, as a rule, the total bodily energy condition deteriorates to the point where cancerous cells, provoked by either internal or environmental sources, form and multiply. In short, Reich stated, "long before the development of the first cancer cell in the organism, there are a series of pathological processes in the respective tissues and its immediate surroundings. These local processes, in turn, are induced by a *general disease of the vital apparatus.*"[28] Eventually, Reich felt, modern medicine would view cancer and other such diseases as representing an integral disharmony in the mind-body system, involving either an undercharge or an unreleased surplus of bioenergy.

THE SOCIAL ROOTS OF DISEASE

Never content to confine his innovative insights to the laboratory or clinic, Reich combined his views of health and illness with trenchant and sweeping social criticism. Although by the 1940s he had repudiated the partisan politics and dogmas of his Communist days, he retained much of his early condemnation of modern industrial society. In the last decade of his life, he argued vehemently that modern "biopathic" illnesses are significant indicators that something is deeply wrong in the lives of multitudes. In his last years, as the struggle with the FDA reached its peak, Reich prophetically warned that unless drastic preventive measures were undertaken, such diseases would in time reach epidemic proportions. In 1948, Reich declared:

> The fight against the biopathies will be one of the most arduous tasks with which humanity was ever confronted. I do not hesitate to contend that no previous revolution nor such achievements as the conquest of the plague of the Middle Ages can compare with this task in magnitude, depth, and danger. . . . As long as education and social conditions are going to produce resignation and muscular armoring en masse, so long is any radical elimination of the cancer scourge out of the question. . . . Cancer, as a special form of biopathy, is inseparable from the social structure of our society.[29]

Today, more than thirty years later, how much more strident his tone might be! One can hear him insist that until the masses begin to express their emotions without inhibition and learn to cherish loving as well as aggressive feelings, there would be no relief from such diseases.

And yet, in the final analysis, Reich was optimistic about the distant future. Though his work on cancer was banned by the federal government and he himself was thrown into prison, he remained convinced that the day would eventually come when his ideas would not only be accepted but wholeheartedly embraced.

INTUITION VINDICATED

What is the evidence today for Reich's bold theories? First, research now clearly suggests that many, if not all, forms of illness have their roots at least partly in emotional or psychological soil. Occasionally there are cases in which an illness is unmistakably due to purely physical causes, such as bacteria found in spoiled food. As physicians and scientists continue their investigations, however, they are finding an emotional component for nearly every type of disease from the common cold to heart attack and cancer. Such findings are being published in highly respected professional journals and debated at the most prestigious national and international conferences.

Some of the most important publications at present include the *American Journal of Epidemiology*, the *Journal of Psychosomatic Research*, the *Journal of Chronic Disease*, *Psychosomatic Medicine*, and the *British Journal of Social Medicine*, all of which publish each year a variety of research papers on the relationship of disease to psychological and social factors. The worldwide Society for Psychosomatic Research sponsors an annual symposium that highlights some of the most exciting work now being done in this field. A sampling of its 1977 papers includes presentations on prenatal events and infant behavior, breast-feeding and its effect on the child, and the nature of mind-body communication. In effect, what Reich and a handful of iconoclasts have been saying for decades is finally being acknowledged within the medical profession. While fragmented and still weak in influence, especially in relation to the allocation of research and health-care funds, this swelling "movement" represents the wave of the future.

Some recent research, for instance, has focused on how heart disease and various forms of cardiovascular illness are related to emotions. Cardiologists Ray H. Rosenman and Meyer Friedman, director and associate director respectively at the Harold Brunn Institute of Mount Zion Hospital and Medical Center in San Francisco, have sparked much of this work. In popular writings, they have dubbed the heart-attack-prone individual a "Type A personality," in contrast to the "Type B personality" who seems relatively immune from the disease. It seems that Type A's push or drive themselves in most avenues of life and are aggressive, competitive, and, above all, give off a pervasive sense of impatience and hurry. They typically speak and eat too fast, interrupt others frequently, and sometimes will finish others' sentences for them. The Type A person also tends to explosively accentuate key words in speech, become enraged when held up in traffic or made to wait anywhere, feel guilt when relaxing, and measure success quantitatively. This echoes Reich's observation that people with a susceptibility to heart disease are explosive, anger-prone characters.

Other research has confirmed Reich's hypothesis that this personality is formed in childhood or early adolescence. It is not inherited but *learned,* often from one or both parents. For instance, Bortner, Rosenman, and Friedman reported in a 1970 issue of the *Journal of Chronic Disease* that adolescent boys whose fathers have the Coronary Prone Behavior Pattern are themselves somewhat more likely to exhibit aspects of this behavior pattern. In another study, Dr. Arthur Butensky and his associates reported in a 1975 issue of the *Journal of Psychosomatic Research* that rural children display considerably less hurry and impatience, though no less desire for achievement, than their suburban counterparts. In a research review of this whole subject, Rosenman emphasized in a 1978 article in *Advanced Cardiology* that while the Type A personality is not a very strong threat alone, it may indeed lead to cardiovascular disorders if it is present with other risk factors such as smoking or high cholesterol intake.

A growing number of health professionals are beginning to treat heart disease and related disorders as psychosomatic disturbances. As we shall see in Chapter 5, rather than simply prescribing medication, they are now involving heart patients in psychotherapy. The goal is to help them modify their explosive, anger-prone, impatient characteristics and become more accepting and easygoing. Of course, only the patient can really make such changes, so once again there is confirmation of Reich's insight that a cure requires personality and character transformation.

Diseases such as peptic ulcer, colitis, asthma, and allergies are being increasingly regarded by the health establishment as somehow related to the patient's emotional state. Little doubt remains that a peptic ulcer is almost always the result of chronic tension. This stress seems to go back to the individual's childhood and is often related to intense unconscious desires to be loved, mothered, and cared for. In a review of research on this disease, Drs. Dan Hertz and Milton Rosenbaum observe, in *Psychosomatic Medicine* (Wittkower and Warnes, 1977), that both depression and a perfectionist makeup are key precursors to the onset of the duodenal ulcer. "In order to develop the proper therapeutic approach," they write, "the physician should make every attempt to determine the life events connected with . . . the illness."[30] It is also now well known that emotional stress often triggers allergies and that many such skin reactions tend to disappear when intense emotional pressures are removed. Health professionals also accept the idea that skin diseases such as acne are heavily affected by chronic, unresolved stress.

Asthma is another illness of a psychosomatic nature. Though the medical evidence is still relatively scanty, a variety of studies suggests that asthma is often precipitated by specific emotional states. Dr. Aman Khan of Northwestern Medical School dealt with this subject in an article published in the *Journal of Psychosomatic Research* in 1976. He hypothesized that at an early age a child who is highly dependent may unconsciously learn that asthmatic attacks bring him or her closer to mother and thereby lessen his or her fears of abandonment. Later on, these same feelings may trigger asthmatic attacks whenever the person is under particular stress. Indeed, in their book, *Psychosomatics,* Harold and Martha Lewis cite several studies suggesting that asthmatics are people who have especially suppressed emotions of sadness and the need to cry deeply and spontaneously. Here again, the problem stems from childhood family patterns, and particularly from the presence of an overprotective mother. The authors observe, "Many parents of asthmatics steadfastly insist that the child's condition is due entirely to an allergy. . . . But the evidence in many cases suggests that the allergic component of asthma is secondary to the emotional."[31]

Other studies propose that migraine headaches are often psychosomatic, as the most typical prelude to migraine seems to be repressed rage. Some conditions may disappear as the patient learns to express anger vigorously and fully. Harold and Martha Lewis note that "a migraine sufferer is typically perfectionist, ambitious, rigid, and orderly. . . . Such people often have an attitude of chronic resentment and are frustrated in not being able to live up to their unrealistic ideas. Faced with an insuperable task, they may come down with an attack of migraine."[32] Once more, the belief seems to be growing among professionals that the most effective form of treatment involves a change in the patient's characteristic forms of emotional expression. Some migraine sufferers are being taught to voluntarily control blood flow through biofeedback techniques so that the migraine can be averted. The success of this approach confirms Reich's view that the mind and body are intimately related, but, of course, this method is basically a palliative since it is not directed toward a cure.

Finally, a growing body of research has begun to suggest that cancer has at least some emotional or psychological predeterminants. As we shall see in the next chapter, some professionals have incorporated psychotherapy into cancer treatment and claim that those patients who participate in it and learn to express emotions such as anger have longer life expectancies than those who do not. Even more strikingly, several studies now suggest, as Reich theorized over thirty years ago, that there may in fact be a "cancer personality."

Actually, theories about psychological precursors of cancer date back to the 1940s, when Reich was actively pursuing his own investigations into this subject. Rapid advances in biomedical research after World War II, however, shifted interest away from these concerns. During the 1950s, one of the lone-wolf pioneers of this area was Dr. Lawrence LeShan. Over the course of several studies, published in such reputable journals as the *British Journal of Medical Psychology,* the *Journal of Nervous Mental Disorders,* and the *Journal of the National Cancer Institute,* he found systematic evidence that persons who develop cancer are generally rather unhappy with their lives, particularly feeling a sense of bleakness that borders on despair. Though in the type of research he conducted he could not prove that these psychological traits *preceded* the onset of cancer, he was certain that such persons had experienced a sense of emptiness and pleasure starvation for years. LeShan found that cancer patients tended to be lonely and isolated during childhood, unable in later years to establish real warmth and intimacy with others.

Another innovator in this line of inquiry during the 1950s was William Greene, an internist and professor of psychiatry at the University of Rochester. As discussed in a 1978 article in *Science* that summarizes the major research relating personality to cancer, Constance Holden reports that Greene tested patients with leukemia and Hodgkin's disease and found that in nine out of ten cases, "the time the disease develops is when a person feels alone, helpless, and hopeless."[33] A recent study cited in the same article was carried out at Johns Hopkins Medical School by a multidisciplinary team of investigators. They found that women who expressed a high degree of anger concerning their affliction with breast cancer had a significantly longer life expectancy than those who appeared resigned to their condition. Dr. Leonard Derogatis, a psychologist who spearheaded the research effort, commented that this finding had not been anticipated and was therefore especially convincing.

In another often-cited body of research, Dr. David M. Kissen of the University of Glasgow has found that cancer victims especially suffer from denial and repression of their emotions as compared with the noncancerous population as a whole. They tend to be extremely unexpressive emotionally and to hold back strong feelings. As Kissen described these patients, they had "poor outlet for emotional discharge." As we have seen, this is precisely how Reich diagnosed such individuals. According to Howard and Martha Lewis, Kissen's work has strongly suggested that the cancer patient's life consistently shows a pattern of childhood family tensions and especially of parental separations. In other words, just as Reich hypothesized, the onset of cancer may actually be preceded by devastating emotional events decades earlier in the person's life. Moreover, scientific evidence is accumulating to suggest that cancer patients may have special difficulty in expressing anger. In 1975, S. Greer and T. Morris at Kings College Hospital in London found that inappropriate means of coping with anger—typically suppression but occasionally intense expression—was related with discovery of breast malignancy in women.

In short, the cancer-prone individual tends to be submissive and inhibited, particularly in expressing anger, or else is consumed with self-pity. None of this, of course, rules out the fact that pollutants in the air, water, or food are contributing factors. Rather, it seems that the interaction of environmental carcinogens with a particular disposition causes the disease. This type of interactive model has already been advanced to explain such other major noninfectious illnesses as schizophrenia, and before long, we predict, will become the dominant perspective on cancer, too.

The contemporary holistic-health movement has not only begun to validate Reich's findings, but also, often unwittingly, has formulated ideas paralleling his on how to attain optimal emotional-physical health. For example, holistic thinking now recognizes that many modern diseases are caused or aggravated by stress. The impressive research of Dr. Hans Selye launched this discovery. In a career that has spanned decades, Selye's work at the University of Montreal has convincingly demonstrated the shattering impact that prolonged stress has on our bodies. A contemporary of Reich's in the 1930s and 1940s, Selye is another brilliant innovator who currently argues for the inextricable link between mind and body. His book, *The Stress of Life,* first published in 1956, is a landmark in the field. His writings, and those of others, emphasize that, in our technological-urban society, we must learn to cope with constant stress. Barbara Brown has argued that it is imperative for us to become aware of our internal states, to feel when stress is mounting, and to develop means of releasing tensions. Biofeedback, meditation, Yoga, and autogenic training are now espoused by growing numbers of health professionals and therapists, especially those in holistic medicine, as helpful in alleviating chronic tension. Although all these approaches are useful in lessening superficial armoring, they do not come to grips with chronic armoring patterns and their characterological correlates. In this respect, they have yet to satisfy Reich's demands.

Holistic-health advocates are also vigorously echoing Reich's assertions that each person must take full responsibility for his or her own health. They point out, as did Reich, that within each of us there exists a kind of natural body wisdom, an "inner voice," that can guide our daily behavior to sustain positive emotional and physical well-being. The well-known author George Leonard, a member of the Board of Advisors of the Association for Holistic Health, has outlined some major principles of this organization. Highly reminiscent of Reich's own views are these statements:

1. Positive well-being, not just the absence of disease, is the goal.

2. The causes of most illnesses are to be found in environment, lifestyle, and emotional sensory balance.

3. Prevention of illness ... lies less in the annual physical [examination] than in the transformation of your life.

4. Healing of many chronic diseases, which are only ameliorated by the Old Medicine, may be possible after all.

5. Responsibility for your health lies not with your physician, but with yourself.[34]

Advocates of this outlook point to research on the ways in which stressful life events affect our health. Most investigators working in this field have followed the pioneering efforts of Holmes, Rahe, and their colleagues. In the 1960s, Dr. Thomas Holmes and his associates at the University of Washington developed a forty-three-item checklist of stressful events. Based on the reports of thousands of interviewees, they assigned each kind of major life event a point value. These ranged from the death of a spouse (100 points), the most devastating occurrence in our culture, to vacations (13 points), the Christmas season (12 points), and minor violations of the law. In a variety of studies, growing medical evidence documents a close relationship between tension-inducing life experiences and physical reactions in the form of diseases. Even "pleasurable" stress—a marriage, an exciting new job—can mount up until it too reveals itself in illness. In fact, it now seems possible to predict, in general terms, the likelihood that a person will develop a given kind of illness within a given time period if he or she is subjected to certain specific stressful events.

In a comprehensive review of the literature in the prestigious international journal *Science* in 1976, Drs. Judith Rabkin and Elmer Struening discussed the impact of life events and stress upon human illness. Based on their work at the Epidemiology of Mental Disorders Research Unit of New York State, they concluded, "The notion of socially induced stress as a precipitating factor in chronic diseases is gaining acceptance among a wide spectrum of scientists. . . . Even susceptibility to microbial infectious diseases is thought to be a function of environmental conditions culminating in physiological stress on the individual, rather than simply of exposure to an external source of infection."[35]

At first, researchers concluded that the greater the life stress, the greater the possibility of serious illness. However, it has been shown that people react very differently to the same anxiety-producing event. At the loss of a job, one person might attempt suicide, turn to heavy drinking, or abandon his or her spouse. Another individual faced with the same trauma might recover within days and enthusiastically resume life. Holistic-health advocates have taken up Reich's view that our basic personality determines how we react to life events, stressful or otherwise.

Another contemporary echo of Reich's ideas is the current recognition of pollutants as major contributors to ill health. During the 1950s, Reich became convinced that environmental pollution was becoming a growing menace to the planet. Ever-growing numbers of people are today realizing that not only do air and water pollutants affect human health on a mass scale, but that food pollutants—used in the artificial processing of most of our food—are equally harmful. The role of grocery chains, food processors, and the vertical integration of agriculture (chain stores owning and operating the farms that grow the foods they sell) is significant in this growing pollution of the national diet. The ecology and organic-food movements are hopeful signs in the face of these trends.

In one area—sociopolitical change and the relation of modern disease to the dominant lifestyle of our society—today's holistic-health exponents have yet to catch up with Reich. The reason that so many people exhibit degenerative diseases is that chronic stress is an insidious fact of life for those living in industrial nations. Though increasing numbers will be helped by holistic methods, which emphasize natural rather than artificial means of healing, we can confidently predict an increase in such diseases unless the major changes that Reich envisioned come about. In support of this comes *Social Stress and Chronic Illness* by D. L. Dodge and W. T. Martin, describing stress, despair, and resignation as common emotional states in urban and metropolitan centers and further linking them to various chronic diseases.

Even if we learn to take control of our health and come to trust the inner wisdom of our bodies, it is Reich's claim that such a development fails to get at the root problem. Reich did not hesitate to declare that unless major transformations occur in how we work, love, manage our families, and interact with one another, modern disease will continue unabated. Significant structural changes are needed in the basic institutions of industrial society: the family and the world of work, medicine, government, science, and the environment. These social policies will be discussed in Chapter 8.

We see grounds for optimism in the fact that, on an ever-widening scale, people are becoming more physically sensitive to and aware of the relative healthfulness of their environment and of elements in their diet. As the trend toward greater acceptance of bodily and emotional expression becomes more pronounced, we can expect increased public concern about how environmental factors—noise, food additives, chemicals, work alienation, all kinds of pollution—prevent us from living in our bodies and to our fullest potential.

It is gratifying to realize that although Reich himself was imprisoned and his books burned because of their radical ideas on health and illness, his work could not be stopped. Now, barely two decades after his death, there is a clamor for alternatives to mainstream medicine. While degenerative diseases continue to affect millions of lives, we see a solid and growing body of health professionals and interested laypeople who are determined to secure the kind of medicine that Reich envisioned. An example of this movement's impetus was the two-day Conference on Total Health held in Toronto in March 1979, which drew more than four thousand persons from a wide spectrum of interests and professions. Although it did not pay explicit tribute to Reich, his spirit was actively there.

CHAPTER 5

Psychotherapies for Healing and Wholeness

Only you yourself can be your liberator.

Now, when the natural streaming of the bioenergy is dammed up, it ... spills over, resulting in irrationality, perversions, neuroses, and so on. What do you have to do to correct this? You must get the stream back into its normal bed and let it flow naturally again.

—WILHELM REICH

Perhaps the greatest recognition that Wilhelm Reich has yet received for his work is in the realm of psychotherapy and healing. Since his first discoveries in that area over fifty years ago, his ideas have attracted serious interest. To be sure, Reich's approach remains outside the bastions of medical orthodoxy. Still, it has both parallels and influences in some of the most popular psychotherapies of our time, including Gestalt therapy, Bioenergetics, Primal therapy, Rolfing, and a host of others. And, advancing even further, many physicians have adopted similar psychotherapeutic methods for treating degenerative diseases.

As we move into the 1980s, more and more people are likely to seek modes of healing to replace those associated with mainstream medicine and psychotherapy. Already this movement has accelerated interest in the treatment practices of Wilhelm Reich. Though some practitioners are still hesitant about being linked to such a controversial figure, his influence is now more readily acknowledged than ever before. No doubt we will witness his continued impact on the development of ways to ameliorate mental and physical illness.

PSYCHOANALYSIS FAILS TO DELIVER

As a young physician under Freud's protective wing in the early 1920s, Reich was at first very excited by and interested in the existing forms of therapy for emotional distress. He was readily drawn to what he perceived as the genius of Freud's insights into personality development, sexuality, and the unconscious and wished to develop them further. He quickly found from his own experience in treating patients, however, that Freud's psychoanalytic technique had many shortcomings.

In essence, Freud relied upon "free association"—encouraging the patient to talk spontaneously about whatever thoughts, images, or memories flitted across his or her consciousness. Eventually, over many sessions, a specific theme emerges from the associations, usually centering on childhood fantasies, often of a sexual nature, and involving the parents. Freud believed that through logically analyzing (hence the term *psychoanalysis*) such long-suppressed thoughts or feelings, the patient could unravel the hidden causes of his or her neurosis. Dreams, slips of the tongue, and other nondeliberate behaviors are like pieces of a puzzle; rational interpretation is the rule.

Another key element in psychoanalysis is known as transference. In the course of therapy, Freud found, the patient typically comes to view the analyst in precisely the same manner as he or she originally reacted to parents or parent surrogates, and a love-dependency relationship springs up. By successfully maintaining a blank screen in front of his or her own personal life, the analyst can draw out the patient's fantasies and wishes, and thereby uncover hidden motivations. For instance, the patient can be made to see that he is behaving toward the therapist exactly as he had behaved toward his mother.

In theory, this was how patients could be healed of their underlying emotional problems. But Reich soon found that the therapeutic reality failed to live up to Freud's theoretical expectations. For a variety of reasons, it seemed, psychoanalysis did not work very well. First, Reich noticed the time span of therapy was gradually lengthening. "When I started out," he reminisced years later, "an analysis of six months was considered long. In 1923, a year was considered a matter of course. The view even gained ground that two and more years would not be bad, considering the fact that neuroses were very complicated and serious disturbances."[1] Today, of course, psychoanalysis may well take many years and even decades, as prominent clients like Woody Allen often concede, with a mixture of embarrassment and humor. This prolongation of a method that had once been viewed by Freud as quick and incisive was proof to Reich that alternatives were necessary. Ironically, though, later in his own career he found that effective therapy often takes considerable time and warned, in fact, against overly quick attempts at cure. Certainly, too, some of the chief neo-Reichian schools of therapy, such as Orgonomy and Bioenergetics, take many months of intensive work in order to effect therapeutic breakthroughs of a lasting nature.

Reich also faulted what he regarded as the extremely passive role that the analyst plays in Freudian therapy. The theoretical concept of transference did not seem to translate well into practice, and the analyst of the impassive facade appeared to be of questionable usefulness to Reich. Indeed, one of his first innovations was to move the analyst's chair alongside the patient's couch so that the patient could actually see whom he or she was dealing with. "Among themselves," Reich wrote,

> colleagues joked about the temptation to sleep during analytic hours; if a patient did not produce any associations for hours on end, one had to smoke a lot to keep awake. . . . Jokes, like that of the analyst who, in the course of a session, awoke out of a deep sleep and found the couch empty, did not improve matters; nor did profound explanations to the effect that there was no harm in the analyst falling asleep, inasmuch as his unconscious dutifully kept watch over the patient. In short, the situation was depressing, and looked hopeless.[2]

Reich was particularly distressed with the emphasis that psychoanalysis placed on talking about one's problems as the way to mental health. Some patients might be able to chat glibly about alleged childhood traumas or fantasies and yet remain mired in their immature and unsatisfying relations with others. People could analyze their past mistakes and misplaced desires in the most minute detail but somehow never connect emotionally with them. There had to be a more direct way, Reich argued.

"The patients were quick to find out the analyst's theoretical expectations," he commented, "and presented associations accordingly. They produced material for the analyst's benefit. If they were sly characters they would lead the analyst astray more or less consciously, e.g., by producing such confusing dreams that no one could possibly understand them."[3]

Reich's insight here has become the mainstay of the Gestalt therapy approach, which has similarly stressed the way in which therapists can be easily manipulated by clever patients. Fritz Perls, who studied under Reich in the 1930s, always declared that his primary task as a healer was to convince the patient that no amount of game-playing would work, and therein almost "compel" him or her into honest disclosure.

In effect, Reich urged a complete overhaul of psychoanalytic treatment. He regarded Freud's insights as brilliant, but, faced with the failure of Freud's healing techniques, he wanted to develop something better.

Reich decried most treatment situations as catch-as-catch-can at best. "There was no order in the material, no structure in treatment, and, consequently, no evolving of a process. Most cases petered out after two or three years' treatment. Occasionally, there were improvements, but nobody knew why."[4]

Unless psychoanalytic leaders were willing to admit their failures and strike out for new methods, Freud's movement was doomed, Reich believed. Some of Freud's inner circle began to adopt Reich's innovations but claimed that they were simply "restatements" of what Freud had said years before. Others flatly rejected Reich's therapeutic methods as incorrect or even potentially damaging to patients. As briefly discussed in Chapter 1, in the late 1920s this rift steadily widened, until 1934, when Reich was formally expelled from the International Psychoanalytic Association.

The infighting eventually became so vicious, in fact, that Reich was slandered by some of his former colleagues, who spread rumors that he had been institutionalized in a mental hospital or was physically violating his female patients. "The organization became more important than its task," Reich observed with bitterness years later. "Many psychoanalysts changed into the worst enemies of their own cause."[5]

In the following section, we will briefly take up Reich's cause, outlining the principles behind Reichian therapy as well as providing some examples of what this healing method feels like from the patient's perspective. Reich's therapeutic approach has engendered a wave of new therapies that go far beyond the limits of psychoanalysis, so an understanding of Reichian therapy is essential to an understanding of the neo-Reichian and parallel therapies discussed in subsequent sections.

REICHIAN THERAPY: A CHINK IN THE ARMOR

In orthodox Reichian therapy, the patient becomes as aware as possible of precisely *how* he or she is suppressing emotions. Using essentially nonverbal techniques, the goal of Reich's bodywork is to restore the emotional and physical health of the individual through the arousal and release of repressed tensions and feelings. Indeed, it is this supreme emphasis upon *experiencing* one's long-denied emotions, rather than simply intellectualizing about them, that defines the essence of Reich's therapeutic perspective and of its contemporary heirs.

Reich believed that there is an energy flow within the body that is inextricably linked to the emotions. In someone suffering from physical or mental illness, this energy flow is in some way impeded or overexcited. Over many sessions, by a careful loosening of chronic tension, the healer helps the patient to discharge the emotions contributing to the energy blockage. In this way, the organs recover their vitality as this energy now flows naturally. For Reich, the presence of what he termed the *orgasm reflex,* in which the individual completely surrenders to the streamings of the bioenergy within, signals the successful completion of therapy. For centuries, Oriental medicine has relied upon a somewhat similar approach, and treatments such as acupuncture derive from it. As we shall see in Chapter 6, recent scientific evidence has begun to amass in support of this view.

Reich considered the first step in healing to be accurate visual diagnosis. Although he did make occasional use of laboratory tests, such as a blood test for cancer or precancerous conditions, he insisted that "the living [organism] has its own specific forms of expression which cannot be put into words at all. . . . As soon as the patient ceases to talk, the bodily expression of emotion becomes clearly manifest."[6]

As part of the body-language approach to diagnosis, Reich insisted that the therapist's ability to feel how his or her own body is reacting to the patient's demeanor should guide the bodywork to follow. For instance, if the patient sits with a frozen smile, the therapist thinks, "Do I begin to feel angry, or perhaps all of a sudden rather tired?" Reich emphasized to his students that such questions helped to get to the root of the patient's condition. "Only when we have *felt* the facial *expression* of the patient are we also in a position to understand it," he said. "It makes no difference whether the emotion is actively mobile or whether it is held back, immobile."[7]

Reich did not subscribe to the dominant medical practice of using Latin phrases to mystify bodily processes. Nor did he attach much importance to the need for explicitly interpreting for the patient the precise nature of his or her problem. "It would be perfectly useless, for example, to try to make the patient understand his condition in terms of, say, physiology," Reich insisted. "We cannot say to him, 'Your masseter muscles are in a state of chronic contraction, that is why your chin does not move in talking, why your voice is monotonous, why you cannot cry.' . . . True, the patient would understand such statements intellectually, but that would not change his condition."[8]

Once the visual diagnosis has been completed—for which the patient is typically requested to strip down to underclothes and socks—the therapist begins the actual bodywork. He or she may ask the patient to try to become as aware as possible of tensions in a particular body area and to *consciously* experience them. The patient may be required to kick or hit, and the physician may begin to directly manipulate the patient's musculature, including pinching or prodding. As various parts of the armor are probed in the Reichian technique of "vegetotherapy," the patient—invariably treated alone rather than in a group—spontaneously begins to relive long-forgotten experiences, and the associated emotions now return in full force. Thus, when the therapist's touch stimulates a particular part of the anatomy, the patient may cry out in anguish, perhaps reliving a parent's death that occurred in childhood. Another patient may be flooded with waves of anger over a painful humiliation suffered at the hands of a former employer. The patient does not talk about the past but actually re-experiences it. As Reich succinctly put it, "The memory of the experience which had originally produced the effect, appears afterward without any effort. . . . This fact cannot be stressed too much."[9]

Eventually, as more and more important emotional suppressions surface, the patient begins to feel a growing sense of physical vitality and aliveness. Initially strange, currentlike sensations run up and down the body. A relatively unarmored person may experience these after several therapeutic sessions. Other spontaneous sensations, often unsettling at first, may include involuntary twitching and trembling of the muscles, a feeling of pins and needles, and hot or cold prickling. In time, these sensations should give way to the sweet, even euphoric experience of wavelike streamings up and down the body. Streamings are typically accompanied by sensual feelings, indicating that the bioenergy, or orgone, has begun to flow freely and that the person's armor has largely dissolved.

Reich identified seven regions, or what he called "segments," of human armoring. These include the ocular region (around the eyes), the oral (around the mouth and jaws), the cervical (the neck, throat, and shoulders), the thoracic (the upper chest), the diaphragmatic (around the diaphragm and organs under it), the abdominal (including the large abdominal muscles, lower back muscles, and rectum), and the pelvic (containing all the muscles of the pelvis and legs). While Reich did not explicitly note it, this physical scheme bears a strong resemblance to certain Eastern concepts of the body, particularly the Oriental system of seven *chakras*, said to regulate life energy flow. (This will be discussed in detail in Chapter 6.) Some contemporary therapists influenced by Reich, such as Alexander Lowen, the founder of Bioenergetics, have explicitly made this comparison.

Reich discovered that each person is armored in a unique way. The healer's task is to focus first on the top, or ocular, segment of the body and then gradually work down through the other segments. As the therapist treats each body segment, the initial pain and subsequent release of emotions make the patient aware that there had been little or no physical sensation in that part of the body. For example, as the muscles of the jaw region are kneaded and pressed, at first there is pain, and then the patient may begin to quiver involuntarily around the mouth or perhaps cry, sometimes uncontrollably. Each step of loosening the armor almost inevitably means the patient will feel some anxiety at the new sensations of physical and emotional freedom that are emerging. For this reason, Reich felt, the armoring must be broken down slowly, over a series of sessions, typically taking place over several months.

As we have briefly discussed earlier, Reich found that among men and women in Western society, the pelvic area usually contains the most heavily suppressed emotions. "Immobility of the pelvis," observed Reich, "gives the impression of deadness. In the majority of cases, this is subjectively felt as an 'emptiness in the pelvis' or a 'weakness of the genitals.' This is especially true in cases suffering from chronic constipation. Thus, the therapeutic task is first that of making the patient aware of the vegetative emptiness in the pelvis."[10]

Typically, Reich started his therapy with the eyes and forehead and left the pelvic area to last. Many of the other bodywork therapies, such as Bioenergetics and Polarity, have similarly stressed that dissolution of the pelvic armoring is the final and most painful step in healing. Apparently we are still armored in very much the same body areas as were our counterparts forty or fifty years ago.

Above all, the key to successful healing lies in the restoration of full respiration. As outlined earlier, Reich believed that few of us regularly breathe fully and deeply. This is traced back to childhood, when we were taught to bury many feelings. Over the course of many sessions of Reichian therapy, patients slowly learn to breathe in a more natural and satisfying way. As physical tensions dissolve and long-pent-up emotions are released, they find they are holding back less. For instance, in an interesting account, Orson Bean related that his initial euphoria after his first session with Dr. Baker led to both physical and mental panic several hours later. "The anxiety was terrific," he wrote, "and I was aware that I was involuntarily tightening up on my muscles to hold myself together."[11] Eventually, every breath taken is deep and full.

Reich found from clinical experience that this approach to therapy was necessary to effect significant bodily changes. Physical exercises cannot fully restore bodily vitality, as the underlying emotions accompanying any physical block must be released. Equally important, the patient must adopt a new lifestyle to eliminate the causes of armoring. "It is perfectly useless to have the patient do exercises with his pelvis," Reich declared. "As long as the concealing and defensive attitudes and actions are not discovered and eliminated, the natural pelvic movement cannot develop."[12]

Reichian therapists continue to practice Reich's orthodox methods, though some of Reich's students have preferred to elaborate special or additional therapeutic techniques. In *Me and the Orgone,* actor Orson Bean provides a vivid description of Reichian therapy from the patient's perspective. He relates his experience as a patient in the late 1960s of Dr. Elsworth Baker of New York City, one of Reich's closest associates and a leading practitioner of the Reichian healing method called medical orgone therapy. In fact, Dr. Baker delivered the eulogy at Reich's funeral in Maine in 1957.

In Orson Bean's evocative account of his first session, he has just removed his clothes down to shorts and socks and has lain down on the doctor's table.

> I fixed my eyes on a spot of water damage near the upper left-hand corner of Dr. Baker's window and breathed naturally. . . . The doctor was feeling the muscles around my jaw and neck. He found a tight cord in my neck, pressed it hard and kept on

pressing it. It hurt like hell but Little Lord Jesus no crying he makes. "Did that hurt?" asked Dr. Baker.

"Well, a little," I said, not wanting to be any trouble.

"Only a little?" he said.

"Well, it hurt a lot," I said. "It hurt like hell."

"Why didn't you cry?"

"I'm a grown-up."

He began pinching the muscles in the soft part of my shoulders. I wanted to smash him in his sadistic face, put on my clothes, and get the hell out of there. Instead I said "Ow." Then I said "That hurts."

"It doesn't sound as if it hurts," he said.

"Well, it does," I said, and managed an "oo, oo."

"Now breathe in and out deeply," he said and he placed the palm of one hand on my chest and pushed down hard on it with the other. The pain was substantial. "What if the bed breaks?" I thought. "What if my spine snaps or I suffocate?"

I breathed in and out for a while and then Baker found my ribs, and began probing and pressing. . . .

"Turn over," said Baker. I did and he started at my neck and worked downward with an unerring instinct for every tight, sore muscle. . . . "Turn back over again," said Dr. Baker, and I did. "All right," he said, "I want you to breathe in and out as deeply as you can and at the same time roll your eyes around without moving your head. Try to look at all four walls, one at a time, and move your eyeballs as far from side to side as possible." I began to roll my eyes, feeling rather foolish but grateful that he was no longer tormenting my body. On and on my eyes rolled. "Keep breathing," said Baker.

I began to feel a strange pleasurable feeling in my eyes like the sweet fuzziness that happens when you smoke a good stick of pot. The fuzziness began to spread through my face and head and then down into my body. "All right," said Baker. "Now I want you to continue breathing and do a bicycle kick on the bed with your legs." I began to raise my legs and bring them down rhythmically, striking the bed with my calves. My thighs began to ache and I wondered when he would say that I had done it long enough, but he didn't.

On and on I went, until my legs were ready to drop off. Then, gradually, it didn't hurt anymore and that same sweet fuzzy sensation of pleasure began to spread through my whole body, only much stronger. I now felt as if a rhythm had taken over my kicking which had nothing to do with any effort on my part. I felt transported and in the grip of something larger than me. I was breathing more deeply than I ever had before and I felt the sensation of each breath all the way down past my lungs and into my pelvis. Gradually, I felt myself lifted right out of Baker's milk chocolate room and up into the spheres. I was beating to an astral rhythm. Finally, I knew it was time to stop. I lay there for how many minutes I don't know and I heard his voice say, "How do you feel?"

"Wonderful," I said. "Is this always what happens?"

"More or less," he said.[13]

In a later session, Bean describes his ability to finally cry and let go of long-held-in frustrations. Though apparently no specific memories were released at that time, the account is representative of what Reichian healing entails.

"Turn over," he said and I flopped over and he began prodding at my back, around my shoulder blades. He found a spot he liked and began to press it. He pressed it hard and I let out a howl. He squeezed and he pinched at it and I lay there and screamed. It occurred to me that I had never really screamed before. . . . It wasn't that it hurt so much, although it did—it was that he had found the "on" button and I had no choice. At least, it seemed that way. The muscles he was loosening were the very ones which I had tightened up on so many years before when it had suited my purpose never to scream again. I had kept them tight for so long that the condition had become chronic and now Baker was unlocking them and all the leftover screams were pouring out.

"Now," he said, "make a fist and hit the bed." I scrunched my hands together and pounded feebly at the sheet.

"Harder," said Baker. I felt like a simp. Suddenly he began gouging at that sore, knotted muscle again and he didn't stop, and then I really hit the bed. . . . I cried harder than I ever had before. Every time I took a breath, it felt like it went right down to the base of my spine and then I'd cry again—wracking, convulsive sobs. . . . Finally, I recovered and turned over on my back.

"How do you feel?" asked Baker.

"I feel fantastic relief," I answered.[14]

This approach, in essence, was the way Reich treated most types of disturbance. He was emphatic that despite its apparent simplicity, the method was powerfully effective. Of course, the more serious a person's emotional or physical illness (it must be remembered that he drew no sharp line between mental and physical complaints), the more rigorous and difficult the course of healing. For instance, someone suffering from impotence would certainly receive different treatment than someone suffering from chronic ulcers or heart disease. A more severe disorder, such as schizophrenia, would necessitate a more demanding course of therapy. The goal, however, remains the same: the gradual loosening of the armor, the release of deeply suppressed emotions, and a restructuring of the person's attitudes and behavior in work and social relationships.

A man whose attitude toward much of life was otherwise characterized by a fiery impatience, Reich did not believe in therapeutic shortcuts. In answer to his critics, as well as to his more hot-headed disciples who sought immediate clinical breakthroughs, he insisted, "It is essentially the slow and thorough overcoming of the emotional blocks in the organism and of the anxieties connected with each single block which secures lasting results."[15] Quick results, he stressed, were likely to meet with only transient success; durability of cure was the ultimate goal.

Reich was especially wary of his treatment methods being used by the untrained; in his later years, he warned that extreme patience was a prerequisite to effective work. Our emotional and physical armor has a very real protective purpose; it must be removed slowly and with the utmost care every step of the way. Otherwise, a person might very well be overcome by the unforeseen force of long-suppressed fears or furies. In such a state, an unstable person could easily be driven to attempt suicide or murder.

As we have seen in Chapter 3, Reich emphasized that the more heavily armored the individual, the more likely he or she is to experience this kind of disorientation and despair in reacting to the bodywork therapy. Persons who vigorously express their emotions on a daily basis are much less disturbed by the sudden free flow of pent-up bioenergy.

Despite Reich's success as a healer, toward the end of his life he became rather pessimistic about the overall effectiveness of his therapy in thoroughly eliminating the armoring of many adults in our society. He never gave up on it, however, and remained firmly convinced that people can indeed make significant changes in their attitudes and lifestyle and recover a sense of well-being. He believed that, with diligent work, the individual could cure even life-threatening illnesses like heart disease and cancer or extreme forms of mental illness like schizophrenia. While he was never very specific about how long a normal course of therapy should take, he apparently believed that within a year or two a person could achieve dramatic breakthroughs in recovering mental and physical vitality.

Reich never really believed in the usefulness of his approach as a *mass* cure for widespread neuroses. He believed in preventing rather than trying to cure people's deep-seated problems. The way to get there was to work with children from the start. Thus Reich advocated measures to prevent the formation of neurosis in infants and young children. Even then, children could be changed only in certain fundamental ways, given our society's restrictions.

It seems that his personal experiences with patients had left Reich disappointed at the slow and erratic progress made in the movement toward total health. Also, once he had developed basic techniques for successful therapy, he felt the urge to conquer new scientific territory. He was never content to rest very long in any one intellectual waystation. But even though it might take many decades, perhaps even a century or more, Reich believed that his approach to healing would finally be embraced, even if there was little hope for significant change in the near future. While he was able to attract a fair number of innovative therapists and physicians during the 1940s and early 1950s, his ideas and techniques were decisively outside the mainstream. He was acutely aware of just how radical his methods were in comparison to the "talking" therapies (psychoanalysis) and to orthodox medicine, with its mechanistic emphasis. It would not be until well into the 1970s, in fact, that the healing profession would even consider Reich's approach, and in 1980 his methods have yet to win wide acceptance. "You always think in too short terms, Little Man," he wrote with obvious bitterness, "just from breakfast to lunch. You must learn to think back in terms of centuries and forward in terms of thousands of years."[16]

THE NEW WAVE: NEO-REICHIAN THERAPIES

While Reich's ideas and techniques on therapy attracted many innovators in the healing profession, these practitioners did not consider his method the inviolate message of a prophet. Rather, Reich's students and followers tended to adapt what they regarded as the most relevant features of his approach in their own treatment of patients. During the 1940s and 1950s, psychiatrists and educators as well as gymnastic teachers and dancers came to study under him, both in his institute in New York City and, later, in the distant hills of Maine. Reich expected a great deal from his students, some of whom could not keep pace with his emotional and intellectual demands.

In the field of psychotherapy the therapist's particular theoretical orientation is often less important than how well it meshes with his or her own personality traits. Hence, in keeping with his blunt and forceful character, it is hardly surprising that Reich evolved techniques to work directly on the body armor and pent-up bioenergy. Various neo-Reichian therapists, therefore, have also developed methods that reflect their own interests and skills, while at the same time conforming to Reich's overall perspective.

The tie that binds the neo-Reichian therapies is their shared belief that the individual must *experience* his or her hidden emotional conflicts, not simply discuss or analyze them. These approaches also make strong use of Reich's insights into body language as the key to our inner emotional makeup and, to varying degrees, they utilize direct massagelike techniques to unblock the feelings suppressed in the musculature. Three representative schools of psychotherapy generally viewed as "neo-Reichian" are Orgonomy, Bioenergetics, and Radix. We will briefly describe their key features and their similarities to and differences from Reich's own approach.

There are numerous other psychotherapeutic methods or healing techniques today, of course, that, while independent of

Reich's influence, have adapted many of his key concepts. These approaches include Gestalt therapy, the Alexander Technique, Primal therapy, Applied Kinesiology, Actualism, and others that emphasize heightened body awareness and the release of emotions rather than intellectual analysis as essential to effective cure. In this chapter we will describe two of the more recently formulated therapies: Polarity therapy and Oriental integration.

Orgonomy

Undoubtedly the most similar therapeutic approach to Wilhelm Reich's today is Orgonomy, named after Reich's orgone energy concept. Its leading practitioner is Dr. Elsworth Baker of New York City, who studied with Reich for eleven years and is probably the most faithful and articulate spokesperson for Reich's own methods as practiced in the 1940s. Dr. Baker heads the American College of Orgonomy and also edits the *Journal of Orgonomy,* a small, professionally oriented publication. Earlier in this chapter, we quoted extensively from actor Orson Bean's description of what Orgonomy, or orthodox Reichian therapy, feels like from the client's perspective.

Baker shares Reich's therapeutic objectives of establishing "orgastic potency" as the goal for each client. He believes that the attainment of this state "brings about very definite changes in the individual—changes which are not properly recognized or understood by most psychiatrists even today."[17] Such potency, Baker claims, includes the capacity for discharging excess energy and thereby maintaining a stable energy makeup. He also believes, with Reich, that as the client learns to surrender to the full orgasm, he or she undergoes significant changes in many aspects of daily life and that attitudes toward work, love, and even society shift to a greater acceptance of bodily pleasure as a human birthright. Moreover, orgastic potency can be seen in the client's enhanced body stance, Baker believes. The body loses its stiffness as the armor is dissolved. The face appears more relaxed and expressive. In short, Orgonomy very definitely adheres to Reich's notions of sexuality and its pivotal role in mental health.

Baker's therapeutic technique also accurately mirrors Reich's method. In one-to-one sessions once or twice a week, the client is required to strip to underclothes and lie down on his or her back with knees bent. The orgonomist is seated alongside. Much of the work is nonverbal, involving body movement and breathing. The client may be required to express an emotion bodily by hitting or kicking, and the therapist may engage in some direct contact with the body, such as prodding tense muscles of the armor. In keeping with Reich's dictum, the work proceeds systematically from the top of the body down, from one segment of the armor to the next. Typically, the client experiences spontaneous outbursts of feeling as long-suppressed memories come to the surface of consciousness.

Orgonomy makes definite clinical use of verbal exchange between therapist and client. Baker subscribes to traditional Freudian concepts, though he adds his own early stage of development—the ocular, involving the area around the eyes—to the oral, anal, phallic, and genital stages that Freud described decades ago. Based on the content of the client's dreams and verbal material, as well as on his or her body language, the therapist classifies the particular personality type displayed. Heavy armoring in the ocular area is viewed as a major sign of schizophrenia, for instance, and is explained in terms of a major disturbance in the infant-mother relationship during the first weeks of the newborn's life. The therapist will also take up the client's resistance to recovery—if such resistance is demonstrated during treatment—for verbal analysis of the precise nature of the emotional difficulties.

According to Baker, the client is considered "cured" when he or she establishes the "orgasm reflex" during the course of therapy. He comments, "To relieve the situation it is necessary to reverse the armoring process by a dissolution of the armor, releasing and draining off the repressed emotions layer by layer, from latest to earliest blocking, until unitary function is restored and natural sexuality is reached. At this point, one sees a spontaneous tilting forward of the pelvis at the end of complete expiration. This is the orgasm reflex."[18]

Orgonomists adhere to the medical model of treatment and

insist that all of its practitioners be licensed physicians. The training is conducted through an organization headed by Dr. Baker, the American College of Orgonomy, established in New York City in 1968. Most applicants are psychiatrists who are well versed in mainstream medical theory and practice. The training is conducted by means of individual therapy sessions under Baker's supervision, which may last at least three years, and weekly training seminars with the group of student orgonomists. In addition, the student is expected to undergo orgonomic therapy under one of its certified practitioners. Like Reich, Baker believes that "only a physician should attempt to use these methods of treatment, and even the physician must be adequately trained in both conventional methods and orgonomy. The tools are powerful and disaster can result if they are mishandled."[19] At present, the circle of therapists who meet Baker's rigorous selection criteria is quite small, only two or three dozen at most in the United States.

Bioenergetics

Another school of psychotherapy strongly influenced by Reich and sharing his emphasis on the body is Bioenergetics. Founded by Dr. Alexander Lowen, who is currently in private practice in Connecticut, this approach maintains Reich's focus on freeing the flow of orgone, or bioenergy, hence its name. Lowen studied under Reich for several years and also underwent therapy with him. Since the 1950s, Lowen has helped popularize many of his mentor's principles of growth and healing and is undoubtedly the most widely read of Reich's students today. His books such as *Bioenergetics* and *The Betrayal of the Body*, as well as numerous lectures and training workshops, have awakened much public interest in alternatives to more orthodox, purely verbal kinds of therapy.

According to Lowen, the aim of Bioenergetics is to integrate feelings with body awareness so that the body comes alive and is in a vibrant state. The body "has a motility independent of ego control which is manifested by the spontaneity of its gestures and the vivacity of its expression," Lowen observes. "It hums, it vibrates, it glows. It is charged with feeling. The first difficulty that one encounters with patients in search of identity is that they are not aware of the lack of aliveness in their bodies."[20]

Through direct dissolution of specific spots of armoring and various exercises, the therapist helps the client regain this awareness and release repressed emotions. "The focus of the bodily intervention is to open blocked areas of the body to the flow of excitation and feeling," Lowen says. "When any part of the body begins to vibrate—it happens in the legs—it is an indication that energy is flowing through that part of the body."[21] This approach is modeled closely on Reich's. However, where Reich insisted on loosening the armor from the eye and forehead segment downward, Lowen works on the legs first and neglects Reich's systematic attack on the armoring and the top down approach.

Lowen includes traditional verbal analysis in the course of therapy during which the client is encouraged to explore dreams, past conflicts, hopes, and fantasies. He or she may be verbally prompted by the therapist to become aware of a particular bodily feeling or localized region of intense armoring. The client's character is analyzed in terms of classic psychoanalytic theory, with its concepts of the oral, anal, and phallic stages of individual development. In this manner, the therapist brings the suppressed feelings to consciousness by both physical and analytic means. Indeed, speaking recently of his personal therapy under Reich, Lowen commented, "When I started back into practice, I realized that I had to make some of the following changes in the Reichian approach: *first,* to do more analysis."[22]

Like the Reichian approach, Bioenergetics emphasizes the importance of body language as a key to the client's inner disturbances. Lowen has made use of Reich's technique of simply letting the client sit or stand for a few minutes in complete silence. Then, relying on his subtle perceptions of and reactions to that person's totality, he makes diagnostic judgments. For example, in *The Betrayal of the Body,* he vividly describes his first impressions of an artist who came to him for help.

> As he sat opposite me, I saw his drawn face, his empty eyes, his tightly set jaw, and his frozen body. In his immobility and shallow

breathing, I could sense his fear and panic. He, however, was not aware of the gauntness of his face, the blankness of his eyes, the tension of his jaw, or the tightness of his body. He did not feel his fear and panic. Being out of touch with his body, he only sensed his confusion and desperation.[23]

Like Reich, Lowen believes that letting oneself go out of control is frightening to most people. Hence, like Reich, he believes that the course of therapy must be gradual. Despite its often dramatic nature, in which clients sometimes experience powerful changes in their self-image in short periods of time, shortcuts are not desirable. Growth takes time. Thus Lowen's therapeutic objective seems less grandiose than Reich's or Baker's, in that he does not strive for "orgastic potency" in the client but, rather, for a more general liberation from neurotic disturbances.

Bioenergetics also differs from these other approaches in Lowen's willingness to use groups in treatment, especially in the supplementary practice of the Bioenergetics exercises. In these techniques, the client is typically required to stay in an upright position and hold physical stances that are designed to free the flow of the bioenergy. These postures are often exhausting and difficult to execute. Particular emphasis is placed on the nature and quality of the individual's contact with the ground. Lowen's focus on this aspect of body language is called "grounding"; it has become a widely used concept in many of the body-oriented therapies that flourish today.

What differentiates Bioenergetics from its parent system is its less systematic approach to loosening the armor, besides a downplaying of Reich's concept of the orgone and its minimizing of cause-and-effect relationships between social or political issues and our inner blocks. Lowen says relatively little about the existence of armoring in Western society as a response to our characteristic way of life.

But in speaking of the joyful body experiences to which we become sensitive as we become more alive, he shares his mentor's dissatisfaction with the emphasis on technology in our civilization. "The amazing thing about our culture is that this is all denied because it isn't objective," he has commented. "If you can't probe it by a machine, it doesn't exist."[24]

Like Baker, Lowen directs a training program derived from the principles of his therapeutic system. It did not get started until the early 1970s, although by then Bioenergetic techniques had been adapted by many practitioners working with clients across the country. Currently based in New York City, the Institute for Bioenergetics mandates a four-year training course for professionals consisting of 160 hours of training therapy, a series of training workshops conducted with groups of students, and twelve hours of personal supervision under a competent Bioenergetic Trainer. At present, the number of certified Bioenergetic therapists is quite small, at most several dozen. Lowen's methods, however, have been highly influential and are used by hundreds of therapists in the United States and Western Europe.

Radix

The third major school of psychotherapy to emerge directly out of Reich's work is known as Radix, meaning "source" or "root." It has been developed by Dr. Charles Kelley, an experimental psychologist who became interested in Reich's work in the 1940s and was first published in one of Reich's own journals in 1951. In 1960, Kelley founded the Interscience Research Institute of Connecticut; the name was changed to the Radix Institute in 1974. Radix is currently based in Southern California. From 1961 to 1965, Kelley served as editor-in-chief of *The Creative Process,* a lively professional journal, now unfortunately defunct, devoted to Reich's legacy. Since the 1960s, Kelley has been active, especially on the West Coast, in disseminating a modified version of Reichian therapy.

Reflecting the background of its originator, Radix is broadly educational rather than medical in its orientation. That is, persons entering into the Radix work are not viewed as "sick" or "ill," and thus are not led to expect a complete "cure" of their problems. Instead, Radix is designed to teach its students, through bodily as well as verbal means, to better express their emotions and thereby experience more satisfaction in their lives. In this respect, Kelley shares the general goals of the human potential movement in that he adheres to an optimistic view of human nature and growth.

Radix differs from both Orgonomy and Bioenergetics in several respects. There is far more emphasis on group work; indeed, Kelley has estimated that perhaps half of all its sessions are done in groups. Under the direction of the instructor, each member of the group assists in the Radix Intensive (the primary technique, which stresses deep emotional release) of the other members, and each one in turn experiences his or her own Intensive. Through various "paired feeling" exercises, in which participants pair off and aid in each other's therapeutic work, clients gradually learn to loosen their body armor. In these exercises, Kelley makes use of guided fantasy, direct body contact between the client partners, and other means to free the flow of their bioenergy. It should be noted that Kelley prefers to use the term *radix* for Reich's *orgone energy*. Having pioneered his therapeutic efforts with persons suffering from visual disorders, Radix also emphasizes the improvement of visual awareness and eye contact as precursors to more general well-being; these "visualization techniques" are a unique feature of the Radix program.

Unlike Orgonomy and Bioenergetics, Radix makes little use of orthodox psychoanalytic theory. As we have seen, both Baker and Lowen interpret the body language of their clients in terms of the various Freudian psychosexual stages of development. Kelley employs a different terminology, "based on whether the student is blocking primarily fear, anger, or pain—or some combination. This new characterology is highly useful in our work, but is new and undeveloped. It will require a great deal more technical work to integrate our findings with the Freudian system of classification."[25] In Kelley's view, a certain amount of character armoring has valuable psychological functions, so his approach does not aim at totally eliminating it.

Kelley's approach also seeks to avoid the established psychoanalytic phenomenon of transference. Radix teachers are instructed to shun situations in which clients may place them in the role of authority figures or surrogate parents. For example, Radix teachers do not give advice or counsel their students about such personal decisions as whether to change jobs or relationships. However, transference has been a readily identifiable occurrence in many kinds of psychotherapy, and Kelley readily admits that this issue remains one of the thorniest confronting his approach.

Like the other major neo-Reichian schools of psychotherapy, Radix provides a comprehensive training program for those who wish to serve as its teachers. Kelley does not require applicants to hold advanced degrees in medicine or mental health, but rather stresses their emotional readiness to direct the inner growth of others. He has observed that "trainees run into difficulties in the training program when they encounter resistances or problems in their own character or development that they are having difficulty working through."[26] Consequently, he insists that intense personal Radix work, typically lasting three years, serve as the foundation for every Radix trainee. At present, the program is certainly rather small, with about twenty certified Radix teachers and over forty Radix trainees.

PARALLEL THERAPIES

Two recent and relatively unfamiliar approaches to healing that incorporate many of Reich's healing principles—especially his concept of dissolving the body armor and restoring the vital flow of the bioenergy—and yet go beyond his initial groundbreaking discoveries are Polarity therapy, established by Randolph Stone, and the Oriental integration represented by Michio Kushi's East West Foundation.

Polarity Therapy

Dr. Randolph Stone is an osteopath, chiropractor, and naturopath. While he does not make explicit reference to Reich's ideas, the similarities are in many ways unmistakable. Born in Austria in 1890, Stone was a contemporary of Reich in time and place and also emigrated to the United States, where he settled in Chicago. Having traveled widely around the globe and currently residing in India, Stone has had firsthand contact with acupuncture, Yoga, and Native American shamanism. The essence of Polarity therapy is, in part, a distillation of the most relevant aspects of these healing traditions.

According to Stone, each human being mirrors the energy structure of the universe. A great many traditional spiritual disciplines have declared that the cosmos includes a duality of opposite and complementary forces, known in the Orient, for example, as *yin/yang*. Stone contends that every living thing is similarly made up of this energy duality. When it is in balance, good health and well-being are experienced. If either the active or passive part of this duality predominates, however, a disharmony results and manifests itself as disease. As we shall see in Chapter 6, Reich articulated much the same view in his theory of the orgone energy. Each person's dual energy patterns are supposedly revealed by the body. The trained observer in Polarity therapy uses indicators such as the shape of the feet and toes, the curve of the spine, the lines in the torso or face, and even scars and birthmarks as important clues to a person's emotional and physical history and health. The resemblance to Reich's emphasis on "reading" body language as a first step in healing is readily apparent.

Many of the Polarity techniques developed by Stone are similar to Reichian methods. Through massagelike strokes, the healer uses pressure and his or her own bodily energies to free up and release energy blockages in the client. A basic goal is to achieve a balance in the client's body between the left and right sides, which are seen to correspond to different personality styles (the left side is intuitive and nurturing, the right is assertive and forthright). These manipulations can be quite painful to the recipient as long-suppressed emotions of anger, sadness, or longing are liberated. Eventually the patient learns to let go of the emotions that are bound up in chronic muscular patterns.

As in Reichian therapy, there are no shortcuts in the Polarity approach. Although Stone does not specifically identify how long the typical healing process should take, a moderately armored person might be expected to spend about a year in regular weekly sessions to experience a thorough regeneration of inner well-being. As part of its complete therapeutic process, Polarity therapy requires daily practice of various physical exercises designed to accelerate the gains in vitality reaped during the healing sessions. The exercises, which Stone has called "polar-energetics," resemble Yoga postures. Full, deep breathing is encouraged in order to discharge stored emotional and physical toxins. As we have seen, Reich placed tremendous importance on the quality of respiration and strove to develop an even, rhythmic breathing pattern in his patients. Going beyond Reich's therapeutic system, however, Polarity therapy also prescribes specific diets for various types of physical and emotional imbalances.

Does the Polarity method really work? In Boston, in 1979, one of the authors, Dr. Hoffman, had the opportunity to undergo a series of Polarity sessions over a period of several months. The experience was a complete confirmation of the view articulated by Reich, Stone, and others that the human being is indeed a subtle energy system in which mind and body are inextricably linked. A brief description of the sessions is provided below. We invite the reader to make his or her own comparisons to Orson Bean's experience in Reichian therapy.

> My introduction to Polarity therapy came at a large "New Age" fair held, ironically enough, in a military practice building in Boston. Nearly all the booths were well attended, but there seemed to be a particularly large crowd around the Polarity therapy one.
>
> After a long wait, it was finally my turn. A slight-looking young woman introduced herself as Donna, and asked me to remove my shoes and socks, then make myself comfortable on the massage table. As I lay down and closed my eyes, she quietly requested that I relax myself as fully as possible.
>
> For a few seconds, I listened to the din of the crowd in the large hall around me. I began to feel the mild pressure of her fingers on my toes, and the loudspeaker noise grew more distant. Within seconds, I felt calmer than I could recall. As I felt myself about to drift into a dreamy haze, a sudden stabbing pain tore through me.
>
> I almost sobbed in surprise and agony. This was no joke, the pain was real and becoming unbearable. Should I forget this whole thing? I heard her voice calmly say, "Let it out . . . go 'aaghhh . . .'"
>
> I was a bit embarrassed to shout in public, but we were off in a

corner of the hall. I imitated her sound, much louder of course, and miraculously, the pain did subside. More feelings of bliss, alternating with more moments of acute pain, occurred, as she continued to apply direct pressure to various points on the soles of my feet.

Next, she applied brief pressure to my temples. I now began to experience a strange, eerie kind of tingling. First, my face began to feel as though I had been hyperventilating. Then, the tingling spread to my neck, shoulders, and at last, my arms and wrists. After a few minutes, the tingling subsided, in a path that retraced the initial onset.

Abruptly, the time was up. I sat up on the massage table, wondering what spectacle I had caused. Two or three people stood impatiently waiting their turn, but that was all. Donna asked how I felt, then responded to my request, offering a brief impression of what she had observed during the session. As a total stranger, she thereupon proceeded to make an incredibly accurate description of my personality, strengths and weaknesses. I thanked her, and, smiling, she turned to the next person on line.

That evening and for a day or two after, I walked around in a kind of daze. I felt much more relaxed, in a strange sort of way, than I could remember. I decided to continue with the sessions on a private basis.

To my amazement, again and again, pressure applied to, say, a specific part of one toe would initiate the electriclike tingling in a completely distant spot like a shoulder or part of the neck. When Donna would continue the pressure, the tingling would spread to other body parts, in a path that gradually became recognizable, and formed a reliable pattern. Many of the pressure points corresponded to acupuncture nodes, and were stimulated to enhance the flow of blocked energy.

Direct pressure of certain body points would suddenly elicit long-buried memories. Just as Reich had declared, nothing seemed to be forgotten by the body. As Donna would exert pressure on a set of muscular tissue that appeared knotted, I would first begin to feel a particular emotion, but without any specific memory involved. For example, one spot on the neck seemed to elicit sadness and longing. Typically, though, continued pressure on the node would lead to the recall of very specific memories from childhood or adolescence. Some of these were of experiences that I literally had not consciously thought of since they occurred, and yet I would find myself weeping uncontrollably.

At other times, the physical manipulations induced tremendous pain. I have never prided myself on my abilty to withstand pain, and this was the most difficult part of the sessions for me. In each instance, as I began to cry out in pain, I was instructed to "Make your sound," that "aaghhh!" shouted with full exhalation. Interestingly, as the sessions progressed, I could see that greater pressure applied produced very little pain, or none at all. This was a sign, Donna would say with satisfaction, that the emotions stored in the bodily area were being released and the muscular tensions therefore dispersed.

Two other special systems of massage that use finger pressure on various parts of the body are Reflexology and Shiatsu. Both are based on Eastern principles of life energy flow that also underpin the ancient system of acupuncture, to be discussed in the next chapter. While Polarity therapy seems to be a more complete healing system, these two other approaches are becoming popular, as they, too, show results in both relaxing the client and freeing up the flow of bioenergy.

Oriental Integration

Another highly integrated approach to healing that relies upon direct work on the armor and a restoration of the flow of bioenergy is promulgated by Michio Kushi, founder of the East West Foundation in Brookline, Massachusetts. He is also the guiding force behind the *East West Journal,* a publication devoted to the latest developments in such areas as natural foods and organic agriculture, alternative community living, individual well-being, and "clean" energy sources.

Mr. Kushi's therapeutic orientation bears certain close similarities to Reich's, yet goes beyond Reich's more generalized conception of the life energy. For example, he defines diseases as a specific imbalance in the polarity of the life energy (*ki* in Japanese) in the human body. Some forms of illness flow from an overly *yin*, or expansive, condition; others are overly *yang*, or contractive, in origin. Of particular importance in the cause of any disease is the individual's diet.

Similar to Reich's rather intuitive perspective, Kushi's therapeutic approach relies on visual diagnosis as a key to discerning deeper internal imbalances. However, Kushi not only makes use of the client's body language to interpret his or her emotional makeup, but also incorporates traditional Oriental medicine, which for centuries has correlated facial appearance with the condition of the internal organs. Based on a coherent system that also underlies acupuncture, the age-old Eastern view has been that direct correspondences exist between certain outer physical manifestations, such as the condition of the eyes, hair, skin, or hands, and the vitality of major organs like the heart, liver, or kidneys.

While Reich did not explicitly make this sort of comparison, he independently arrived at one key conclusion that is basic to traditional Oriental healing: that specific emotions, such as anger, fear, or longing, seem to affect the functioning of particular organs in the human body. "Each organ has its own mode of expression, its own specific language," he cogently observed.

According to Kushi, before one can direct the flow of ki in the body, it is necessary to determine which organs are out of energetic alignment. A careful, accurate visual diagnosis is always regarded as the first step to restoring mental and physical harmony.

Once the visual diagnosis is completed, the healing program is carried out simultaneously on several fronts. Depending upon the particular bodily imbalance and specific organs afflicted, a special diet may be prescribed. In addition, the person may be placed on a regimen of daily physical exercises to restore the proper flow of the bioenergy. Like Reich, Kushi believes that vigorous daily exercise is needed to establish health. Finally, the client is encouraged to engage in a thoroughgoing self-analysis, ideally under the guidance of an older, more spiritually attuned helper. Meditation and prayer are considered essential components of any genuine return to well-being.

Kushi has not yet amassed an indisputable body of evidence for his innovative approach to healing. As is true of Reich, he has tended to rely upon intuitive observations rather than rigorous scientific validation. At the 1979 East West Foundation's Cancer Conference, however, Dr. Anthony Sattilaro, president of Philadelphia's Methodist Hospital, presented his own case history, fully documented. Not only did he cure himself completely of terminal bone cancer by following Kushi's recommendations, but he substantiated each stage of his path to total cure. In other publications of the East West Foundation, emphasis is now being placed on medically corroborating, whenever possible, the often dramatic effects reaped by this approach.

Kushi, like Reich, guarantees no immediate recoveries. The individual must accept absolute responsibility for his or her return to inner balance. Summing up his healing philosophy, Kushi observes, "If you want instant, impressive results, you are looking in the wrong direction. On the other hand, if you are ready to take a long, slow, but steady way, you can be your own doctor and change yourself into whatever you would like to be."[27]

PSYCHOTHERAPY FOR DEGENERATIVE DISEASES

Reich may have been unduly pessimistic in his predictions of how long it would take for Western medicine to advance. In the last few years, once-ridiculed techniques such as meditation, autogenic training, and Yoga are now within the field of study of top researchers at major clinics, from the Harvard Medical Center in Boston to the Langley-Porter Institute in San Francisco. The needle-and-pill path to cure has not disappeared, but it is waning in influence. Especially among the most talented and innovative health professionals, there is widening interest in methods that emphasize the inherent unity of mind and body. To be sure, the majority of these scientists are undoubtedly unaware of Reich's work. It is in some ways a historical irony that he advanced his sweeping criticisms of mainstream medicine at a time when it was enjoying tremendous confidence from nearly every quarter. More and more frequently, however, major illnesses today are being dealt with along the lines that Reich suggested decades ago.

For example, there has been marked interest of late in treating heart disease and related cardiovascular disorders through psychotherapy. Drs. Ray Rosenman and Meyer Friedman, of San Francisco's Mount Zion Hospital and Medical Center, have made pioneering efforts in this field. Their approach to heart disease parallels Reich's and utilizes a similar kind of treatment.

People who are prone to heart attacks by virtue of their hurried, impatient attitude to life are carefully trained in deep muscle relaxation. "Drills" in motor deceleration and in progressive relaxation are recommended to reduce the tension that begins to surface unconsciously in stressful situations. Even more to the point, such persons are taught to observe themselves constantly throughout the day. They learn to monitor their own daily actions, "the way they hurry through the working day, the struggle and tension manifested by brusque motor movements, hostile grimaces and frequent verbal explosions, as pent-up irritations are vented," observes Rosenman. "The resultant shock of recognition affords an incentive to change."[28]

Even more indicative of this new trend is their recommendation that Type A individuals participate in both group psychotherapy and some form of meditation in order to change their self-destructive behavior. Much as Reich did, Rosenman and Friedman insist that the patient integrate the suggested exercises into the entire therapeutic process. They add that medication is of little value, for the patient must learn to personally restructure his or her behavior and orientation to life.

They echo Reich's sentiment that heart-attack-prone persons must above all learn to discharge their emotions in a healthy, satisfying manner rather than through short and abortive bursts of anger or impatience. Closely paralleling Reich's social sentiments as well, they have emphasized that our industrial, work-oriented society actually *encourages* the development of heart-attack-prone individuals. They not only estimate that over 50 percent of the American urban population now exhibits Type A behavior, but point out that most cardiologists and internists appear to be "Super A's." Until Western society alters its definitions of success and achievement, we can expect little progress in combating this twentieth-century "epidemic."

Another twentieth-century epidemic is cancer, certainly the most dreaded of all modern diseases. In the last few years, there has been a surge of interest in alternative approaches to cancer, from fasting to laetrile, in recognition of the fact that orthodox medicine has utterly failed to stem the cancer tide. Although the

United States alone has spent billions of dollars on cancer research, there has been no significant lessening in its spread.

As we saw in Chapter 4, Reich firmly believed that one day cancer would be recognized as having an important emotional component. In *The Cancer Biopathy*, he emphasized repeatedly that cancer was a disease in which the individual's life energy gradually becomes depleted through emotional resignation. He viewed the chronically poor respiration of such persons as the key contributing factor to the illness, and contended that "the respiratory disturbance is characteristic of all known malignant tumors."[29]

Working with cancer patients in the early 1940s, Reich therefore stressed the necessity of teaching them to vigorously express anger and other negative emotions. To help them establish full, natural breathing and thereby stimulate the flow of bioenergy in their bodies, he would encourage them to shout, strike pillows, or "throttle" his arm as though it were the throat of an enemy. In other cases, he encouraged highly repressed cancer patients to fully release long-repressed sexual frustrations. At the very least, he argued, they should be able to masturbate freely and without guilt. If physical strength permitted, they were prompted to engage in sexual intercourse and enjoy the strong physical pleasures of sex in daily living.

The best prognosis for recovery, he found, lies with those who adopt a fighting attitude to the disease, who refuse to surrender. Often, though, the patient would be so resigned to the course of the disease that very little could be done. Reich railed against those who gave up on life and refused to mobilize their inner forces for health. If at all possible, he sought to get the cancer patient to *feel*, and to achieve some *joie de vivre*.

Not surprisingly, Reich was denounced as a quack or lunatic for adopting this theory and approach. He lacked impressive scientific evidence to substantiate his views, relying mainly on intuitive observations. "How could any serious disease, particularly one as dangerous as cancer, be related to how happy one is in life?" his critics asked. "What good would psychotherapy do for someone with cancer?" Amid a veritable barrage of ridicule and censure, Reich's view was summarily dismissed.

Today, however, not only are many innovators in the cancer field acknowledging the link between mind and body, but therapeutic efforts along the lines suggested by Reich are being carried out. One of the most promising of these approaches is represented by the work of the well-known radiologist and oncologist Carl Simonton, M.D., and his wife, Stephanie Matthews-Simonton, described in their recent book, *Getting Well Again.* Directors of the Cancer Counseling and Research Center in Fort Worth, Texas, they have developed a nationally focused training program for health professionals who work with cancer patients. Their methods resemble Reich's but also go beyond his particular techniques.

Independently confirming Reich's seminal observations, the Simontons have found that the predisposing personality characteristics of the cancer patient include a poor self-image and a marked tendency to hold in resentment and indulge in self-pity. Moreover, such persons find it difficult to form intimate relationships, sexual or otherwise. In line with Reich's perspective, the Simontons use a combination of techniques, including meditation, progressive relaxation, and visual imagery, in conjunction with group psychotherapy (Reich never utilized group treatment in his approach to cancer or other forms of illness) to stimulate a change in the emotional makeup of the cancer patient. The patient's reaction to stress and its effect on the development of cancer are key areas for discussion. As Reich did, the Simontons encourage the cancer patient to accept responsibility for recovery, and emphasize the self-curative powers of the human mind-body; however, they urge the patient to continue with regularly prescribed medical treatment such as radiation therapy or chemotherapy, types of healing that Reich viewed as dubious.

Today, more than thirty-five years after Reich first began to use psychotherapy to treat cancer patients, this approach is gathering momentum across the country. The link between cancer and emotional health is being confirmed in current research; and, equally important, practitioners are now realizing that intensive psychotherapy can effect significant changes in the course of the disease.

CASTING A CRITICAL EYE

While Reich would certainly find much to applaud in the many new therapies his work has spawned, he would undoubtedly be critical of some that lay claim to his influence, either directly or indirectly. Certainly, he would be uncomfortable with the pervasive emphasis they attach to ventilating emotions, often without much regard either for the effect this may have on others or for the proper time and place. While Reich argued forcefully for honest and full emotional release in social relations, he did not believe that simply expressing anger, hostility, or sexual desire was an indicator of mental health.

As a matter of fact, he was acutely aware that in years to come his ideas might well be misinterpreted or misconstrued by overzealous followers. In his prophetic book, *The Murder of Christ*, he warned that his therapeutic system might be distorted and thereby cause further damage to society's well-being. He was especially afraid that new, rigid ideals would be imposed to regulate emotional health and that all persons would be expected to conform to them; he particularly feared that everyone would be encouraged simply to rage at others for the sake of supposed "emotional release."

Shortly before his death in 1970, Fritz Perls expressed similar concerns about the misuse of Gestalt therapy. "We are entering the phase of the turner-onners," Perls wrote. "Turn on to instant cure, instant joy, instant sensory awareness. We are entering the phase of the quacks and the con men, who think if you get some breakthrough, you are cured—disregarding any growth requirements."[30]

Today, a decade later, the sensible cautions of Reich and Perls seem even more valid and compelling. In the mad rush and restlessness that characterizes so much of daily life in America, it is easy to be fooled by the fancy claims of those who purport to "transform your personality in forty-eight hours" in the same way an auto mechanic might advertise the quick replacement of a worn-out muffler.

We believe that one major criticism Reich would undoubtedly make in regard to many of the new therapies is their extreme lack of social consciousness. Throughout his life, Reich insisted upon connections between the individual and society, politics and sex, economics and mental health. While recently developed bodywork techniques have unquestionable value for many people, the leaders of these therapeutic systems often speak and write as though we live in a social vacuum. Some spokespersons pay brief lip service to the need for "self-expression" or "self-fulfillment" but seldom get very specific about the political and social realities that stifle human creativity in our bureaucratic and technological society.

During the years when he was actively training therapists in the 1940s, Reich was extremely critical of those students who seemed to lack his social concern, and he was particularly incensed by practitioners whose main motive appeared to be a lucrative private practice. It is an unfortunate characteristic of some of the leading therapeutic approaches today that they are so clearly aimed at the upper middle class. From the beginning of his career, Reich went out of his way to provide low-cost assistance to those unable to afford private sessions. As we have seen, he helped found several "people's clinics" for precisely this purpose. Year after year, he also poured much of his income into research to more fully validate and develop his discoveries. It is a sad fact that many therapists who declare their allegiance to Reich's methods and views have thus far refrained from making even a semblance of such a commitment, even though some of them have extremely successful private practices.

Reich emphasized that individual therapy could not possibly solve the growing dilemma of mental and physical illness. He became increasingly convinced that complete individual healing could not even take place within the context of mainstream society. There were simply too many forces that cause armoring—and, indeed, Reich readily conceded that without their emotional and physical armoring, many persons would become sadly vulnerable to the harsh realities of modern industrial life.

Thus, in his later years, as recounted in Ilse Ollendorff's biography, Reich was seized with the vision of a therapeutic community, a kind of healing kibbutz, on his remote farm in Maine. He hoped that it would one day encompass a treatment clinic, infant-care program, dormitories, and scientific research quarters. He saw it as a kind of model for Western society, to be guided by shared decision making and devoted to peaceful pursuits. In such an environment, Reich believed, farsighted thinkers could quietly study the process of human healing and its relation to the natural world. During the 1940s and 1950s, recalled his former wife, "Reich would walk again and again over the property, carrying little wooden markers and designating the spots where he saw the buildings in his mind."[31] While the farm did eventually include a small laboratory and living area, most of the vision remained unrealized.

But even though Reich was not able to implement this dream, it did inspire others. In 1969, Fritz Perls began plans for a similar enterprise in British Columbia. Several of his associates became involved in the quest for a Gestalt community, but the death of their leader later that year curtailed their activities. More recently, such therapeutic systems as Polarity are developing integrated communities in which bodywork therapies are only one part of a complete way of life designed to promote emotional, physical, and spiritual well-being. The Findhorn community in Scotland, though less clearly influenced by Reich's ideas, provides another example of this type of venture. Its members, many of whom have benefited from bodywork therapy, participate in a small-scale rural society based on egalitarian values and open and honest communication with one another. In such a manner, true breakthroughs in healing may take place.

As Reich prophetically observed over forty years ago, "These model institutions will be the nuclei from which the principles of the new order will spread to society as a whole."[32]

CHAPTER 6

Orgone:
The All-Embracing
Life Energy

Because armored man is rigidified, he thinks predominantly in terms of matter. He perceives motion as being in the beyond or as supernatural.

The same energy that guides the movements of animals and the growth of all living substances indeed also guides the stars.
—WILHELM REICH

C ertainly the most controversial aspect of all of Wilhelm Reich's work was his theory of an undetected, subtle energy that is present in all living things and, indeed, throughout the entire universe. Developing his notion in the 1940s, through both his clinical practice and laboratory experiments, Reich became convinced that he had stumbled upon one of the most important discoveries of modern times. Because he lacked formal, rigorous training in biology or physics, however, he was not able to influence many orthodox researchers. In fact, as he continued to insist upon the validity of his concept, some of his closest supporters confided that they could no longer totally agree with his conclusions, which they found too fantastic.

As his legal battles mounted, Reich interpreted the persecution as a sign of the brilliance of his discoveries. At the time of his death in 1957 and for ten to fifteen years after that, Reich's claims for the life energy theory were viewed, at best, as the sincere but misguided efforts of a great intuitive genius. At worst—and there were many who adopted this view—the whole concept was ridiculed as the obsession of an unbalanced mind. By the late 1960s, many farsighted scientists could easily acknowledge the significance of Reich's insights on sexuality, women's rights, child care, or holistic health. But the life energy theory seemed to be another story, one better left forgotten.

Then, in 1972, President Nixon made his historic visit to China, inspiring an explosion of interest in things Oriental, including acupuncture and acupressure. Once relegated to obscure back-alley walkups in the Chinatowns of New York or San Francisco, these ancient practices were suddenly brought to worldwide attention. The American Medical Association quickly lobbied for legislation to prohibit their use except under the supervision of a licensed physician, but the proverbial cat was out of the bag. Before long, popular books and professionally oriented articles began to appear on the subject.

In the 1970s, the blossoming of interest in Eastern mysticism in the West drew attention to the concept of a fundamental life energy, still foreign to our scientists. From American Indian shamanism to esoteric Judaism, this concept had predominated for millennia. As it has now become clear, Western civilization is virtually unique in history in its failure to recognize each human being as a subtle energy system in constant relationship to a vast sea of energies in the surrounding cosmos. Today, in laboratories around the world, studies are slowly confirming this age-old notion. Suddenly, Wilhelm Reich's last years no longer look so outlandish: it now turns out that he had independently arrived at a perspective similar to that held by Eastern thinkers for many centuries.

In this chapter we will briefly sketch out the orgone theory, how Reich stumbled onto it, how it is related to similar Eastern concepts, and how several scientific figures in Europe's past had arrived at similar concepts. Current research tends to confirm and even extend Reich's fascinating notion of the orgone energy, so we will further explore this—the tomorrow that Reich dreamed of.

During the yesterday in which Reich worked, he developed his theory of the life energy by a rapid-fire progression of ideas over a few short years. Fundamentally, the concept was originally developed from Freud's idea of libido. Reich extended this rather ethereal notion, drawing on individual bodywork therapy with patients and small-scale laboratory studies carried out under his private direction. As indicated earlier, he preferred a somewhat independent method of scientific investigation, working with a small team and not expecting immediate confirmation for these findings from the larger scientific community. Certainly, however, because of the extremely innovative nature of his theories, it is doubtful that mainstream university researchers would have shown much interest in his proposals even if he had sought such support.

For more details on the precise experiments that led to Reich's conclusions, we refer readers to Edward Mann's book, *Orgone, Reich, and Eros.* Suffice it to say here that Reich personally financed the studies, using the best equipment he could secure. In fact, once he became convinced of the importance of his research, he devoted nearly all his income to it. True to his nature, he set up the experiments quickly, one after the other, following wherever the trail led. Because of lack of time, he rarely replicated them more than a few times, and in any case it was just not his style to repeat the same experiment hundreds of times. Moreover, in his descriptions of this work, he wrote in an impassioned style, liberally mixing findings, interpretation, bold theorizing, methodology, and even social criticism. It is little wonder that other scientists, accustomed to precise, dry, emotionally detached articles and books that moved from experimental procedure to cautiously worded conclusions, tended to dismiss him as a misguided or impractical dreamer.

THE ORGONE

Between 1940 and 1950, Reich became convinced that a subtle biophysical energy permeates all living things. This energy, he claimed, is akin to such physical energies as electricity , magnetism, or radiation but is distinct from them. Its characteristic color is blue.

One impetus for his view came from clinical work with patients. From character-analysis therapy, he discovered numerous individuals who reported feeling tinglings, energy streamings, or currents at certain breakthrough points in the therapy. The undulating character and slower movement of these sensations implied that they were like, but not the same as, electrical currents.

The other and more exact source of the orgone theory was experiments Reich conducted in Norway in which grass, earth, and other substances like ocean sand were pressurized and steam-heated in a vessel called an autoclave. This process led to the production of tiny blue bladderlike cells called *vesicles*, observable microscopically at a magnification of 2,000 to 3,000 X. Under certain conditions these tended to clump together in protozoalike formations. Reich called them *bions*, suggesting thereby that they were the smallest unit of living matter. He found that those made from ocean sand, called SAPA bions, emitted radiation. Attempting to understand this strange radiation effect, he put some sand into a windowed metal box and observed a bluish-gray glowing. Later, he found the same type of glowing when the SAPA bions and all other residue had been removed. After many other laboratory experiments, he labeled this energy the *orgone*.

In a series of experiments that went on for many months, Reich developed an understanding of the main properties of this bioenergy. Subsequent scientific work by him and other investigators has served to confirm these conclusions. Psychologist-researcher Dr. Charles Kelley has summarized these properties in a ten-point statement that is printed, with his permission, in Appendix D. Let us note briefly here that the orgone is mass-free; permeates all of space in different concentrations; is in constant motion, either pulsating or flowing along a curving path; is responsible for all forms of life; is taken into the body through breathing; is present in all cells, including red blood cells; is especially drawn to water; and forms units, both living (bions, animals, humans) and nonliving (for example, clouds). These units are "negatively entropic"—that is, they acquire energy from their environment.

During the 1940s, Reich elaborated his theory in further work with patients. For one thing, he found that some mentally ill persons felt this electriclike current running through them but mistakenly attributed it to external forces. Thus, it is common for many schizophrenics to insist that they are being "bombarded with rays" or "attacked by influences in the atmosphere." The frequency of such reports helped convince Reich that the strange sensations his healthier, less sensitive patients experienced in therapy were, in fact, quite real. Late in his career, he argued that a schizophrenic will lapse into utter disorientation when his or her self-perception is overwhelmed by strong sensations of orgonotic streamings; the healthy individual will feel well and happy under the impact of the streamings. The schizophrenic perceives the bioenergetic flow within, but misinterprets it.

Reich clearly differentiated this bioenergy from such other energies as electricity, X-rays, or magnetism. For instance, orgone energy pulsates in a slow, smooth, wavelike fashion, characteristics observed by Reich in the orgone accumulator. It is especially present in several "power centers" in the body, and particularly in such nerve clusters as the solar plexus (stomach), hypogastric plexus (lower abdomen), and lumbosacral plexus (lower back). As we shall see later in this chapter, some of these body areas have been identified in the East for centuries as generators of an instinctual psychospiritual force. Furthermore, Reich found that this energy flows in the body in a spiral, or figure-eight, pattern rather than in simple vertical or horizontal lines.

Based on his work with the chronically ill, notably cancer patients, Reich emphasized that all diseases could ultimately be best understood as imbalances in the orgone energy system. "If we wish to comprehend the cancer disease in a simple fashion," he declared in *The Cancer Biopathy*, "we must acknowledge the existence of a basically new cosmic energy, which I call orgone."[1] Health is characterized by the vital and complete pulsation of this energy in all the organs; various diseases represent either under- or overcharges of specific organ systems. As we noted earlier, Reich viewed cancer as a systematic, long-term shrinking of this energy resulting from chronic feelings of self-pity or resignation about one's life. Conversely, he saw heart disease as an overexcitation of life energy brought about by chronic frustration and pent-up anger.

Reich was also convinced that every living thing exudes an energy field, which then surrounds it. "A fish, for example, shortly after death, still shows an orgonotic field around its body, but the reactions are weak and disappear soon. Dead branches, in contrast to living ones, show no orgonotic field," he observed. "This means that the dying organism loses its biological energy. First the orgone energy field shrinks, and then the tissues lose their orgone."[2] Kirlian photography, which we will discuss later in this chapter, is helping to confirm this notion.

The human energy field, Reich contended, operates at a distance. People are usually unaware of how their field both affects and is affected by others. In the 1960s, our language became steeped in various references to this concept, as millions of young people began to speak of a person's "vibes." Phrases like "He gives off bad vibes" or "I like her vibes" became popular expressions. Years earlier, Reich had argued that we indeed unconsciously respond to the energy forces of others and not simply to body-language cues of appearance and gesture. In fact, he believed that authentic healers and charismatic figures like Jesus naturally give off this life-enhancing force in large amounts.

The "healing power" of Christ, later on so badly distorted into cheap exploitation by armored individuals, is a well-understood and easily observable quality in all men and women who are endowed with natural leadership, Reich declared vigorously. They exude a bioenergy that can enliven the sluggish energy fields of the unhappy and neurotic, who experience this "donation" as calming and tension releasing. It may even convey a sweet glow of authentic love to an unhealthy person. When conveyed to someone sickly it can expand blood vessels, improve the blood supply to tissues, accelerate wound healing and even stay the effects of what he called "stagnant orgone."

Reich emphasized that such a transfer or donation of orgone between persons in close physical contact is a fact of human existence. It explains why people like to be around some persons (the unconscious donors) and stay away from others who are unwitting "takers." He believed that healthy children are particularly sensitive to the "vibes" of others and almost instinctively turn away from armored people. In fact, they are somehow able to detect simulated attempts at affection or friendliness. He observed that an unarmored person approaching someone who is armored may suddenly experience a "hemmed in," "rejected" feeling.

The failure of modern medicine to detect this energy could be attributed to its methods of studying health and disease, Reich believed. He labeled its approach "mechanistic," a concept we will explore in Chapter 8. The practice of dissection forces orthodox research into what is essentially a blind alley, as it makes the analysis of dead tissue the primary means of learning about living processes. "Dead tissue, in contrast to living tissue," Reich contended in *The Cancer Biopathy*, "shows no changes in bioelectric potential. Dying tissue gives only negative bioelectric reactions; the source of biological energy becomes extinguished."[3] Amidst a barrage of ridicule and censure, he contended that *natural* science research, focusing on the flow of biological energy in living organisms, was essential for the advancement of knowledge. So long as medical scientists persist in studying dead tissue, he insisted, our understanding of health will remain limited and our treatment of illness, including epidemics of noninfectious diseases like cancer, will remain fragmented. The key principles of his conceptual approach, Reich maintained, are motion and energy processes rather than structural form or dead matter.

Reich's laboratory experiments on the life energy soon led him into the realms of physics, engineering, and eventually meteorology and weather control. In a sense, this gradual shift of interest was a logical extension of his intuitive thinking: orgone energy, he found, appeared to fluctuate significantly with changes in humidity, time of day, season, and other atmospheric and cosmic influences. Hence, he sought to unravel the elusive relationship between inner and outer forces in nature. In so doing, he turned away from his earlier focus on the specific qualities of the bioenergy as it courses through the living body.

By the late 1940s, then, he had already begun to explore other areas. As a result, Reich's excursions into biophysics during his last years seem less orderly and methodical than his earlier pursuits. He spread himself thin—he started his own publishing house, turning out books and a succession of differently titled journals; he ran a number of annual conferences at Orgonon; he invented devices to accumulate orgone energy; and then, after 1950, he began his unique weather-control operations.

By a serendipitous process similar to that by which penicillin was discovered, Reich uncovered a method of accumulating orgone from the atmosphere. As we have already mentioned, while investigating the properties of SAPA bions he stumbled onto the fact that a metal-lined box "produced" or accumulated this new energy. Through the use of layers of organic and metallic materials, more bioenergy was accumulated inside or above the box. Reich appropriately called his collecting device an "orgone accumulator," more popularly known as the *orgone box.* Basically it is a rectangular box about 5 feet by 2½ feet by 2½ feet in size, made of alternating layers of sheet metal and an organic substance such as wood. (Details on construction appear in Appendix E.)

The main purpose of using the box is to gain additional orgone, which Reich found to possess healing potentialities. Sitting in such a box for an hour led many people to experience electriclike tingling sensations, or to feel more energized, although heavily armored people or those with little vitality usually felt nothing during initial sessions. Eventually Reich began manufacturing the box and rented out several hundred at $10 a month to physicians and psychiatrists for experimental purposes.

Later in the 1940s he invented adaptations of this device: the shooter, which directed orgone—via a metal funnel—to an area of the body needing healing, and an orgone blanket, made of alternating layers of wool and steel wool. The blanket is usually put over one's body. Dr. Mann, his family, and friends have all made use of the orgone blanket to gain energy and accelerate healing. Their experiences are described vividly in Chapter 17 of Dr. Mann's earlier book, *Orgone, Reich, and Eros.*

Apart from its healing effects, which skeptics ascribe to either suggestion or spontaneous remission, the chief proof that orgone is accumulated in such devices is increased heat. The scientific assumption is that, having controlled for all other variables, if the temperature inside the box, the body temperature of the person in it, or the temperature under the orgone blanket increases, then such a heat difference indicates the presence of an energy. Reich found temperature increases of .1 to 1 degree centigrade, especially at midday on sunny days, and at one point credited the sun as being the source of orgone. Sometimes he even found negative temperature differences— that is, the temperature inside or over the box is lower than that outside—or no differences at all. Since the 1950s, researchers in Italy, Britain, the United States, and Canada who have repeated the experiment have found heat differences. Numerous articles describing these temperature effects written by accredited scientists have appeared in various journals and Institutes devoted to Reichian researches; their names and addresses appear in Appendix C.

While it is too early to be certain that the orgone accumulator actually concentrates a new and fundamental energy as Reich hypothesized, we believe that his initial experiments and their partial confirmation merit careful replication by qualified independent researchers. One such replication was carried out in 1966 by the United States Testing Company, Inc., at Hoboken, New Jersey. The company's researchers treated two types of carcinomous mice with orgone. In each case the mice in the treated group were significantly different (in size or weight) from the controls up to the 95 percent confidence level statistically. Those treated with orgone had smaller tumors and their weight was also significantly less than those left untreated. In short, orgone seems to have slowed down the tumor growth. Experiments performed on cancerous mice during the 1960s by biologist Bernard Grad of McGill University in Montreal also showed that significantly fewer of the orgone-treated mice died of cancer.

In any event, Reich pursued his research on aspects of life energy up until the time he was imprisoned, whether he was working with this energy in the atmosphere, in his weather research, or in people's bodies. The legal battles against him, which culminated with his death in prison in 1957, must have affected him daily, however, and hindered his creative output in his final years. Some of his chief disciples—notably Alexander

Lowen, Elsworth Baker, and Charles Kelley—have developed bits and pieces of their mentor's therapeutic system in the years since his death. Only a handful of researchers have carried out systematic experimentation on the orgone accumulator, and most of these men were not active until late in the 1960s. Because of a lack of research funds, many of Reich's former colleagues have been unable to pursue this aspect of his work. Undoubtedly the virulence with which the Food and Drug Administration sought to stop Reich's work and the use of the orgone accumulator must have dampened their enthusiasm.

AN ORGONOTIC LINK WITH THE EASTERN ANCIENTS

With the powerful surge of Western interest in ancient Eastern disciplines, it has become clear that Reich's concept of a subtle life force has been a familiar Oriental notion for centuries. All postulate an underlying energy but do not see it in exactly the same light. Though the name of this energy varies according to the particular culture and historical period, there has been remarkable consensus among highly diverse traditions about the nature of this force. Indeed, while laboratory scientists methodically explore its nature, adepts of Yoga, tai chi, and other Eastern systems like aikido or Rajneesh meditation speak frequently of "feeling the energy" in and around the body. It is not uncommon for some to claim, in fact, that they actually begin to see energy emanations or an aura around the human figure.

In the Jewish Kabbalistic tradition, this force, known as *ruah*, is said to underlie inner vitality, and disappears at physical death. In esoteric Jewish teachings, ruah may be influenced by special body postures and controlled-breathing techniques. Although little has been written about this energy in the American Indian cultures, oral sources suggest that it is considered a part of all living things and that a medicine man can impart it to help restore health to the sick. The Islamic mystics, called Sufis, speak of a subtle force, *baraka*, that may be transmitted from teacher to disciple to effect subtle changes in consciousness. The Sufis also believe there are seven centers of *latifa* (bioenergy) in the body that influence mental and physical conditions.

Reich's home at Orgonon with roof-top observatory. 1949.

Reich at his desk in his Forest Hills, New York, home. This is his favorite photograph of himself. May 1946.

All photos by Anthony Obert.

Inside the historic lab at Orgonon. 1948.

Early orgone devices for experiments at the research lab in Reich's Forest Hills, New York, home. From left to right: electroscope, pulsation meter, and small accumulator. 1947.

Reich putting in the long hours at his desk in the Forest Hills home. May 1946.

Two close friends, Wilhelm Reich and A. S. Neill, share a happy moment at the "lower" cabin at Orgonon in Rangeley, Maine. 1947.

Above, *Reich's fashionable Forest Hills, New York, home, one block from the Forest Hills tennis stadium. 1946.*

Right, *poised for action: the cloud buster, Reich's unique weather control device, located near the student lab at Orgonon.*

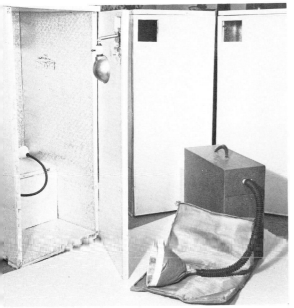

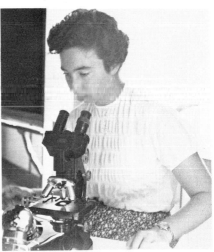

Below, oldest daughter, Eva Reich, M.D., following in her father's footsteps: looking through the microscope in the lab. 1949.

Above, on the far left is a sit-in orgone accumulator with an orgone shooter on its seat. In the center we see a portable black accumulator with a shooter resting on an orgone blanket.

Below, Reich's study in his home at Orgonon overlooking the woods, with six-year-old son, Peter, at the window. 1950.

Medical colleagues experimenting with microscopes and other instruments in the Orgonon lab, while Reich's second wife, Ilse Ollendorf Reich, observes on the right. August 1949.

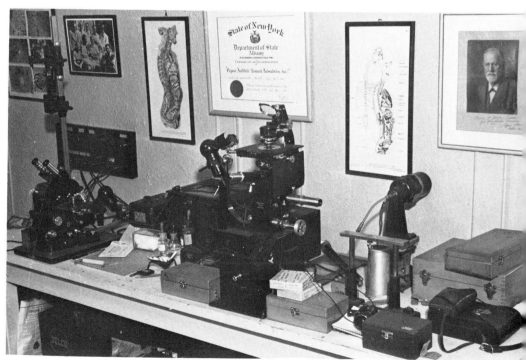

Workbench in the research lab at Orgonon. Sigmund Freud, Reich's early mentor, is watching from his place on the wall, far right. 1947.

Full view of the student lab at Orgonon, nestled in a wooded area. This is where much of the basic experimental work went on. 1949.

Inside the metal-lined orgone room at the Orgonon lab. Although many accumulators are square, there is also a small cylindrical one on the left. A Geiger-Müller scaler is attached to the orgone accumulator on the right. 1948.

Perhaps the most widely known Oriental psychospiritual traditions that focus on the life energy are the Indian and Chinese systems of thought. While there is no evidence that Reich was directly aware of all these disciplines, he did refer to Hindu yogic practices on several occasions and was apparently fairly well acquainted with them.

According to ancient Sanskrit tradition, seven energy bodies, or *chakras*, exist in the human body. They are located along the spine, and each, when awakened through specific methods, governs and stimulates particular physical, emotional, and spiritual functions. Each chakra is said to have a characteristic color, which appears as a surrounding ring or aura of light when observed through nonordinary perception. Furthermore, each chakra is believed to be affected in turn by special colors or sounds.

In Hindu thinking, the universal energy that permeates everything and is important to health is called *prana*. It is drawn into the body through breathing and is apparently associated in the atmosphere with the oxygen molecule. This pranic energy is described as coursing through the body via a network of fourteen main channels and thousands of tributaries. Through its subsidiary aspects, it affects each of the chakras in specific ways. Yogi adepts learn to control the flow of prana in order to directly energize mental or physical aspects of their being. Disease in this system is viewed as a breakdown in the integrated interaction of the various energy centers and channels, and healing is aimed at restoring a harmonious flow through the person's system. The parallels in thought between this approach and Reich's are striking, especially as Reich secured his by scientific experimentation.

In recent years, several notable works have examined the yogic tradition from the standpoint of Western medicine, seeking to synthesize these seemingly contradictory approaches. The best of these efforts are written by researchers who are both rigorously trained in psychology or medicine and intimately familiar with Eastern esoteric knowledge. In *Yoga and Psychotherapy,* and example of this perspective, the authors observe, "In yoga . . . the entire spectrum of energies is included. The internal energy pattern which is experienced results from

the merging of mental energy with the physical energies. . . .
The two find a common meeting ground in the phenomenon of
prana."[4]

Another major Oriental healing system that has attracted a
good deal of interest in recent years is acupuncture. As with the
yogic traditions, it postulates that the human body is a vast and
complex network of subtle energies that underlie our daily
health and vitality. The life force, known as *chi* (*ki* in Japanese
thought), is said to run through the body in twelve major
meridians, ten of which correspond to organs and two of which
are concerned with the regulation of the entire organism rather
than any particular organ. Each meridian has specific points that
most accurately reflect different aspects of its health status.
Disease is always viewed as an external manifestation of an
inner imbalance in this energy system. Each organ is considered
to be closely related to overall physical vitality as well as relating
to specific emotions. It is believed that long before a visible
disease occurs, the meridian system will show the underlying
disharmony, a signal that preventive healing should be initiated.

In traditional Chinese healing, various methods are used to
diagnose the functional condition of the meridians. Some practitioners rely upon the sense of touch and recognition of various
pulses throughout the body. Others may make slow passes over
the body and attempt to "feel" irregularities in the flow of chi. In
acupuncture and related methods of treatment, the goal is to
restore the natural harmony of the chi network. Through physical manipulation of specific acupuncture points, the healer
carefully re-establishes a smooth, regular energetic charge
throughout the body. Some illnesses are viewed as representing
too much energy flow in particular organs, while others are
diagnosed as constituting an inadequate amount of the life force
in certain body areas.

The similarities to Reich's orgone theories are vivid and dramatic. These systems all accept a universal energy that permeates space—that is, it is everywhere, is basic to all living
forms, flows throughout organisms in a definite path, is highly
significant to the health of the organism, and can be passed or
"donated" from one person to another. Certain systems, such as
acupuncture, provide details about the precise flow of the life

energy within the human body that Reich did not deal with, but, overall, there are no contradictions. Reich's special contribution in this area was to present scientific evidence for the existence of this life force: its color (blue), heat effects, presence in the human body, healing powers (in cancer, for example), its affinity to water, its effect on a geiger counter, its antientropic quality, and so on (see Appendix D). Later in this chapter we shall look at some of the current scientific evidence that supports these ancient Oriental concepts of health and life energy and validates Reich in yet another area of his wide-ranging thought.

BIRDS OF A FEATHER: EUROPEAN FORERUNNERS

Wilhelm Reich was not the first Western thinker to discover evidence for a life energy. He was preceded by several influential innovators, the most important of whom were Anton Mesmer and Baron Karl von Reichenbach. Both initially exerted strong influences on their times and then, under establishment pressure, retired into obscurity. Now they are once again being taken seriously by some thoughtful scientists.

Franz Anton Mesmer (1734–1815) popularized the concept of *animal magnetism* throughout Europe and eventually the United States. The thesis of his doctoral dissertation, "The Influence of the Stars and Planets as Curative Powers," presented in 1773, was that gravitational tides exist in the atmosphere and affect everything on earth. These tides issue from the planets in the solar system in the form of an invisible force governed by natural laws. This energy, he argued, is similar in some ways to magnetism and flows within living organisms, hence the origin of the phrase, "animal magnetism."

As a practicing physician in Vienna, Mesmer applied this theory to the treatment of disease and found that putting a magnet over stricken parts of a sick person often effected a cure. Later, in working with "nervous" patients, he observed that they exhibited peculiar physiological effects, such as jerks and spasms, which led him to believe that the magnet was mainly serving as a conductor of some "fluid" that emanated from his own body. Accordingly, he postulated the existence in the human body of a healing force that is activated by magnetism. He viewed this force as permeating all of nature. Eventually he insisted that animal magnetism penetrates bodies, operates at a distance, and interacts in various ways with light and sound. Interestingly, he also explored the effect of hypnotic or trance states on the human body and believed that remarkable hidden powers, such as mental telepathy or clairvoyance, could be released in some people through altered states of consciousness.

Mesmer was forced to leave Vienna when he became the focus of hostility from the orthodox medical establishment. He took up residence in Paris, where he cofounded a clinic for the "Mesmeric" treatment of various illnesses. Almost overnight, he attracted a wide following, especially among the wealthy. Before long, the animal-magnetism theory swept through France. In 1784, responding to pressures from the French medical establishment, a royal investigatory committee was set up, not unlike the recent American committee that investigated laetrile. The verdict was damning and concluded that the effects of Mesmer's elaborate healing techniques could be attributed entirely to the power of suggestion.

Although the official position toward Mesmerism hindered organized research, the theory of animal magnetism never completely died out in Europe. Mesmer himself denied the accuracy of the royal committee's findings, tenaciously insisting that animal magnetism was a physical fact and that his cures had little to do with imagination or suggestibility. Mesmer's direct influence on the development of hypnotism has long been recognized. While Reich acknowledged no intellectual debts to Mesmer, the similarity of their theories is leading to a renewal of respect for Mesmer's medical work.

Another forerunner of Wilhelm Reich was the German industrialist and scientist Karl von Reichenbach (1788–1869). After taking a Ph.D. in science, he opened a factory and soon became wealthy. Later, he showed skill in chemistry, discovering creosote and three lesser-known substances. In 1839, he was made a baron and began to devote himself to special scientific investigations. Like Mesmer, he began his work with magnets and spent twenty years developing a more sophisticated universal energy theory; he wrote a total of eight books about what he called the *odylic* force, or *od* (from the Viking god of thunder, Odin). He launched his investigations after discovering that a magnet with a ten-pound pull would often produce unusual sensations in individuals when passed along their bodies. The emotionally disturbed, it seemed, were most strongly affected, and many reported seeing luminous auras as well as experiencing strange pulling or drawing bodily movements. Reichenbach was convinced that these sensations were real and that magnetic currents did indeed exert influences on humans. Over the years in Vienna, he subjected several hundred psychic sensitives (at least a hundred of whom were men of scientific education) to experiments designed to establish the properties of od.

Reichenbach distinguished odic energy from heat and ordinary magnetism, though he acknowledged that they might prove to be interrelated. He first observed that magnets and crystals produced detectable energy effects on the human organism, and then later was convinced that all living substances give off variants of the odylic force.

Reichenbach concluded that the energy he had discovered was distributed universally but in varying concentrations. He believed that it could be transmitted from one person to another and that objects could be charged with it. Moreover, he claimed that every living organism has a surrounding energy field and that the nature of this field at any given moment signals its health or disease.

Unfortunately, Reichenbach was not able to win the support of the scientists of his day. When skeptics came to witness his experiments, he could not always duplicate his findings. His use of psychic sensitives inevitably produced uneven results. The odic theory came to be regarded as the regrettable eccentricity of an otherwise brilliant scientist. In recent years, however, Reichenbach's speculations on odic energy are being reassessed by scholars studying healing energies and parapsychology. Reich was aware of Reichenbach's work and quotes this predecessor in *The Function of the Orgasm*. He would, however, have been critical of Reichenbach's reliance on psychics as scientifically unsound.

CLOSER TO REICH: BURR, RAVITZ, AND STEINER

Though a number of farsighted scientists have pursued research on life energy in the twentieth century, perhaps the outstanding figure, in the field of biology, was Dr. Harold Saxton Burr. Over a twenty-five-year period, from 1935 to 1960, Burr produced increasing evidence for the presence of bioelectrical activity in organisms. A biological researcher at Yale University, Burr published his findings in nearly sixty scientific articles and yet, like many others, made little impact upon his mainstream-science colleagues. Though Reich was definitely aware of Burr's exciting investigations and referred to them briefly in *The Cancer Biopathy*, the two innovators never met, and it is doubtful whether Burr ever read of Reich's orgone theory. In 1972, the year before his death, Burr gathered together his decades of research on what he called L-fields in a book entitled *The Fields of Life*. The L stands for life, so in a real sense Burr was investigating life fields, or life energy. He did not use the term *life energy*, probably because of mainstream (mechanistic) science's longstanding prejudice against any theory of vital energies (vitalism).

In essence, Burr found that living organisms give off or are constituted by an electromagnetic field that can be measured in millivolts and varies widely according to environmental influences. People cannot see or feel such fields, although perhaps some who claim to see auras are actually perceiving these energies. But in a biology laboratory, highly sensitive modern voltmeters have measured the differences in electric potential between different parts of the body. Burr's team of researchers experimentally verified that L-fields are true fields of energy. One proof was that electrodes placed a few inches from the surface of the body—that is, not in direct contact with the skin—would register readings of voltage gradients.

Burr's team discovered that there is a characteristic L-field for every kind of living thing, from trees to mice to humans. For instance, when they measured the L-field in frog eggs, they could determine the future location of the frog's nervous system, showing that it is the L-field that somehow structures the body of the frog. By measuring the L-fields of seeds, they found it was possible to predict how healthy the future plants would be.

In partial support of Reich's bold ideas, Burr's coworkers found that every organism's L-field is strongly affected by environmental forces. Not only are animals, plants, and humans permeated by bioenergy, but all are linked to atmospheric energies as well. It was discovered, for instance, that the electromagnetic field of all the trees in a given neighborhood fluctuates similarly according to the activity of sunspots, the presence of storms, and changes in daylight and season. Many people, of course, also report noticeable differences in their emotional outlook depending upon electrical storms and other natural events. Burr's research seems to confirm these intuitions quite impressively.

Burr's team also found that detectable changes in the typical L-field may take place before physical signs become manifest. In studies with animals and humans, the team discovered that ovulation in the female is preceded by a sharp rise in the L-field voltage. All a woman needs to do to determine her ovulation phase is to dip the index finger of each hand into two small dishes filled with saline solution and connected to the voltmeter. The team also found that women with cancer (men were not studied) show noticeable differences in their energy fields compared with their healthy counterparts. For example, those with cervical cancer showed zero voltage at the cervix. Like Reich, Burr was convinced that cancer could best be understood as a breakdown in the living organism's organizational field. He urged physicians to develop better means of measuring this energy field in order to predict and avoid the onset of cancer.

While measurements of L-fields can be useful in diagnosing such physical conditions as cancer, they can be equally valuable in assessing the condition of the mind. As far back as the late 1940s, Dr. Leonard J. Ravitz, one of Burr's most eager pupils, found that mental states can actually be measured indirectly through the L-field. For instance, as people experience altered states of consciousness, such as hypnotic trance, they exhibit marked changes in voltage gradient. Furthermore, once one's characteristic L-field pattern has been identified over time, changes in that signal will indicate emotional instability or undue stress.

The significance of these findings, which Ravitz reported in long articles in established medical and biological journals, is that they point to Reich's insight into the *functional* identity of body and mind. Both physical and mental changes can be detected electrically; hence they are functionally identical. More specific information about Ravitz's work can be found in Dr. Mann's earlier book, *Orgone, Reich, and Eros.*

Another German thinker far ahead of his time, and someone who exercises a powerful attraction to some Reichians, is the philosopher-clairvoyant Rudolf Steiner (1861–1925). Beginning as a student of the poet-philosopher Goethe and then becoming a leading theosophist in Germany, Steiner founded his own branch of occult studies, called *anthroposophy*. Before his death in the mid-1920s, his creative mind had produced an amazing number of innovations in architecture, medicine, agriculture (biodynamic farming), education (the Waldorf schools), philosophy, dance (eurythmics), and physical science. All these undertakings were informed by a profoundly spiritual approach to nature and life, which has been called *objective mysticism* and which combines scientific, rational, and intuitive approaches. Although Reich apparently had no knowledge of Steiner, his latter-day excursions into religion and science, as will be described in Chapters 7 and 8, suggest that he was moving inexorably toward a similar philosophical standpoint.

In terms of the orgone theory, it is Steiner's physical notion of four "etheric energies" that merits a brief discussion here, since it seems to imply that cosmic orgone is but one of four very fundamental energies. These four energies—which he called the warmth, light, chemical and sound, and life ethers— supposedly are engendered sequentially, one out of the other, and together account for the creation of all matter and living organisms. Each ether possesses not only its own distinctive properties and functions but those of its "ancestral" ethers as well. (These ethers are not to be confused with the stationary ether postulated by classical physics; rather, they constitute the motive power of nature giving rise to life in all its various forms.) The ethers apparently function rhythmically or in a pulsatory way, like the orgone. Put very simply, the warmth ether corresponds to the heat state, light ether to the gaseous state, chemical ether to the fluid state, and life ether to the solid state. The warmth and light ethers tend to act centrifugally whereas the chemical and life ethers act centripetally; each also characteristically tends to create different-shaped forms: circles, squares, and so on.

It may be that the orgone corresponds to one of these four "etheric" forces, although at this stage of our understanding it is difficult to say precisely which one. However, Trevor James Constable, a prominent student of Reich and a leading practitioner of Reichian cloud busting (see Chapter 8), feels that the orgone is equivalent to the chemical ether. On the other hand, there also seem to be suggestions that orgone is akin to the life etheric force since this force comes from the sun, as Reich once posited orgone does, and is responsible for the rhythms of day and night and of the seasons, variations that Reich also ascribed to the orgone energy envelope (the atmospheric orgone ring surrounding the planet). For an interesting attempt to integrate Reich's ideas with those of both Rudolf Steiner and an American exponent of radionics,* Ruth Drown, the reader is referred to Trevor Constable's book, *The Cosmic Pulse of Life.*

Until recently, followers of Steiner who have written about the four ethers, such as Guenther Wachsmuth (*Etheric Formative Forces in Cosmos, Earth, and Man*), have failed to produce impressive empirical evidence. The situation was somewhat changed with the publication in 1976 of an exciting book by British physicists Denis Milner and Ted Smart called *The Loom of Creation.* Milner and Smart are at the University of Birmingham and were visited by author Edward Mann in August 1979. Based on many years of work with a form of Kirlian photography, their book features beautiful photographs of "auric" shapes around materials, such as leaves and magnets, that possess the types of shapes predicted in the Steiner four-ether theory. For instance, some photographs show a collection of circular forms, while others have a "sunburst" structure. The former are considered to be

---

*A fairly new field of study which, asserting that all matter radiates, attempts to both diagnose and treat illness by detecting "radiations" from "samples"— a blood spot, for example—of a patient.

warmth ether manifestations, the latter to be signs of the light ether. To get these photographs, a photographic plate is exposed to one pulse electricity (one brief shot of electricity) in a dark room; the object being studied is sandwiched between two metal plates opposite another glass plate with a gap in between that is created by a cardboard spacing frame. A charge from 5,000 to 20,000 volts is applied across the plates for a short period of time. Significantly, one photograph shows a raylike emanation when *nothing* was sandwiched in the device; this accords with the precise description of orgone radiation that Reich claimed to see in an orgone box in total darkness. In other photographs of empty space, pulsating energy globules, which are very suggestive of prana or orgone, are seen. Milner and Smart write, "An essential feature of these and further experiments . . . is that they convey the impression that space is not emptiness or nothingness, but that it is comprised of a substance or an ether."[5]

When Milner and Smart placed a dead leaf next to a live one and "photographed" both of them, the resulting picture showed the live leaf donating an auric energy, visible as a whitish glowing, to the dead one. In another photo, where a dying leaf is juxtaposed with a piece of wet filter paper, one sees a drawing of auric energy from the filter paper to the leaf, supporting Reich's idea that water possesses orgone and that it has life-giving properties.

According to their own testimony, these two scientists began as strict materialists and became convinced of the appropriateness of Steiner's concepts only through their experimental work. They conclude: "Results . . . seemed in many instances to provide evidence for the existence of invisible subtle forces. Thus it was found that it was not the physical leaf that was being recorded, but some sort of 'energy system' that only registered if activated. Flow patterns were registered around leaves at certain periods during the day and night. . . . Interactions were obtained between compass needles and leaves, as though they had something in common. . . . These phenomena suggested that there are forces at work in nature which are not yet embraced by the established laws of science."[6] Working quite independently of Reich, the tireless labors of these two men and their Ph.D. assistants add additional support for Reich's orgone theory.

As Theodore Roszak indicates in his recent book, *The Unfinished Animal,* "Steiner remained to the last a faithful student of Goethe's nature philosophy, which posited that esthetic and visionary experience would eventually join empirical observation and provide a new world view which sees beauty, form, and meaning as really present in nature."[7] Milner and Smart, Wachsmuth, and a few others are trying to give this approach an empirical base. If, as suggested by Thomas Kuhn in *The Structure of Scientific Revolutions,* a new paradigm (theoretical model) emerges in physics, it is possible that it will follow something like Steiner's formulation, in which Reich's orgone theory may be a valued component.

BEYOND REICH: "CURRENT" EVIDENCE FOR LIFE ENERGY

Measuring the body's electrical gradient—and how it is influenced by forces in the atmosphere—is two steps away from mechanistic science. Perhaps just one step away, but still controversial, is the research on bioenergy currently being carried out by Dr. R. D. Becker, a highly reputable surgeon on the staff of a Philadelphia Veterans Administration hospital. Becker has indirectly followed up on some of Burr's basic research to show that one to three millimicro amps (a tiny amount) of electrical DC current can accelerate healing. Noting that, unlike most animals, salamanders can regenerate lost limbs through an additional electric charge, Becker finally proved that weak DC currents applied by electrodes can also stimulate bone regeneration in humans. In over sixty published medical and scientific papers, Becker has outlined how an induced DC current promotes the healing of bone fractures, skin ulcers, and burns as well as producing general anesthesia, and how it can stimulate partial multitissue regeneration and nerve functioning.

Other innovative researchers have pursued similar work. Dr. David Wilson of Leeds, England, has demonstrated experimentally that pulsed electric signals cut down by 50 percent the recovery time of patients with severely sprained ankles. Neuro-

surgeon Norman Shealy of LaCrosse, Wisconsin, has shown
that pain can be greatly diminished by electrical stimulation. At
Necker, a leading hospital in Paris, anesthesia is now being
applied successfully by a small electric current fed through
electrodes. For several years, electrosleep, the inducing of sleep
by passing a tiny electric current through the head, has been
used in medical practice in the Soviet Union. The therapeutic
value of this technique is now being widely recognized in the
United States as well, particularly in studies at the University of
Texas Medical School. "So great is the interest now in exploring
the full potential of electricity in medicine that a Neurological
Society made up of physicians, engineers, and others has been
formed to further such investigations," the author of a recent
report on this field commented.[8] While such research is still far
from accepting an orgone theory of bodily energies, the fact that
it even *begins* to view the organism as an electrical or energy
system means it is moving toward a holistic perspective and
eventually may accept a life energy model. Thus it looks as if
Reich was at least on the right track.

KIRLIAN PHOTOGRAPHY: PROOF POSITIVE OF REICH'S THEORY?

Kirlian photography may throw a brilliant new light on Reich's
vision. This brand of electrical photography—named for its
Russian inventors, Semyon and Valentina Kirlian—is a sophisticated technique in which high-voltage electricity is sent
through an object (just about any kind of object—animal, vege-
table, or mineral—such as a finger, a leaf, a coin) that has been
placed in direct contact with film. Somehow, and no one really
knows how, a picture is thus produced without camera, lens, or
other photographic paraphernalia. What is even more strange,
such Kirlian photographs reveal not only the object itself in
vivid detail but also colorful coronas—faint glows—and flares
surrounding the object.

What *are* these coronas and flares? Controversy rages over
what they mean. Some scientists claim they are nothing more
than electrical artifacts, or corona discharge (after all, electricity
is sent through the object photographed). Other scientists

maintain that the coronas simply reflect the amount of moisture in the object, the amount of electrical resistance, the ionization of the air, or some other physical variable. A few avant-garde researchers espouse the more esoteric idea that what is revealed through the coronas and flares is a reflection of "bioplasma" (or the "bioenergy" that Reich discusses).

Since no one yet has satisfactorily demonstrated proof of any of these hypotheses, research continues around the world.

In Russia, according to Ostrander and Schroeder's *Psychic Discoveries Behind the Iron Curtain*, the Kirlians showed that "illness, emotion, state of mind, thoughts, fatigue, all make their distinctive imprint on the pattern of energy which seemed to circulate . . . through the human body."[9] Verified in repeated research, this finding lends support to Reich's view that our energy fields continually reflect our deepest inner feelings.

Other areas of research have been confirmed in different countries. For instance, studies in Czechoslovakia, Russia, England, Germany, Brazil, and the United States have found reliable changes as apparent effects of spiritual, or psychic, healing (as in the "laying on of hands"). In the United States, parapsychologist Douglas Dean, working with healer Ethel DeLoach, regularly found that flares from her fingertips increased dramatically during healing. Dr. Thelma Moss, of UCLA, repeatedly observed that with such healers as Dr. Olga Worrall, Dr. Hans Engel, and Jack Gray there is a considerable increase in the patient's corona after a healing treatment, and that during the actual treatment the healer shows an emission of a brilliant red-orange color, which is then transferred to the patient.

Confirmation of this healing effect is provided by the research of Brazilian engineer Jarbas Marinho of the Institute of Psychobiophysical Research in São Paulo. Marinho reported in the Proceedings of the Second International Congress on Psychotronic Research that he took Kirlian photographs of healer and patient before, during, and after the healing sessions. Fingertip coronas showed that the healer emanated an energy that the patient seemed to receive in visible form as an increased corona. (This lends total support to Reich's claim that vital organisms give off a strong orgone charge.) Marinho cautiously concludes his paper: "We are not prepared to assert here that the Kirlian Effect shows the action of bioplasma [another term for life energy] on the etheric body. Yet we feel that this effect reveals more than merely the result of ionization of air by an electrical discharge between metal and biological electrodes."[10]

Appearing in the same Proceedings is a study done at UCLA by Dr. Thelma Moss and three collaborators, in which eleven patients with various medical problems were treated by "magnetic passes" (a technique developed by Anton Mesmer for donating life energy to a patient). Of the eleven patients, three did not respond and dropped out, two responded initially and then regressed, and six showed considerable improvement, confirmed by their doctors. All the patients routinely underwent Kirlian photography, and "consistently the Kirlian pictures show a dramatic increase in flares and emanations posttreatment."[11] Although none of the six showed instantaneous recovery, in at least two cases there was improvement their doctors had thought impossible. The researchers conclude, "We believe that some form of bioenergy is being transferred, a bioenergy that perhaps is made visible in Kirlian photography. But the nature of that energy which apparently has therapeutic value remains an unsolved mystery."[12]

This is a cautious statement, as it should be. For there remains much uncertainty about just what Kirlian photography reveals. However, the research it has engendered (now in more than twenty-five countries around the world, with remarkable progress made by Dr. Dumitrescu of Romania) lends support to the Reichian theory of orgone energy.

VALIDATION FROM THE EAST

Recent experimental research in Japan has begun to dramatically confirm another concept discussed earlier in this chapter— the energy lines, or meridians, and the chakras, said to generate life energy in the human body. Dr. Hiroshi Motoyama, a physician and acupuncturist, has had a long and lively interest in unconventional approaches to medicine. After studying parapsychology under Dr. J. B. Rhine at Duke University, Motoyama returned to Japan, where he has conducted research at the Institute for Religion and Psychology in Tokyo. From his extensive experience, he writes: "When a yogi awakens a chakra through prolonged meditation, then it becomes more active and powerful than in the average person and can bring in more prana. This prana is in turn converted into physical or nervous energy and sent to the ... central spinal tube where it seems to be stocked ... for future use. This prana is also distributed throughout the body to each tissue and internal organ through the meridians. [Once] a chakra is ... awakened a person can control the receiving and ejecting of energy through the chakra by mental concentration. This energy ejected from the chakra is very strong and can make a great change in an electromagnetic field in terms of frequency and potential."[13]

In recent years, Motoyama has designed a device capable of measuring the electrical field surrounding a person's body without the need to attach any electrodes to the body. The device, called a chakra machine, must be housed in a specially designed, lead-shielded room. It can detect the intensity as well as fluctuations in the electric field around anyone's body. "The 'Chakra Machine' consists of an electrode box somewhat resembling a telephone booth, with two copper electrodes on the top and bottom and a sliding square panel with electrodes attached on all four sides, which is free to traverse up and down the structure so as to be positioned at any part of the subject's body. An electromagnetic field is set up between the electrodes, and as the subject stands inside the box, with electrodes positioned 30–40 cm from his body, any energy ejected from subject's body can be detected as a change in this electromagnetic field. A special preamplifier [designed by Motoyama] with an impedance of near infinity allows even the most subtle energy ejection to be picked up and recorded. The preamplifier in turn sends the measurement information to various amplifiers and analysers outside the lead-shielded room where the data is recorded on a highly sensitive chart recorder."[14] Utilizing the device, Motoyama has found evidence for the existence of the chakras, since the strength and frequency of the energy field at the chakra sites tend to be greater than in other body areas. The intensity of its signal, moreover, shows marked differences before, during, and after meditation.

Later, with another device, Motoyama found experimental verification for the existence of the meridians and nodes postulated by Chinese medicine. The machine, called an "Apparatus for Measuring the Function of the Meridians and Corresponding Internal Organs" (AMI for short), is used to diagnose energy imbalances anywhere in the human organism. It consists of an electrode box, computer interface, calculation computer, and data printout machine. Special electrodes designed by Motoyama are covered with antipolarization paste and attached to the twenty-eight meridian seiketsu end points—well verified now by Westerners studying acupuncture—on the patient's fingers and toes. Next, three volts DC are charged through the electrodes and the machine measures skin current values (GSR) at each seiketsu meridian point just before and after the body reacts to the charged voltage. This reaction of the subject's body to a definite voltage, an action of the homeostatic, or balancing, function, is called "polarization." By measuring the skin current before and after the above reaction, Motoyama can diagnose the function of the meridians and the corresponding internal organs. Roughly speaking, if the skin current values before and after the reaction are less than a standard—already determined on the basis of data on over two thousand persons tested at that specific meridian point—he assumes that the function of the meridian and sometimes the corresponding organ is underactive. If the skin current values are more than the standard value, however, he assumes that the function of the meridian is overactive.

After measuring over five thousand persons with this machine and comparing the findings with the results of orthodox medical examinations of the patients' symptoms, Motoyama constructed a table of standards for normal energy flow and symptomatology. These standards were computerized so that after testing a patient it is now possible within minutes to pinpoint on the computer printout any abnormality in the individual's meridian energy charge. Though obviously still in the experimental stage, the AMI is already in use in medical settings in Japan and the United States as an inexpensive and painless diagnostic tool. Insofar as it accepts the human organism as an intricate energy system, it confirms Reich's basic stance.

The electrical aspects of body energies are perhaps most dramatically illustrated by electronic types of acupuncture, which were first used in Germany and Japan some ten to twenty years ago. An article in the 1975 issue of *Psychoenergetic Systems* highlighted a Japanese approach called ryodoraku acupuncture therapy. The object of this method is to "tune" the autonomic nervous system on all meridians in a given patient. This is done by adducing a slight electrical stimulus through a low-voltage needle application device at the acupuncture points. The points focused on are indicated as either stimulation points for under-active meridians or sedation points for overactive meridians. In this manner, a great many medical complaints have been definitely eased, as well as the patient having his or her whole system impressively made more vibrant. Similar to Dr. Moto-yama's AMI, the device used by the ryodoraku acupuncturist measures the electrical resistance present at each of the test points bilaterally. It supports Reich's view that persons can be either under- or overcharged energetically and that either of these conditions implies poor health.

In the last few years, Russian investigators of the bioplasma energy theory have carried out similar research. In 1973, Professor V. M. Inyushin presented a paper at the First International Conference on Psychotronics at Prague entitled "The Study of Acupuncture Points' Electro-Bio Luminescence With and Without the Action of Laser Radiation." In this article, Inyushin described his efforts to treat fifteen patients with toothaches or other facial pain. He established that the illumination or bioluminescence was greater in every case at the pertinent acupuncture points than in other nearby points. In other words, his findings have added experimental weight to the conclusion that there is indeed a measurable difference in electrical resistance or conductivity at the acupuncture points on the body.

Most recently, in Germany, a laser device has been perfected that detects the exact acupuncture nodes, indicates their presence by means of an audible signal, and then calculates whether the flow of energy there is within normal range. Here again is confirmation of Reich's claim that ill health is related to under- or overcharge in the organism.

SPARKS: THE SCIENCE OF THE FUTURE

As we look in retrospect at Reich's orgone theory, we hardly find it the work of a wild dreamer or paranoid. Rather, we are confronted with many essentially correct intuitions of a thinker decades ahead of his time. This is not to say that he made no errors or didn't oversimplify the situation. Rather than a single life energy, there may actually be many subtle biological energies, all interrelated in some yet-to-be discovered manner, but distinct from one another. Yet Reich's fundamental instincts about body energies seem on track.

What is significant is that in recent years numbers of innovative and often brilliant scientists—in areas ranging from medicine to physics—have begun to converge on the general theme of energies and organism, sometimes called psychoenergetics, sometimes psychotronics. These refer to scientific study of energy-psyche interactions. The *International Journal of Psychoenergetics,* launched in 1974, highlights this interdisciplinary realm and is headed by Dr. Stanley Krippner, past president of the Association for Humanistic Psychology. In 1977, along with John White, he edited a groundbreaking book devoted to this topic, entitled *Future Science: Life Energies and the Physics of Paranormal Phenomena.*

In forty articles, scientists and scholars on both sides of the Iron Curtain examine the breakthroughs, discoveries, and newest theories in the study of life energy and paranormal phenomena. Thus, in an article by innovative physicist Victor M. Inyushin, we are told, "We have obtained evidence that a fifth state of matter, bioplasma, exists . . .[consisting] of ions, free electrons, and free protons. . . . At times, it may extend considerable distances from the organism, raising the possibility of its involvement in telepathic and psychokinetic phenomena."[15] Other articles show how healing energies have been scientifically validated, examine psychotronic generators (energies associated with specific geometric forms such as pyramids and cones), or discuss—as one title puts it—"Quantum Physics and Paranormal Events." In the six sections of the book, reputable physical scientists comment on and take seriously the facts and theories put forward by the various authors. Three articles, one of which is by coauthor Edward Mann, outline the orgone theory. The significance of this book and the international journals now devoted to psychotronics and psychoenergetics is that mainstream science is now having to admit there is impressive evidence for a life energy theory as a basic component in the explanation of unusual healing and psychic phenomena.

In the next few years, the medical field—including psychosomatics, physics, and biology, besides the burgeoning study of parapsychology—will give more attention to life energy theories and their implications. Evidence from acupuncture and Kirlian photography, only a tiny fraction of which we could note here, will oblige medical scientists and those doing psychosomatic studies to carry out experiments on the functioning of bioenergy in health and disease. Developments in physics, including fresh understandings of quantum theory and of the neutrino (an almost mass-free element that, like the orgone, can permeate everything), will lead some mainstream physicists to look into the orgone theory and chakra energies. Professor William Tiller, a physicist at Stanford University, is already establishing a reputation for exciting theorizing in these realms. Biologists may soon be willing to replicate the many careful experiments of Dr. Grad at McGill, and may come up with confirming data. But, particularly among interdisciplinary scientists and those studying parapsychology and psychoenergetics, we can reasonably expect very significant studies supporting and enlarging our understanding of life energy and its implications for organisms.

One of the more promising developments here is the biennial meeting of an international congress devoted to psychotronic research, the first of which occurred in Prague in 1973. Every two years since then, several hundred qualified scientists, many of them dedicated to life energy studies, have met, reported on, and compared their findings, moving gradually toward a more precise understanding of bioenergy and its effect on people and vice versa. Their impact is eventually going to affect mainstream scientific thinking.

Most of these endeavors will ultimately be predicated upon a more intuitive approach to nature and to life than has been accepted heretofore. It will unite Western to Eastern thought.

As Reich observed, "We find the accent on life thousands of years ago—in the ancient thought systems of the great Asiatic religions such as Hinduism, certainly in early Christianity, and in the beginnings of the natural sciences in antiquity."[16] The revival of interest in the powers inherent in the human energy system represents a return to humanity's deepest understanding of life and the cosmos.

Perhaps the most compelling aspect to all these discoveries is their philosophical implication. For centuries in the West, we have been taught to believe that human beings occupy an isolated, separate place in the cosmos, somehow apart from the rest of the natural world. But what these findings demonstrate is that we live in constant interrelationship with both animate and inanimate forces, that a universal harmony exists, and that, as the mystics have been insisting all along, everything around us is unified into a whole.

CHAPTER 7

Spiritual Reawakening

I do not believe that, in order to be religious in the good and genuine sense of the word, one has to ruin one's love life and has to become rigid and shrunken in body and soul.

The basic truths in all teaching of mankind are alike and amount to only one common thing: to find your way to the thing you feel when you love dearly.

—WILHELM REICH

Wilhelm Reich underwent a fascinating and at times bewildering transformation in his attitude toward religion and spiritual concerns. As we have seen on many other intellectual issues, he seldom remained stationary. Originally holding a rather cynical, Marxist view of religion, Reich gradually became increasingly tolerant and even friendly toward religious sentiment. In his later years, in fact, he turned from social analysis to deeper, more philosophical concerns, until the question of religion occupied a central position in his life. Because Reich's particular metamorphosis may in some way represent a prophetic trend in Western medicine and science in general, it should prove interesting to examine his ideas and their development in detail.

Little information remains about Reich's childhood and adolescence, especially about the role that religion may have played in it. From his own scattered reports and those of his family, it seems that he was raised in an almost wholly secular and assimilated Jewish environment, receiving no formal religious training. At home, his parents conversed in German, unlike the majority of Jewish families of the nation, who spoke mainly in Yiddish. It appears that his own family, not unlike others in Western Europe, sought to merge as closely as possible into the dominant Christian culture.

Reich's own attitude toward Judaism was a curious mixture of indifference and antipathy. In her biography, Ilse Ollendorff, his former wife, indicates that Reich claimed a famous rabbi among his ancestors but otherwise rarely alluded to his religious or ethnic origins. Unlike his mentor, Freud, who opposed orthodox religion but identified strongly with Jewish traditions and values, Reich preferred to view himself as an enlightened scientist and "citizen of the world," standing above any particular ethnic or religious allegiances. Unlike Freud and many of Freud's closest disciples, Reich at times seemed to express an almost active disdain for Jewish values, viewing them as repressive and guilt-ridden. Ironically, as we shall see later, Reich's general unfamiliarity with his ancestral religion blinded him to potential insights Judaism might have offered him through its historical teachings on love, sexuality, and the body.

OPIATE OF THE MASSES OR NEUROTIC ESCAPE

Reich's earliest public statements on religion came during the late 1920s, when he was closely involved with first the Socialist and then the Communist movements. At this time, he adopted the conventional Marxist attitude toward religion: one of general contempt. He believed that religious feeling was indeed the opiate of the masses and one of the chief means by which the ruling class maintained its hold. Faced with the specter of worldwide economic and social unrest combined with rising political violence, Reich regarded orthodox religion as simply a major social institution by which political revolution was repressed. "To be sure," he wrote in *The Mass Psychology of Fascism*, "mysticism's function is clearly articulated: to divert attention from daily misery, 'to liberate from the world,' the purpose of which is to prevent a revolt against the real causes of one's misery."[1]

Once political and social justice were won, Reich contended, the need of the masses to believe in an afterlife or a vengeful, repressive God would vanish. The abolition of war and economic suffering would eliminate the necessity for blind faith and religious irrationality, for dull patience and forbearance in the midst of injustice. "What religion calls freedom from the outside world really means fantasized substitute gratification for actual gratification," he declared.[2] He saw religious institutions as, at best, guided by sincere but politically naive individuals; more typically, he felt, such organizations were directed by cynical and manipulative figures working in close association with economic rulers.

During the 1920s and 1930s, Reich basically agreed with Freud's analysis of religion and mysticism, although he was never as totally negative as the latter. Despite Freud's emotional and cultural loyalties to Judaism, he was a confirmed atheist and bitterly cynical about religious sentiment or the mystical experience. In such works as *The Future of an Illusion, Moses and Monotheism,* and *Civilization and Its Discontents,* Freud fully developed such contemptuous opinions.

Essentially, Freud said, all religion is based on illusion. The religious-minded are persons who are emotionally immature and derive their beliefs in an omnipotent deity from the child's image of a father as all-wise and all-powerful. Accordingly, Freud saw all religion as a regression to infantile needs and fantasies, and, therefore, as invariably neurotic. The emotionally healthy individual, Freud contended, did not need to postulate the existence of a deity any more than he or she needed to view parents as omniscient and omnipotent. As stated in *Moses and Monotheism,* one of his last published writings, "I have never doubted that religious phenomena are to be understood only on the model of the neurotic symptoms of the individual."[3]

Furthermore, Freud viewed the mystical or transcendental experience itself as an expression of mental illness or imbalance. He regarded the "oceanic experience," the feeling of peace and oneness with the universe reported by mystics down through the centuries, as an immature, regressed state of consciousness. Just as the newborn baby presumably has difficulty in differentiating itself from its external environment and must learn the boundaries of its own body, so Freud believed the mystical experience is a reliving of an original, infantile situation. In Freud's view, no amount of ecstatic raving or poetic description could alter an experience that was ultimately a sign of mental weakness and immaturity.

Freud also denied that humans possess any intrinsic need for compassion, altruism, or empathy. Yet, despite this contempt for the very basis of religion, Freud remained an ardent Zionist and a lifelong member of the Vienna B'nai B'rith, the Jewish fraternal organization.

During his early years, Reich adopted many of Freud's attitudes toward religion and mystical experience. Like Freud, he saw faith in God or a hereafter as an immature response to a world that promised no easy answers. Like Freud, too, he felt that mentally healthy individuals did not require an elaborate cosmology of angels and devils, realms of heaven and hell, in order to enjoy productive, loving lives. Nor did mature persons require a belief in eternal reward or punishment in order to behave morally and help their fellow humans. Essentially, Reich agreed with Freud that religion was at best a kind of psychological crutch.

On the other hand, Reich did accept the legitimacy of the mystical experience. He believed that this is often an authentic experience, but that people mistakenly attribute its subtle, almost indescribable sensations to supernatural influences. He was convinced that such oceanic feelings were internal and biological or sexual in nature. Thus, they were not to be disparaged, but their origin and nature should be clearly understood and demystified. In other words, he viewed "religious ecstasy" as often being a distorted form of sexual release.

Reich was aware, too, that within the Roman Catholic Church, for example, some priests, monks, and nuns frequently experience self-transporting moments of great exaltation. Devout lay people can also experience a great sense of unity with Jesus Christ, often peaking at certain points in the Mass. Reich's conviction, clarified in the 1930s, was that this unitary experience presented a close parallel to sexual union. Unable to express themselves sexually in the natural way, such persons may simply displace sexual sensations onto religious symbols. Still later in his life, Reich regarded all mysticism as a mistake, a detour from the more authentic and satisfying experience of physical-emotional love with another human being.

By the 1930s, in *The Mass Psychology of Fascism*, Reich combined both Marxist and Freudian approaches to evoke a deeper understanding of how religious attachment arises among individuals. He was perhaps the first thinker to wed psychological and sociological methods in seeking to unravel this issue. Above all, Reich was concerned with religious dogmatism and fanaticism, asking such questions as, "How can seemingly intelligent and rational people believe the most illogical and preposterous things in the name of religion?" Again, "How can they be guided to commit destructive or self-serving acts against even their best interests?" Faced with the rising menace of Nazism in Europe, he also asked, "How can this totally irrational and ideologically mystical system capture the minds of so many millions? In what ways are mystical dogma and fascism interrelated?" Working out the answers to these questions, far from being an abstract, academic exercise, was necessary for comprehending and then successfully combating these movements, Reich insisted.

The reason so many individuals are drawn to authoritarian, fascist, and antilife religious beliefs, Reich declared in the 1930s, lies in the makeup of the traditional, authoritarian family, especially as exemplified by the lower middle class. In such families, order, obedience, and a pervasive suppression of emotional life are the rule. Children are raised to fear the father, who governs the family with a harsh hand. Women are subordinated to men in decision making. Even more critical, the outward expression of almost all vital feelings, particularly anger and sexuality, is heavily discouraged. Strict obedience is the rule, and exacting discipline, often of a physical nature, is quickly meted out to any who violate parental dicta.

In this atmosphere, Reich argued, children would almost inevitably mature with a tremendous sense of personal guilt centered around sexual feelings. And here religion came in.

> The sexual inhibitions and debilitations that constitute the most
> important prerequisites for the existence of the authoritarian
> family . . . are compassed with the help of religious fears, which
> are infused with sexual guilt-feelings and deeply embedded in the
> emotions. Thus we arrive at the problem of the relation of
> religion to the negation of sexual desire.[4]

After all, Reich pointed out, didn't one's parents say that
sexual thoughts were a sign of moral weakness or degeneracy?
Not surprisingly, individuals from such a background would
probably adopt a very strict, guilt-ridden religious orientation.
God would be regarded as a stern, forbidding father figure, ever
ready to smite his children for the slightest improper act or
thought. Through the suppression of joyful and playful emotions, though, the individual *could* behave morally and thereby
expect reward from God. Reich stressed that in this repressive
religious system, sexuality is a rigid taboo: "The struggle to
resist the temptation to masturbate is a struggle that is experienced by every adolescent and every child, without exception.
. . . Every form of mysticism derives its most active energy and,
in part, also its content from this compulsory suppression of
sexuality."[5]

In recent years, a variety of books have discussed the way in
which organized religion, from fundamentalist groups to fringe
cults, often serves this purpose. Though such critics have not
argued, as Reich did at that time, that religion plays *only* this
repressive role or that all spiritually minded people are emotionally and sexually neurotic, many psychological studies have by
and large confirmed Reich's analysis. That is, persons who are
highly dogmatic and authoritarian in their view of life are often
drawn to rigid mystical systems of thought. There is also evidence that, just as Reich insisted, these individuals tend to come
from cold, strict families in which emotionality and physical
affection are stifled. Morton Schatzman, for instance, in *Soul
Murder*, documents how the late-nineteenth-century German
family, in its almost obsessive emphasis on order and cleanliness
in childraising, may have directly contributed to the generation
that embraced Hitler and Nazism. It seems fair to conclude that,
certainly for the time and place on which Reich focused, organized religion and most religious mysticism represented a destructive antilife force in the society.

The other fundamental question is the role that mystical ideology per se played in Nazi or general authoritarian movements of the time. Reich painstakingly sought a connection between mystical thinking and the Nazi ideology. He insisted that, rather than serving as isolated or fringe features of the Nazi system, fervent emotional-religious sentiments were at its foundation. Moreover, they were almost inevitable consequences of a childrearing and family structure that demanded of males a violent suppression of all tender emotions. As a result, the individual could easily be led to focus pent-up frustrations against a specific group, identified as "dirty," "beotial," or "per verted" and characterized as almost devilish. This was how Nazi ideology portrayed the Jews and, to a lesser extent, all non-Aryans. Additionally, the worship of the "Führer" as all-powerful and all-knowing leader was attributable to the individual's need to identify with a father figure perceived as totally good and beyond all sin. "The more helpless the 'mass-individual' has become, owing to his upbringing, the more pronounced is identification with the Führer, and the more the childish need for protection is disguised in the form of a feeling at one with the Führer," observed Reich.[6] Written several years before the Nazi sweep across Europe and the "final solution" to the "Jewish problem," Reich's analyses were all too accurate and prophetic.

For these reasons, even in his later years Reich remained extremely wary of any phenomena that were at all tinged with psychic or occult overtones, including the budding science of parapsychology, which studies psychic occurrences. He had a blind spot here, but we must also remember that apart from a few isolated researchers like Dr. Rhine at Duke University, there was not that much solid evidence for parapsychology in Reich's day as compared with today. Unlike his contemporary, Carl Jung, Reich was never willing to consider the validity of information that could not be gained in the clinic or laboratory. He had an almost obsessive belief in the uselessness of knowledge within mystical or mythological traditions.

Undoubtedly these biases were heavily influenced by the cultural and social climate in Vienna, where Reich lived in the 1920s. During this period, the city was a hotbed of various occult systems then being pursued in Austria and elsewhere in

Europe. Apparently there lay below the surface of conventional social life a seething mass of fascination with black magic, astrology, and mystical legends. Several recent books have documented that many leading Nazis, including Hitler himself, had been deeply immersed in the occult and a form of astrology, and were totally entranced with a mysterious "spear of destiny." The legend attached to this spear, kept in a museum in Vienna in the 1910s, was that its owner would reign over all of Europe. Hitler, on taking over Austria, seized it. Hitler also belonged to a mystic brotherhood in Germany called the Thule Society. Apparently, it played a very dynamic role in his self-image and obsession with power. Other occult groups refused to admit the growing reality of Nazism and continued to toy with bizarre and esoteric rituals.

What this meant was that people with a strong moral sense, like Wilhelm Reich, became very critical of any idea of secret powers from above, or of occult wisdom, or studies of psychic phenomena. Out of these experiences Reich turned totally against both the psychic and the occult for the rest of his life. At best, he viewed interest in such matters as foolish and misguided; at worst, he associated it with irrationalism, racism, and sadism. However, if he had lived on into the 1970s or 1980s he would probably have changed his mind on this issue, for he kept moving intellectually.

NATURAL RELIGION

During the 1940s, after fleeing war-torn Europe and coming to the United States, Reich became increasingly sympathetic toward certain spiritual concerns. Perhaps this change in his life can be attributed in part to his move to the remote wilderness of northwest Maine, an area lush with natural beauty. Having been born and raised in the country, Reich undoubtedly felt this resettling as a liberating experience—a return to roots. For a few years, too, he was relatively free from political and mass-media harassment and was able to pursue his scientific interests and familial needs in peace. Photographs of him in this period, some of them in the photo section, typically show him as content and self-confident.

By the late 1940s, Reich had come to fashion a kind of personal spiritual outlook on life. It was intertwined with his growing involvement in holistic health and life-energy research and difficult to categorize, as is any genuine encounter with the transcendent. Although he never declared a formal belief in any particular religion and was still contemptuous of religious dogma, Reich developed more and deeper interest in the spiritual issues. In his latter-day writings, such as *The Murder of Christ* and *Ether, God and Devil*, questions such as "What is the meaning of life?" "How can one lead the most worthwhile possible life?" and "What are good and evil, and why do they exist?" emerged as central concerns.

As Reich's thinking matured, he began to differentiate more clearly between authoritarian, antilife religion and what he termed genuine or natural spirituality. He now increasingly emphasized that *some* religion might not only be unharmful, but might in fact have a liberating function. It is this metamorphosis in Reich's views that is of interest today, perhaps heralding a significant trend among health and scientific professionals. While some such professionals have been impressed by the bold theological thinking of the famous theologian Paul Tillich, who has lately been joined by other Christian thinkers concerned about human liberation, it is humanistic psychology—and parapsychology—that has led other scientists to reassess their earlier rejection of all religion.

Various psychological studies in particular have examined altered states of consciousness and have provided new credibility to certain basic religious experiences, as well as indicating their therapeutic benefits. It seems as if scientific data are gradually going to validate the reality of many basic spiritual truths.

For Reich, authoritarian or mystical religion is represented by values that hinder or even stifle natural human emotions and physical needs. "In order to realize the power of mysticism, one has only to think of the murderous conflict between Hindus and Muslims at the time India was divided," he commented.[7] He maintained that originally before the rise of patriarchal or male-ruled societies, all religions had involved essentially *natural* spiritual traditions, which emphasized the power and beauty of the natural, observable world. Humanity was then at harmony with

its own emotional and physical makeup; religious rituals typically sanctified our physical being and the world of nature. Thus
primitive religions, said Reich, were essentially erotic in nature.
What scholars today contemptuously refer to as "fertility cults"
and "cult prostitutes," he claimed, were often in the beginning
extremely spiritual, uplifting practices. For participants in such
ceremonies, their relation to the unity and mystery of nature
was affirmed in a deep and meaningful way. These ancient
peoples appropriately regarded sexuality and the body as holy.
"The common principle of sexuality and religion is the sensation
of nature in one's own organism," Reich argued.[8] "In primitive
religion, religion and sexuality were one."[9]

Furthermore, Reich suggested, ancient religions were far less
patriarchal or male-dominated in their orientation than those
that followed and formed the basis for modern civilization. This
conviction was derived mainly from Reich's acceptance of
Bronislaw Malinowski's study of the Trobriander society in
Polynesia. This study pointed to an original matriarchal social
structure antedating the arrival of Western travelers. Although
few other reliable studies corroborated the notion of matriarchy
as being predominant before the rise of patriarchal civilizations
(4000–3000 B.C.), Reich was certain that Malinowski's researches provided a sound basis for this notion. In fact, on the
one occasion that coauthor Edward Mann visited him in the
early 1950s, Reich insisted on this point and could not be budged
by sociological or anthropological arguments.

Reich did not provide a full explanation of *why* the change
occurred from matriarchy to patriarchy but insisted that it
signaled a serious retreat in our acceptance of our own physical
beings as part of the natural world. A variety of recent articles
and books have provided supportive documentation for Reich's
theorizing, which at the time had little archeological evidence to
back it up. We now know that women were often the spiritual
leaders or seers in various ancient religions. Even more striking
in such religions, the deities themselves tended to be female or
hermaphroditic in nature. As Reich correctly concluded, the
"God-the-Father" image of Western religion is a fairly recent
historical development. All over the Orient, figurines and
statues have been unearthed indicating that scenes depicting
sexuality and intercourse were common to such religions and

often adorned temples and altars. In her recent book, *When God Was a Woman*, Merlin Stone states, "Judging by the continued presence of the Goddess as supreme deity in the Neolithic and Chalcolithic societies of the Near and Middle East, Goddess worship, probably accompanied by the matrilineal customs, appears to have existed without challenge for thousands of years."[10]

With the shift to patriarchal social structures, the major religions became increasingly male-dominated. The gods were now warriors and were portrayed as stern and forbidding. They were made in man's image: disciplined fighters. Sexuality became taboo, and gradually more moralistic religious dogmas were introduced. For Reich, this shift to an obsession with guilt, moralism, and shame was ultimately exemplified in the "rampant mysticism of the Church in the Middle Ages."[11] He argued that Christianity had replaced the nature-accepting animism of our early history and the powerful vision of Jesus with a mystical theology far removed from nature and the roots of life.

Reich was convinced that Western society's obsession with evil and the devil arose from its suppression of natural emotional and sexual expression. For him the realm of the devil was nothing more than the sensual and erotic world converted into something horrible and tortured through the repressive mechanisms of negative religious indoctrination. Religion in the West, he contended, has perverted living functions into something mystical. It labels the basic instincts, especially sex, as bad and their source as the devil. Good morals come from God. Thus Christian theology talks of God fighting the devil, who is constantly tempting poor mortals to go against Him.

From this line of reasoning, Reich focused directly on the life and teachings of Jesus Christ. More a literary and philosophical work than a scientific treatise, Reich's book *The Murder of Christ* was published in 1953. A. S. Neill viewed it as among Reich's best pieces of writing. In this book, Reich insisted that Jesus had come to liberate the Jews and other peoples of the time from religions that had become oppressive and inimical to life, that had diverged from their original sources of love for humanity and the natural world. Reich suggested that Jesus was eventually trapped by the adoring attention of his disciples and other fervent followers, who mistakenly believed he was the Messiah.

Propelled by this image, Jesus marched on Jerusalem to meet certain death. Reich observed, "Christ did not pose as a saint. . . . He just lived in a way dreamed of by his fellow man as being the truly saintlike way of living."[12]

Reich's basic sociological insight here was that many great leaders, like Jesus, are victimized by the extravagant expectations of their followers. Once his disciples had defined him as the Messiah and he had accepted this, he felt obliged to carry out the self-sacrificial messianic role pictured by the prophet Isaiah. Reich believed that Jesus could best be understood historically as a proclaimer of natural love and emotional freedom, acceptance of the body, and respect for one's fellow humans:

> Christ's ways lend themselves as the seeds of a future religion. It is, essentially, a religion of love. Love encompasses *every* kind of love: The love of your parents, the love between man and woman, the love of your neighbor and of your enemy, and the child. . . . One cannot cut apart love and say: You may let your love stream in this, but you must not let love stream in that.[13]

For Reich, then, the extent to which any religious or spiritual system accepted or denied our natural life expressions determined whether it was ultimately beneficial or not. The simple teachings of Jesus, he felt, became hopelessly distorted and mystified through centuries of Church rule. As have others, he saw Paul, or Saul of Tarsus, as the first of many to turn Jesus's teachings upside-down by condemning the natural world and the body as sinful and evil. Thus was a religion of love turned into one of authoritarianism and dogma, capable of preaching eternal punishment for simple physical pleasures.

Parenthetically, it is fascinating how many different thinkers through the centuries have each seen Christ as the model of his or her particular social or political theory. Socialists have seen Jesus as a Socialist; Communists have portrayed him as the first true Communist; Spiritualists have seen him communing with the spirits—for example, speaking with Moses and Elijah on the Mount—and now Reich saw Jesus as an exponent and practitioner of natural emotions and acceptance of the body. In these late writings, Reich seems to have expressed with fervor a kind of natural mysticism—and looked to Jesus as its prime exemplar.

DIFFICULTIES WITH THE TRANSCENDENT

It should be pointed out, of course, that Reich did oversimplify matters considerably in his comparisons of antilife with natural religions. Recent archeological evidence suggests that some ancient religions were indeed concerned with an afterlife or transcendent realms of existence. Some ancient religions practiced human sacrifice, while others condoned bizarre sexual rituals that Reich almost certainly would have considered sadomasochistic. Nor does his interpretation of Jesus seem quite accurate. Though evidence is obviously not conclusive, it does appear that Jesus emerged from a locale and an era in which asceticism was advocated as a pathway to God. We must conclude that while Reich's analysis of religion and natural man, briefly summarized here, had some brilliant insights, it was certainly not infallible.

It is crucial to our understanding of Reich's religious orientation to note his conviction in later years that sexuality itself might be a tremendously powerful spiritual force. In particular, he seemed to see the full orgasmic experience as possessing a tremendous transforming power, capable of shattering an individual's feeling of isolation and alienation from the world. Essentially he was suggesting that the full orgasmic experience has the capacity to change, perhaps permanently, our daily human consciousness. From early in his career he had apparently been moving toward this notion: "The longing for the genital embrace is profoundly expressed in the belief in a 'universal spirit,' in 'God,' 'the creator,'" he declared.[14] It is through the sexual orgasm that man and woman most closely experience the oneness with the cosmos that all religions speak of, he asserted.

Two ironies surround Reich's later views on mysticism and religion. First, he was certain that his beliefs on human fulfillment and spirituality were scientifically valid and had an *empirical* basis. He was often angry and impatient with those who could not accept this. This insistence upon the empirical validity of his ideas and insights lost him more supporters than he won. Reich often defended his position by arguing, by way of analogy, that there could not be two or three or twenty principles or guidelines about how to best care for a baby who lies crying for maternal warmth, or for a child who begins to handle its genitals for the first time. In a statement which brilliantly summarizes his own rebuttal to critics, he argued that one can declare philosophically that a union of nature and culture is impossible or undesirable. But, he insisted, it was no longer possible to maintain that our dichotomizing human existence into animal and cultural aspects "does not destroy his [the human's] joy of living [and] stifle his initiative."[15]

On the other hand, a belief or disbelief in a personal God, an afterlife, or a transcendent dimension to human existence, is clearly *not* something that can be reduced to psychological analysis or evaluated scientifically in a laboratory. Reich consistently denied any transcendent meaning to human presence in the cosmos, and flatly regarded those who believed in a supernatural world as neurotic and in need of therapy. For him, the meaning of life was to live, to function healthily—that is all. Of course, he was hardly the first innovative thinker to mistakenly attempt to clarify religious issues and assumptions by strictly logical and scientific methods of inquiry. He could have learned from a scientist like Albert Einstein, who, despite his deeply intuitive and philosophical searching, wisely refrained from claiming that his scientific discoveries qualified him to draw firm conclusions about the ultimate meaning of the human enterprise. But Reich was true to his nature and determinedly impatient to exercise such judgments on the basis of scientific data and findings. He thus alienated many potential allies by insisting upon the scientific basis to *all* of his ideas and discoveries. He used his intuitive powers—what his daughter Eva describes as his "orgonomic first sense"—but he looked for common processes at work in nature, basing himself in natural science.

The other major irony about Reich's religious metamorphosis is that he failed to take notice of the longstanding spiritual traditions that his ideas closely paralleled. His lifelong rejection of Jewish teachings seems to have stemmed from a dislike for the legalistic or Talmudic outlook that had indeed dominated much of Judaism. Even within this tradition, though, a strong emphasis on love and sexuality as spiritual concerns has long existed. For example, Talmudic teaching, besides stressing the place of love between marital partners, states that within marriage it is the duty of the husband to give his wife sexual pleasure. Thus, at least within the family, sex is not just for procreation, as is true in Christian thought, but for mutual pleasure.

The Kabbalah, an esoteric offshoot of Judaism, has for centuries upheld a primary interest in the body and the erotic. Originally derived from the Hebrew root-word "to receive"— suggesting that it was received from God—the Kabbalah has long been shrouded in historical myth and uncertainty. While there exists much Jewish writing on mysticism, the Kabbalah is generally defined as encompassing four main bodies of work. These include the *Sefer Yetzirah* (Book of Creation), believed to have been written about the third century A.D.; the various commentaries on this work; the *Zohar* (Book of Splendor), which first appeared in Europe in the thirteenth century; and its various commentaries. Though the Kabbalah was decisively rejected by the Jewish religious establishment by the nineteenth century, it has never lost its popular appeal. Freud himself, in fact, had a complete set of the *Zohar* in his private study, and some scholars feel it influenced certain of his concepts.

Central to the Kabbalistic tradition of the individual's realization of God is the belief that sexuality is an extremely potent spiritual force. Not only is celibacy discouraged among its disciples, but the Kabbalah repeatedly emphasizes that sexual intercourse, in conjunction with intense mental concentration, is a highly valued means of liberating the deeper aspects of self. In fact, loving sexual union is regarded as among the most powerful experiences available to alter the daily functioning of the conscious mind. The *Zohar* itself states, "Hence, a man should be as zealous to enjoy this joy [of sexual intercourse] . . . as to enjoy the joy of the Sabbath, at which time is consummated the union of the sages with their wives."[16]

Another passage of *Zohar* says:

When is one . . . a man? When he is male together with female and is highly sanctified and zealous for sanctification: then and only then he is designated one without mar of any kind. Hence, a man and his wife should have a single inclination at the hour of their union, attaching her to himself in affection. So conjoined, they make one soul, and one body.[17]

Later in his career, Reich clarified his own views in an interview. "It's not the embrace in itself, not the intercourse. It is the real, emotional experience of the loss of your ego, of your whole spiritual self."[18] The similarities between this view and that of the Kabbalah, which sees sexuality as a self-transcending experience, are readily apparent. This conception of Reich's illustrates a basic aspect of his natural mysticism.

Another spiritual system that closely parallels Reich's partly developed religious views is that of Tantric Yoga. Like the Kabbalistic tradition, this ancient spiritual discipline emphasizes the importance of physical love and emotional release. It views sexuality as a particular expression of the individual's life energy, or *prana.* The Tantric way does not condemn the body, but rather states that *through* the body and the emotions doors are opened to other states of awareness. To become accepting and at peace with one's bodily needs and sensations is regarded as the first essential step, the basic prerequisite for true spiritual development.

One leading contemporary Tantric thinker is Bhagwan Shree Rajneesh, whose ashram is in Poona, India. He makes explicit reference to Freud, Reich, Jung, and other such Western psychologists in writings intended for Western audiences. In *The Psychology of the Esoteric,* Rajneesh states, "Sex has so much appeal because in sex you become one for a moment. . . . But the more you seek it, the more conscious you become. Then you will not feel the bliss of sex, because the bliss comes from the unconsciousness."[19]

The goal in Tantric Yoga is to avoid the artificial splitting of the person into spirit and body, good and bad. Emotions are to be acknowledged or expressed; only in this way, says Rajneesh, can one begin to actually transform lower emotions, such as anger, jealousy, greed, and hatred, into higher states of awareness. Certain elements of Gestalt therapy appear central to his thinking. Again, in language that sounds very much like Reich, he explains, "Beginning with a division between you and the body leads [only] to suppression. So if you are for transformation, you should not begin by dividing. Transformation can come only from an understanding of the whole *as the whole.* . . . The more you suppress the body, the more frustrated you will be."[20] These are but brief allusions to the powerful thought of Rajneesh, whose books are now numbered in the dozens and who, according to a 1978 interview in *Time* magazine, has recently emerged as a growing influence on leaders of the Esalen Institute of California.

INERTIA IN THE EAST

While critical of Western religion, Reich was hardly friendly toward Eastern spiritual approaches. It is difficult, of course, to assess what his attitude might have been had he lived long enough to encounter the recent influx of Oriental philosophies and practices from India and Tibet. Reich's general distaste for Oriental religions often comes as a surprise to those interested in his work today, as they often expect Reich to share with them an open curiosity or interest in both parapsychological phenomena and the insights of certain Eastern religions. He did, however, acknowledge that Eastern disciplines, such as Buddhism and Yoga, contain kernels of wisdom about our relation to the cosmos, and stated, for instance, that there are great insights in such religious teachings, even if they have been misinterpreted. But, for a variety of reasons, he saw serious shortcomings in such approaches.

First, as both a social theorist and a former political activist, Reich was put off by the extensive passivity and indifference to human suffering apparent among the masses of the East. He viewed the tremendous social inertia in such societies as at least partly strengthened by the dominant religious doctrines, which tend to foster a fatalistic outlook. He believed that the Hindu and Buddhist religions are woefully lacking in any conception of political or social improvement because only the individual seems to matter. And, Reich believed, while the goal for the individual might be to personally transcend his or her society, such religions generally promote an acceptance of existing social conditions. As a result, such doctrines have served to keep Eastern societies stagnant and impervious to the breath of change. A major exception here is the work of Gandhi, who struggled to improve the lot of untouchables and the mass of Indians. Of course, Gandhi was influenced not only by Hinduism but also by Western political and Christian thought.

Over twenty-five years ago, Reich prophetically observed in

The Murder of Christ that the patriarchal structure of the Eastern societies formed the framework within which the massive bodily denials were created. Simple physical love, he felt, had been distorted and placed out of reach by the main religious systems.

Reich also maintained that the dominant Oriental religions of Hinduism and Buddhism support a repressive and grossly exploitative treatment of women. He noted that women under such religious systems are treated far more cruelly than in the West and that the Asian masses are at least as armored in their bodies as their Western counterparts. In recent years, a variety of observers and visitors to the East have supported the accuracy of this view. Historically, women in Chinese and other Oriental cultures were generally subservient to their husbands' demands, and even contemporary China has a long way to go to achieve sexual equality. It also seems to be moving toward a new puritanism, in which holding hands and kissing in public is considered a social offense and dangerous to the general morality. It is a sad fact that in some Eastern countries today women are still treated as virtual slaves.

Reich believed that in these societies women would eventually awaken to the vast cultural changes sweeping across the West and challenge centuries-old patterns of sexual and social repression. He warned, however, that the massive social repression in such societies made them particularly ripe for authoritarian revolutions, which would promise too much and attempt to change things too quickly. Recent revolutions in Vietnam and Cambodia with their mass evacuations and killings bear this out. While Reich may have overestimated the influence of formal religion in supporting authoritarian Asian systems, he was clearly very sensitive to the way in which religious ideology can be used to manipulate and mold family, political, and social life.

More specifically, he believed that spiritual systems such as Buddhism and Hinduism are essentially artificial and sterile in nature and outlook. Their latent goal is to harden or deaden individuals to the social suffering surrounding them. Many of their sophisticated techniques of self-development seem designed to achieve a kind of mummification of the emotional and energetic life. In fact, Reich explicitly criticized certain esoteric breathing methods of Yoga (where, for example, one breathes in and out to a count of four or eight) and specific meditation disciplines, arguing that they serve to *increase,* not lessen, the individual's armoring. The basic point is that these mentally controlled breathing rhythms kill the spontaneity of this natural process. Rajneesh, the Tantric master, has similarly criticized Transcendental Meditation's mechanical repetition of a mantra because of its tendency to deaden the feelings and creativity of the practitioner and lead to an artificial sense of inner calm and tranquility. Reich believed that these methods induce a numbing of the senses, warding off genuine excitement and natural emotional expression, whether anger, sexuality, or joy. Speaking of them in the early 1940s, Reich observed:

> They necessitate the overcoming of emotionality altogether, pleasure as well as suffering. This is the essence of the Buddhist ideology of Nirvana. This ideology also provides an insight into the breathing exercises of the Yogas. The breathing technique taught by Yogas is the exact opposite of the breathing technique we use to reactivate the vegetative emotional excitations in our patients. The aim of the Yoga breathing exercise is to combat affective impulses; its aim is to obtain peace.
>
> That the Yoga technique was able to spread to Europe and America is ascribable to the fact that the people of these cultures seek a means of gaining control over their natural vegetative impulses and at the same time of eliminating conditions of anxiety.[21]

While all of Reich's criticism may not be legitimate, it is noteworthy that some of the more reputable Eastern philosophers today have offered quite similar comments. Thus, contemporary thinkers like Rajneesh, Krishnamurti, and Idries Shah (a leading Sufi thinker) have warned Americans and other Westerners to be extremely wary of simplemindedly adopting the spiritual practices of the Orient. They point out that many yogic or other Eastern traditions are culture-specific, reflecting the climate and lifestyle of the populace involved as well as unique social, historical, and physiognomic conditions. Like tropical plants admired for their beauty and transported to North America, where they may flower spectacularly at first only to die later, such disciplines may well fail to meet many of the exciting expectations that they originally aroused.

Moreover, as some of the more reliable Eastern philosophers insist, many of these esoteric techniques assume that the individual is relatively unarmored and free of serious tension. A number of Westerners, it is reported, have suffered unhappy or even physically adverse reactions while attempting advanced yogic positions or meditative breathing techniques without having had skillful preparation or guidance. It was Reich himself, after all, who discovered that intense stimulation of the physical armoring is likely to bring up repressed memories, emotions, or fears. Lacking the guidance of a well-trained counselor, the most well-intentioned person may suddenly experience disturbing anxieties during the practice of Yoga or certain Eastern breathing techniques. Especially for those who are chronically tense and armored, and therefore likely to have an already strained respiratory or cardiovascular system, intensive forced breathing exercises may prove quite dangerous to the heart. In a case known directly to one of us, a man in his thirties died during one such exercise. Thus, while Reich may not have explicitly emphasized it, yogic exercises and similar practices are clearly not useful in dissolving character armoring, although they may be helpful in reducing surface emotional and physical tensions.

FURTHER ALONG THE SPIRITUAL PATH

Reich's contribution to humanity's spiritual development may well lie more in his therapies and techniques than in his specific ideas on religion and society. From natural childbirth to holistic health, the intent of methods in these areas is to loosen and then eliminate the armoring that separates us organically from nature and from other people. They help us emerge from the trap of anxiety and alienation into a dynamic aliveness and full embodiment in the everyday world.

While we do not argue that Reichian therapeutic methods lead automatically to spiritual growth, his basic goals—acceptance and enjoyment of the body, vital emotional expression and physical health, and a pervasive sensitivity of one's relation to the natural world—have been identified in many diverse traditions as prerequisites for mature spiritual development and activity. It is significant that Reichian therapists and those whose therapy has brought them close to orgastic potency typically have no time for orthodox religious systems. For them, Reich's intellectual-therapeutic achievement was the naturalization of religion. This naturalization provides the individual with access to happiness, health, a humane ethical code, and bodily joy that others seek in formal religion.

On the other hand, some people who have been exposed to bioenergetic or Reichian types of therapy—but have not completed them or achieved orgastic potency—are found to be receptive to one of several of the Oriental systems of consciousness raising, including the Indian guru Muktananda, Rajneesh, and Sufi teachers. These spiritual leaders all talk of energy and of vibrations, and have evolved ways—be it mantras, shaking or shouting to music, or whirling-Dervish dancing—to reduce surface armoring and liven up the organism. In this way they function as therapeutic systems and at the same time provide participants with a sense of communal fellowship and belonging.

For instance, at the Rajneesh ashram in Poona, India, Westerners are encouraged to participate in a number of vigorous physical exercises, such as free-expression dancing and jogging, that pave the way for inward, quieting meditative states. Two of the more popular of these are kundalini and dynamic. These exercises are also conducted in Rajneesh Centers outside of India, where participants jump up and down, shake the whole body, and dance spontaneously to tape-recorded Indian drum music followed by passive meditation. The immediate effect is to shake up one's entire musculature, especially around the neck and shoulders, promote deeper breathing, release tensions, and charge up the organism. Participants are also encouraged to shout or cry aloud so that some of their repressed feelings are expressed. There is an obvious similarity here to certain Reichian therapeutic techniques. (For a full discussion of these and other Rajneesh active meditation techniques, see his book, *Meditation: The Art of Ecstasy.*)

After these active exercises, participants usually move into a quiet meditative state in order to get more in touch with their deeper feelings and needs and to feel a sense of greater unity with each other and with nature. In his teachings, Rajneesh discourses on universalistic religion, accenting major themes from the naturalistic Chinese religion of Taoism and Indian Tantric thought. He integrates these with selections from Buddha, the teaching of Christ, and others.

An encouraging trend that was predicted by Reich is the growing challenge to male domination within some major Western religions. Many of the most influential and well-established religions, such as Judaism, Methodism, and Episcopalianism, are finally, although very slowly, permitting both women and avowed homosexuals to be ordained. In other religious groups, men and women now share equally in duties and responsibilities in religious services. Recently a number of books and articles have appeared arguing against a strictly male or "God the Father" deity and the accompanying rigid sex-role stereotyping. Still another reflection of the gradual religious transformation anticipated by Reich is the growing interest in non-Western, *pre*-Christian religions: shamanism, animism, and white witchcraft, most of which wholeheartedly emphasize our interdependence with the natural world, including the erotic, and celebrate the joys of dancing and the powers of energy donations.

Clearly, we live in an era of tumultuous social and religious upheaval and transition. The current proliferation of various power-hungry cults underscores Reich's prediction of over forty years ago when he observed, "Helplessness in the face of natural forces and elemental social catastrophes is conducive to the development of religious ideologies in cultural crises. . . . The formation of religious cults is not dependent upon the will of the individual. They are sociological formations."[22] As the pace of change escalates, we can expect an increasing proliferation of new, along with a renaissance of old, religious systems. Specifically, new self-appointed gurus or religious leaders will appear with teachings that accent particular notions of Tibetan or Indian philosophies or combine these teachings with beliefs about sex, the body, and self-transcendence borrowed from Reichian therapies or transpersonal psychology. Other new teachers will revive the ancient philosophies of stoicism or hedonism and, by dressing them up in a renovated terminology or by combining them with insights from modern psychological findings, will gain a following, especially among the young and the alienated. The vacuum of meaning that is occurring now with the collapse of established political and national systems relentlessly seeks to be filled. Thus the pages of a magazine such as the *New Age Journal* are filled with ads promoting exotic gurus and new institutes, techniques, or disciplines designed to help us find health, happiness, inner peace, or a new direction in life.

It is ironic but not surprising in the light of Reich's analyses that some of these "new age" religious cults, while promising freedom and enhanced fulfillment, are even more rigid, authoritarian, and patriarchal than the groups they criticize as outmoded and out of date. Their leaders, like the infamous cult led by Reverend Jim Jones, demand total obedience from their followers as they attempt to build up a powerful organization. From a Reichian standpoint, they may often be seen as "freedom peddlers." Their followers find it easier to yield power and responsibility to such patriarchal figures than to deal directly and painstakingly with their dependency neuroses and armored bodies. In a sense they are merely replacing one psychological trap with another.

Our understanding of Reich's emphasis on sexual and bodily release and increased sensitivity to nature can help us appreciate why many people are pursuing "secular" activities with a religious zeal and thereby are finding varying degrees of self-transcendence. Among joggers, for example, are some who run miles every day and twenty-six miles on Sundays with a group of friends. They often experience a transporting high and let nothing, even the worst weather, interfere with their jogging routine. Others pursue tai chi, aikido, or judo with similar zeal, finding physical release and a kind of religious communal feeling in the company of their fellow practitioners. These and similar intense physical activities can take us out of ourselves and bring us to nature and to the company of peers—all basic religious experiences.

Many earnest seekers in certain psychotherapeutic groups that emphasize bodily release, like Primal therapy or est, also develop a religious zeal—and a binding sense of community. If most of their friends soon turn out to be from such a group and some seek new converts with the dedication of a Jesuit missionary, the theories and practices of these groups nevertheless help their members deal with life, and certain activities are experienced as self-transporting.

One can even see that rock music, with its orgonous bodily movement and its focus on certain rock stars, can be energy-releasing, self-transporting, and life-directing. We might argue that, along with evangelical and pentecostal Christianity, with its choirs and hand-clapping or foot-stamping to the music, rock bands are the newest mass religion. The evangelicals also use music and vigorous bodily movement—or shouting and "speaking in tongues"—to successfully discharge some pent-up energy. At certain rock concerts one might even loosely speak of collective orgasms. The key is that they first charge up and then discharge bioenergy. The sexual component is often only thinly disguised.

From a Reichian perspective, as our culture continues to induce increasing tension and armor buildup, we can expect new social forms to emerge that either overtly or covertly arouse excitement and serve to discharge surface tensions, thus making everyday life more tolerable—without basically affecting the armoring.

While Reich's orgone theory provides few insights into current religious trends, his overall perspective will help us to distinguish false from true religious expression.

CHAPTER 8

The Liberation of Humanity

Humanity is trying to get at its core, at its living healthy core. But before it can be reached, humanity has to pass through this phase of murder, killing, and destruction.

Human culture does not even exist yet.
—WILHELM REICH

It is in his dreams and visions for human society that Reich stands out as an exciting thinker. While Freud took a very realistic—some say pessimistic—view of humanity's future in his later writings, Reich remained an optimist to the end. He wanted for us the maximum of freedom, creativity, equality, and harmony, and he knew they were ours for the taking if we respected the flow of biological energy, or orgone, within ourselves. Fundamentally, he felt that if this energy were allowed free and loving expression in sexuality and in daily work, men and women would be basically happy and negative emotions of hate and anxiety would not build up to explode in sadistic violence or wars. His goal was liberation of the human being, not basically by one-to-one therapy but by the transformation of the social conditions of life—and especially of the lives of infants and children—so that all of us can realize our potential. The full development of his vision was a libertarian philosophy of enormous scope and appeal.

What makes his vision of society different and more compelling than most current views is that it is grounded in a profound understanding of human character *and* of the social and political transformations of the twentieth century. And, on a more personal level, it flowed from an overwhelming moral passion, a powerful feeling for nature, and a deep love for humanity.

We have seen that, working closely with Freud and his inner circle in the late 1920s, Reich pioneered a whole range of insights into character, character formation, and its roots in the suppression of bodily impulses. These ideas are still widely respected in contemporary psychoanalysis. The aim of these discoveries was to enable patients to work themselves free of their armoring so as to make possible an uninhibited, guilt-free sexual existence and a productive work life. During his rather brief Marxist period (1928–1934), Reich had assimilated the basics of that philosophy, and he now tried valiantly to marry it to his renovated, optimistic version of Freud. He championed equality of the sexes, women's rights, the freedom of adolescents to a full love life, and, for workers, a nonexploitive work situation. His conversion to socialism was tied to a belief that it promised freedom from economic anxiety even in the face of such contingencies as illness, accident, and old age.

Living through the rise of Naziism, Reich became acutely aware of the denial of freedom by all-powerful governments. Before others were aware of it, he perceived that fascism's success was rooted in authoritarian attitudes and the programming of both the masses and their leaders. He delineated the basic outlines of the fascistic character structure and of fascistic groups and trends, regardless of the label. And as a political activist, he struggled against Hitlerism and put his life on the line in the fight, vain though it was, to halt its expansion.

Reich's optimistic version of psychoanalysis rejected Freud's universal death wish and Freud's belief that sexual repression was necessitated by the structure of every type of civilization. In 1928, Reich became acutely aware of the class conflict, the oppression of the working class by capitalists, and the way the industrial system basically enslaved workers. He saw that a radical change in society was required in order to make economic freedom possible—because without it, bodily freedom would not be possible. In short, his social conscience had been awakened.

Reich saw deeply into the problems of social freedom. He held that to proclaim freedom to the masses without rooting this freedom in an unarmored biophysical structure was to invite disaster. For example, he insisted that if rigidly armored persons suddenly gained a great deal of new political or psychological freedom, it would either make them irresponsible and giddy or very anxious. (He called this freedom "giddiness.") We see examples of this in the street riots during the political upheavals in France in 1789 and in Russia in 1917. A sudden access of psychological freedom often turns from sheer excitement to deep panic, as we saw in the excerpt from Orson Bean's *Me and the Orgone*. And, even before Erich Fromm (*Escape from Freedom*), Reich noted a pervasive fear of freedom in the masses. He has said, "If freedom means first of all the responsibility of every individual for the rational determination of his own personal, professional, and social existence, then there is no greater fear than that of the establishment of general freedom."[1] By this he was referring to the fact that emotional insecurity is deeply rooted in the masses, and thus there is a profound fear of experiencing freedom, which inevitably involves responsibility for one's own fate. The great majority of people will yield up their self-determination to a leader, a religion, drugs, or an ingrained habit so that they can blame whatever "bad" that may happen on this external person, thing, or institution. This emotional insecurity, often sensed as uneasiness or recurrent anxiety, is, of course, the psychic or characterological symptom of physical armor. Thus, in a word, the armored cannot tolerate real freedom.

Forced to flee Germany, Reich rather naturally wound up in Scandinavia, whose people are known for their passion for human freedom. Here for a time his thinking took on a social-anarchistic tone. In common with libertarians, he shared the belief that groups—schools, factories, communities—could and should develop their own rules for social living, and that their members would voluntarily respect these rules, thus eliminating the need for governments. This notion was developed further in his concept of work democracy, discussed later in this chapter.

But it was only when he came to the United States, whose political system he grew to love, that he found an attractive and congenial philosophy of scientific and political liberty. He now totally disavowed his earlier Marxism; in his later years, in fact, he was impressed with Dwight D. Eisenhower and apparently voted Republican. In the meantime, he gradually abandoned faith in politicians, calling them parasites.

Then, eschewing the political approach to meaningful social change, Reich articulated a program of democratizing the family and children's upbringing, the school system, and daily work. Liberation was possible, he declared, without waiting for novel or radical political legislation. During his last ten years he waged a campaign against the entrenched medical and psychiatric profession, the drug industry, the nuclear industry, and other institutions that in his view were enemies of human welfare or freedom. He also campaigned for a new nonmechanistic kind of science and an appreciation of the earth's ecology and atmosphere, decrying atomic power and air pollution years before the environmentalist movement was to emerge.

Reich's approach was revolutionary but neither socialistic, simplistic, nor easy to grasp. It was not laid down comprehensively in any one book, but can be seen through what he called a thin red line of connecting ideas, expressed in his many books and articles. Its basis was that human beings are pulsating, energy-filled organisms constantly fired by impulses, feelings, and urges, and that only as our institutions and customs take this fact fully into account can they facilitate growth, creativity, and happiness. At present, our institutions are structured so that physical and emotional movement, full breathing, and creativity are constantly curtailed or denied. They must all be reshaped.

Reich was totally disillusioned by the naked power-seeking of Communist political leaders in Russia. He had come to believe that politicians, whether of left, center, or right, were—with their devotion to state policies; their authoritarian concern for law, order, and discipline; their rhetoric about the ideal of family, national, and economic interests; and their maintenance of "free enterprise"—actually antithetical to productive work, social justice, and the general welfare.

Having abandoned the political process as *the* way to secure important social change, in the 1940s Reich turned his attention to children and the family as the hope of the future. He recognized the importance of proper upbringing and of the rights of children some thirty-five years before UNESCO declared the Year of the Child. And since the most formative influence on the child is the family, Reich's program of social transformation began with how to liberate the family.

THE FREE FAMILY

We have already discussed how Reich criticized the traditional family structure, which he saw as patriarchal and authoritarian. He held that the trouble begins when marriage is made a socially compulsory goal and a lifetime commitment, because forcing our biological energies into a fixed mold inevitably limits freedom. The institution of marriage should be optional, he felt, and if couples do get married they should be allowed to take vows for limited time periods. If their love dies—and with living, pulsating, growing beings this is quite likely—then divorce should be easy, cheap, and swift.

Reich realized that it was the patriarchal nature of marriage that bred armoring, because of its authoritarian base in male dominance. He argued that a marriage system in which the husband-father is all-powerful imposes both physical and psychological pressure on the wife and on all women—as well as on children—to obey the dictates of male authority figures. Because women and children have little or no freedom to express their true feelings, these pressures produce suppression, which in turn causes armoring. In addition, patriarchy in the family is allied to authoritarian religions and political systems that rule by means of fear and physical or psychological violence, so men too are armored.

Historically, Reich felt that the beginning of patriarchy coincided with the heavy armoring of the masses. Evidence for this connection, Reich believed, came from the work of anthropologist Bronislaw Malinowski, long a student of the primitive

Trobriander tribe of New Guinea. In his book *The Sexual Life of Savages*, Malinowski had contrasted two types of marriage systems within the Trobriander society, which were connected with two types of childrearing and linked to varying degrees of patriarchal organization, one sex-negative, the other sex-positive. The former (the sex-negative and patriarchal) was related to a dowry practice that gave an economic advantage to the bride's parents. Reich generalized from this and other ethnographic studies of marriage and sex, including that of Engels, and claimed that Malinowski's study

> demonstrates irrefutably that common property, a lack of rigid family organization, sexual freedom for children and adolescents, and openness and generosity in character structure are just as interrelated as private property, patriarchy, asceticism in children and adolescents, enslavement of women, rigidity in family and marriage, character armoring, sexual perversion, and mental illness, all of which are ever-present symptoms of sexual suppression.[2]

In brief, Reich felt that matriarchal societies were neither authoritarian nor sex-repressive, and that this was because they didn't link private property to the marriage practice. He held, therefore, that the rise of patriarchy was somehow associated with the replacement of communal property rights by private property rights.

In his *Sexpol* writings, Reich clarified how the power relationships in the patriarchal family pave the way for children to accept an extensive system of authoritarian, male-dominant relationships in other institutions: school, business, politics, and religion. In short, patriarchal attitudes embedded in our compulsory family system expand to ensure female inequality throughout our whole society. Reich's analysis of the 1930s thus foreshadowed the concern of today's feminists with women's rights, the abolition of sex stereotyping, and sexism in all its varied manifestations.

In the liberated family envisioned by Reich, the children are reared in an atmosphere of freedom to be themselves. Individual differences are respected, and neither parent browbeats or dominates the children. Parents love, teach, and lead their children rather than imposing on them their superior power, knowledge, or will. They respect the inner wisdom within each of their children by recognizing his or her unique rhythm of growth, learning, and development. The ideal is a democratic family in which the freedom of each person to grow is the major goal. Absolutely basic to the successful family functioning is the practice of self-regulation as opposed to acting in accordance with the wishes or orders of others.

SELF-REGULATION FOR CHILDREN

The theory of self-regulation was apparently first formulated in an article by Tage Philipson, a close coworker of Reich's. It was published in a journal Reich edited in Denmark and then republished in his *Journal of Sex Economy and Orgone Research* in 1942. The concept emerged from Philipson's observation that healthy organisms show a natural capacity for rational morality, which grows spontaneously as the organisms satisfy their basic biological energy needs.

Essentially, both Philipson and Reich recognized that every growing child is heir to internal rhythms and needs, and that the democratic way to bring up children is to allow them to respond naturally to these rhythms and needs in all the basic life processes, such as eating, eliminating, sleeping, and playing. The challenging task for the parent is to trust the child, permit spontaneous expression, and protect the child's natural capacity for bodily pleasure in all the above functions. Boadella notes: "If the child's fundamental needs are gratified he will much more readily accept the inevitable frustrations and accommodations involved in the process of living than the child who has learnt to suppress his natural feelings."[3] Self-regulated children demonstrate unusual self-assurance and self-reliance and are better equipped to cope with the strains and disappointments of life. In addition, since they are in touch with their primary feelings, they enjoy life more and retain their natural exuberance and freedom of movement.

The key is sensitivity to the infant's needs. If the parents are anxious, very tired, and lack self-confidence—or are heavily armored—they will probably fail to read the baby's signals correctly. With the raising of his third child, Peter, born to Ilse

Ollendorff, Reich directly faced the inherent difficulties in grasping the infant's needs. As he admitted in a letter to A. S. Neill, "It took me several weeks to understand what the boy wanted when he cried."[4] He discovered that a given cry can indicate one of a variety of needs. Out of this experience, Reich perceived a basic issue: "The problem still remained unsolved as to how much of these first and most spontaneous activities in a wordless human interrelationship can be taught to mothers and fathers, nurses and doctors at large."[5] Eventually, he made elaborate plans for "preventive-psychiatry" clinics where mothers could receive help in handling their infants correctly. These plans revolved around the Orgonomic Infant Research Center, launched in 1949 at Orgonon and growing out of meetings and discussions that had started in 1940. Reich first reported on its aims in August 1950 at the Second International Orgonomic Conference at Rangeley. The services it planned to provide included (1) care of pregnant mothers in the prenatal period, (2) supervision of the birth and the early weeks of the infant's life, and (3) recognition and prevention of armoring during the early years. Reich also hoped to do follow-up studies on adolescents who had gone through the center as infants. Unfortunately, only the first two parts of the plan were put into practice, mainly because of the pressure of other research and the heavy attacks on Reich's work in the 1950s. He considered this issue so important that the profits from his books and writings were to be used, according to his will, to finance an Infant Trust Fund for the care and support of children and adolescents who suffer any kind of distress and for basic research to help children. In his autobiography, Neill quotes Reich as saying, "All the damage is done to a child before it can speak."[6]

Neill raised his only child, Zoe, according to self-regulation and wrote a book, *The Free Child,* about the experience. In it he confessed that he and his wife had few problems but were occasionally concerned that Zoe, if allowed, would run about naked in all kinds of weather. They had to "bully" her into wearing suitable clothing. She enjoyed good health and at the age of five met Neill's highest expectations.

When Zoe was two, the English press subjected her to intense but congratulatory scrutiny. A reporter for *Picture Post* who visited Neill's home said Zoe was "bright-eyed, strong-limbed, and unafraid of people. Her movements have a steadiness rare in such a young child." Another reporter found her "happy, healthy, and uncomplicated and mentally and physically in advance of many children of the same age."[7]

Early on, Reich spoke out strongly for nursery schools where trained personnel would uphold the self-regulation practices of the parents. In such an environment young children learn the give-and-take of living with others as well as experiencing the capacity to move around freely, play, and develop manual, artistic, and social skills. While there are numerous nursery schools in the United States, few are run on a self-regulation basis.

Other countries, however, are somewhat more enlightened. In many Israeli kibbutzim, care of young children is entrusted during the day to several parent surrogates while the parents work, and the children sleep in peer cottages. Parents are friends, rather than authority figures, so there is not as much patriarchal control or maternal coddling, as a rule, as there is in American homes. While the concept of self-regulation is not always consciously promoted, the structuring of the child-parent interactions and the general kibbutzim concern for the free growth of the personality help many of the children to exhibit a considerable degree of self-regulation. The independent spirit, vibrancy, and self-expressiveness demonstrated by such children have been described in various journals and magazines, including an article by coauthor Edward Hoffman in the journal *Energy and Character.*

In the United States, the major spokesman for some of these ideas has been Dr. Benjamin Spock, and his best-selling *Baby and Child Care* inadvertently expressed many of Neill's and Reich's ideas. Neill described it as the "best book on babies I have come across. . . . It is nearer to self-regulation than any book I have seen."[8] Spock urged parents to feed the baby on demand, favored breast-feeding, advocated letting the child eat what he or she preferred, disapproved of strict bedtime rules, and in other ways expressed faith in the self-regulatory capacities of the infant's organism. Writing for and lionized by middle-class parents, Spock's light touch usually won ready agreement, and it helped to usher in a whole generation of youth more in touch with their feelings.

In the jungles of Venezuela, an isolated Stone Age tribe, the Yequana, demonstrates striking confirmation of Reich's idea of self-regulation. In *The Continuum Concept,* author Jean Liedloff describes infants who, besides being breast-fed, are casually carried by their mothers all day on the hip until they are old enough to crawl. All their needs are met, and they constantly receive warm, loving attention as they are being carried. At the crawling stage, they are allowed great freedom of movement, which is much extended when they can walk. Observation shows that they exhibit a natural caution in regard to heights and other dangers. The adults stand by to help if asked but don't interfere, coax, praise, or cajole. The author, who visited and lived with this tribe on five expeditions, writes:

> . . . The object of a child's activities, after all, is the development of self-reliance. To give either more or less assistance than he wants tends to defeat that purpose.
>
> It is assumed that the child is social, not antisocial, in his motives. What he does is accepted as the act of an innately "right" creature. This assumption of rightness, or sociality, as an in-built characteristic of human nature, is the essence of the Yequana attitude toward others, of any age.
>
> A child's curiosity and desire to do things himself are the definition of his capacity to learn without sacrificing any part of his whole development. Guidance can only heighten certain abilities at the expense of others, but nothing can heighten the full spectrum of his capabilities beyond its in-built limits. The price a child pays for being guided into what his parents think best for him (or themselves) is the diminution of his wholeness.[9]

The unusual happiness, sociability, and skill of the children in this remote tribe attest to what would be possible if nursery schools were run on self-regulation principles—and if parents had from the beginning allowed the child enough scope to develop along his or her own path.

After thirty years as a practicing therapist, Reich saw its many limitations and urged parents and teachers to give priority to the self-regulated raising of children. He saw them as the hope of the future. He believed that only if we adhere to his approach in our homes, nurseries, and throughout a child's schooling, will we have a world free of sadism, violence, and self-destruction.

THE FREE SCHOOL

There is a direct line from Reich's early emphasis on sexual freedom and an open genital character structure to his interest in the free-school movement. While Reich did not originate the free-school approach, which began with A. S. Neill's Summerhill school in Britain, in his writings he certainly influenced and heartily supported this concept. Its democratic and permissive foundations accord totally with his outlook. In such schools, children are free to take up whatever studies they feel drawn to. They are not forced to attend classes or show deference to the teachers, and they participate with the teachers in all decisions on curriculum and school policy. Students in these schools are generally freed from observing conventional moral codes in such areas as swearing or sex. At Summerhill, however, adolescents were not permitted to have sexual relationships. This was merely because, as Neill explained to them, the school would be closed if they didn't observe some of the conventions.

Before meeting Reich in 1937, Neill had been operating Summerhill for over fifteen years, using educator Homer Lane's ideas as a model and drawing attention to himself by the school's progressive posture and liberal ideas on sex education. After coming under Reich's influence, and doing therapy with him, Neill took seriously Reich's sex-economy and prolife ideas. From Reichian therapy, he gained the emotional freedom and integration to advance his educational activities, eventually becoming the international spokesman for the free-school movement. According to Neill, "Summerhill aims at a new democracy of free citizens who will not follow any leader. Until children are no longer molded into castrated sheep, democracy remains a fake and a danger. This is no theory; it is founded on long observation of children who have self-government."[10]

Neill has now taken his place alongside Pestalozzi, Montessori, Fruebel, and others as an innovative educator. Especially since publication of his book *Summerhill,* which sold two hundred thousand copies in one year, the free-school idea has become a force in education. However, free schools usually have high tuition rates and attract only middle-class children, and their numbers are still rather small. It is significant that education at the primary level, especially, has moved in the direction of Neill's goal. In Britain, this has been documented in Roy Hemmings' *Children's Freedom,* published in 1973, which describes the results of a questionnaire sent to a hundred English headmasters. A large number (the exact percentage depending on the precise question) admitted to being significantly influenced in thought and practice by Summerhill. A slow but readily discernible movement toward free-school ideas and practices exists there.

In Canada, too, while there are few replicas of Summerhill, there are many schools that are oriented to goals that are important at Summerhill, such as curriculum flexibility, teacher-student equality, abhorrence of physical coercion, and sound sex education. Some of these schools, such as in Toronto, are part of the public-school system and can be justly thought of as semi-free. The emergence of alternative schools that embrace some of Neill's and Reich's ideas is an important social trend today. In 1979 there were a dozen such schools in Toronto.

In the United States, the educational scene is in a state of enormous flux. The more thoughtful teachers and educators are often drawn to free-school principles, though many of them are frightened of going the whole way. A key problem is how to prepare children for the world of specialized employment while maintaining Summerhill principles. While 100 percent free schools are not likely to expand quickly, one can predict that many of their basic ideas will gain popular acceptance in certain areas and among humanist and progressive elements. Even if it is not the last word in education, insofar as Summerhill stands for the extension of freedom, human happiness, and authentic democracy, it clearly represents, philosophically, the wave of the future.

WORK DEMOCRACY: OF THE PEOPLE, BY THE PEOPLE, FOR THE PEOPLE

One of the most far-reaching of Reich's social concepts was work democracy, a philosophy of shared decision making from factory to executive suite. In proposing real, functional democracy in the workplace, Reich put forward the notion that our daily work itself can fulfill a necessary biological function by providing us with deep satisfactions. It can contribute to a healthy bioenergetic flow, which, for Reich, is the indicator of inner well-being. With both biological and emotional factors in mind, Reich recommended that work be so structured as to minimize authoritarianism.

Beginning with a pamphlet in 1937, Reich developed these ideas in two articles on natural work democracy published in 1939 and 1941. (They were later incorporated into newer editions of *The Mass Psychology of Fascism.*) He argued that work democracy aims at eliminating the split between work and pleasure. The energy used in work is the same as that manifested in sex, and, where the conditions are right, daily work brings its own kind of sensual gratification. The process is not without difficulties: "It is a matter of changing the structure of the working man in such a way as to liberate this natural work democracy from the incumbrances of bureaucracy and to help it to develop its own forms and organizations."[11] Reich noted that wherever people get together to do work, there is a natural tendency both for leadership to fall by mutual consent to the most qualified and for the evolution of a cooperative spirit that recognizes individual needs and rights. Work democracy is thus against permanent authorities or power divisions and stands for the allocation of authority according to the function being performed.

During this period, as he was turning aside from dogmatic Marxism, Reich moved in the direction of social anarchism. As Boadella notes, "He shared with them [social anarchists] the belief that social living could be based on voluntary respect for rational rules made by the members of the community itself, and that self-government of schools, factories, and other organizations was a practical possibility."[12]

Unlike the anarchists, however, Reich did not regard work democracy as requiring political implementation but as something natural that would emerge as workers became free of their armoring and formed self-governing, self-directing groups aimed at honest, productive labor. (His definition of "worker" was anyone who performs vitally necessary work.) In *Ether, God and Devil,* he added that work democracy had a biological base, inasmuch as the human "organism as a whole forms a natural cooperative of equivalent organs with different functions."[13] Neither the head nor any other organ in our bodies dominates, but "function itself regulates cooperation."[14] While the brain and its work are dominant in a technological society such as ours, it is just such domination that creates tremendous strains leading to physical and psychological illness. In Reich's view, it is people who listen to their bodies, pay attention to their senses, and respond to people, events, and situations from the core of their being—from the guts, in the vernacular—who live a whole and satisfying life.

Reich linked resistance to the idea of work democracy to the characteristic outlook of the armored organism. To begin with, armored persons are fearful, irresponsible, and want someone to give them orders and take responsibility for their actions. Just as, in the body, the head seems to be the executive part, so the armored organism feels a need for authority or leadership and wants direction from a boss or manager. Basically, then, Reich viewed opposition to work democracy as related to the workers' character structures; free genital characters and those close to this ideal would spontaneously take to the idea. The rest would be frightened and critical or see it as a plaything to take up casually; consequently, their projects would soon fail. Reich did not expect work democracy to be successfully implemented on a mass scale for a long time.

In recent years, Reich's notion of self-government in factory and office has found growing, though still limited, acceptance in a number of nations. Various gradations of worker control exist in Communist countries, welfare states, and capitalist lands. Yugoslavia has led the way, starting at the highest level. The idea of worker control or self-management is backed by federal legislation and extends to most of its industry. The workers elect their own managers and participate in certain major decisions. The Communist Party, of course, tries to influence the selection of these plant managers. In Sweden there is a widespread system of worker participation, which means that in many plants the workers are involved in decision making along with union and management. In parts of West Germany there is a system of codetermination that gives workers voting rights in some decisions while leaving major power in the hands of management. Some kibbutzim in Israel practice a form of worker participation in decision making, but there is no full-scale commitment to Reich's concept. It is encouraging to see that, in certain nations, the workers are gaining more power over their daily activities and are able to arrange their workday so that they find a certain level of pleasure in their productive activities. Clearly, full implementation of work democracy is a goal that it will take a long time to reach.

Implicit in the work-democracy concept—though Reich did not discuss it—is the advocacy of decentralization, both political and economic. For only in relatively small groupings can direct democracy succeed. Decentralization has been popularized recently in the writings of British economist E. F. Schumacher, especially in his book *Small Is Beautiful,* which has had a wide circulation. In it he argues for smaller-scale, inexpensive, intermediate technology as opposed to the huge centralized technological systems rampant today. He feels that by keeping technological development subservient to real human needs, it will cease to dominate the social scene. Especially in Third World countries, where technology has yet to "take over," there is some hope that Schumacher's ideas may see some implementation.

An influential American spokesman for sociopolitical decentralization was Paul Goodman. An authority in many fields, including Gestalt therapy, Goodman responded favorably to a great deal in Reich's outlook and social philosophy, although in conversation with one of the authors he kept a critical distance from such basic Reichian concepts as the orgone. Goodman opposed compulsory schooling as it existed, supported the free-school concept, and, in one book—*Compulsory Mis-Education and the Community of Scholars*—extended a Reichian type of critique up to university education. In this book, he also suggests various detours around the conventional system of schooling, including decentralization: "Decentralize an urban school . . . into small units, twenty to fifty, in available storefronts or clubhouses. These tiny schools, equipped with record player and pinball machine, could combine play, socializing, discussion, and formal teaching."[15] This book teems with similar unconventional suggestions that, in a sense, flesh out both Neill's and Reich's views on education. Goodman's impact, which was substantial in the 1960s, has subsided somewhat, but his many books remain a source of wisdom on architecture, ecology, the community, and social policy, and take up Reich's insistence on freedom, human scale, and being in harmony with nature.

LIVING IN HARMONY WITH NATURE

It is understandable that Reich should champion the conservation of the natural environment and that, very early, he drew attention to the threat of industrial and other atmospheric pollutants. After 1945, living as he was in the lake and farming area of Maine, Reich was in a strategic position to observe the gradual deterioration of the atmosphere and wrote about this threatening development. Around 1950, he became overwhelmingly concerned about the purity of the earth's atmosphere, and in particular about preserving the atmospheric orgone "envelope." He was referring to the layer of orgone that surrounds the planet, which he felt to be the chief support for life on earth. Any large-scale deterioration of this layer would threaten the continuance of all life, including human society. Its protective function was therefore basic, because without orgone all organisms would die.

After Reich had observed various phenomena, including the aurora borealis (the "northern lights"), Paul Ritter noted: "Reich was led to deduce that the earth and each planet has an orgone energy envelope that rotates faster than the planet; that planets swim in a common galactic orgone energy stream; and that celestial functions such as sunspot cycles, aurora borealis, hurricanes, tides, and major weather phenomena are expressions of the interplay of two or more cosmic energy systems and all show the spiral forms of superimposition."[16] These far-ranging speculations about space and the galaxies were spelled out in an imaginative book, *Cosmic Superimposition*. We don't have the space here to discuss this book except to say that on several occasions Reich attempted to direct East Coast hurricanes out to the Atlantic Ocean via a "cloud buster," and that he claimed success for his efforts.

The dropping of the atomic bomb in 1945 made Reich realize how vital it is for humankind to find some protection against nuclear radiation. This in turn led him to consider whether concentrations of cosmic, prolife orgone might be utilized to nullify, or at least reduce, dangerous antilife nuclear radiation. Because of his conception that orgone is supportive of life, he intuitively felt that it might counteract or nullify nuclear radiation.

He finally decided to test this idea, and in 1951 carried out "Oranur," which was his most ambitious and dangerous experiment, since it brought orgone face to face with nuclear material. This experiment consisted of securing a shielded container of two milligrams of radium and inserting one (shielded) milligram into a powerful twenty-layer orgone accumulator in his lab for one hour a day, for a week; the other milligram, the control, was placed in a garage a good distance away.

The hypothesis—that the orgone would effectively nullify the deleterious effects of nuclear radiation—was not borne out; rather, some unknown force, seemingly quite different and more powerful than radium, ran amok, making lab workers and others nearby very sick, killing experimental mice located in the lab, changing the color and disintegrating the surface of rocks up to several hundred yards away, and eventually, so it seemed, even affecting the atmosphere above Orgonon. Dull black clouds hung in the sky for days and took the sparkle out of people, animals, and plants. People said there was "something wrong in the air." Reich called these clouds *deadly orgone* (DOR), since they seemed to immobilize positive life pulsations and even cause illness in people's chronic weak spots. They were antilife.

The long-term consequence of the Oranur experiment consisted of peculiar effects on limestone rocks several hundred yards away. Not only did their color change, but their surfaces became pockmarked and then slowly disintegrated, the crumbling producing small, unusual rock particles. Another apparent effect of the experiment was the appearance of an unusually high background ionization count—measured on Geiger counters by independent observers—within a radius of 300 to 600 miles from Orgonon. This evidence of a radiation effect occurred three weeks after the experiment. A recent duplication of the Oranur experiment, in a college over a hundred miles north of New York, is reported to have produced a similar aftereffect. Other accounts of attempts to duplicate the Oranur test, which cannot be verified, include similar chilling effects. At this writing, it seems difficult, if not impossible, to ascertain just what are the predictable consequences of an Oranur experiment. Few researchers, understandably, want to risk what happened at Orgonon.

One result, however, is notable—and fascinating. The emotionally depressing effects of the black DOR clouds led Reich to attempt to dislodge them, and inadvertently he happened on a device that he subsequently called a *cloud buster*. Looking something like an elaborate rocket launcher and connected to flowing water by flexible metal cable, this device (see the photograph section), once perfected, gradually enabled Reich to dissipate clouds and even to bring rain to drought-stricken areas. (Details on its construction and experimental confirmation are given in Dr. Mann's book, *Orgone, Reich, and Eros.*) Since writing that book, Dr. Mann has tried out a simplified cloud-busting device on numerous occasions with surprising results, but as yet he has not undertaken exacting experiments. For example, using the cloud buster it was usually possible to clear up overcast weather. Various articles by persons who have tested the device in many parts of the United States and even in Australia—both to disperse clouds and bring rain—suggest that it is quite effective.

The most recent confirmation of the cloud buster is a masters-thesis study carried out at the University of Kansas Department of Geology and Meteorology by James DeMeo. The thesis abstract says:

> A Reich cloud buster was field-tested for its reported ability to modify the weather. Photographic analysis of tested cumulus clouds revealed an increased rate of decay as compared to a control group. NOAA [National Oceanic and Atmospheric Ad-

ministration] weather data indicated, on the average, a *decrease* in percent cloud cover and precipitation over Kansas following precipitation *abatement* tests run during rainy periods. Summarized precipitation *enhancement* tests revealed an *increase* in percent cloud cover and precipitation following onset of testing. The increase in precipitation was, on the average, the largest amount to occur within a week encompassing the test dates. Many other interesting phenomena were observed and minimally documented. Natural weather conditions could not fully explain all of the effects noted. While a high degree of statistical significance was not achieved in this preliminary study, the data and phenomena observed do fit comfortably with a positive interpretation of the device's efficacy.[17]

DeMeo is now proposing, as a Ph.D. experiment, to test its rain-making capability in desert areas of Arizona.

The invention and use of this device is another example of Reich's path breaking. Since the early 1950s, cloud seeding to bring rain and other weather-modification procedures have been perfected in the United States and elsewhere, but Reich was the first to speak of weather control and to draw attention to the dangers of hasty or indiscriminate attempts to change weather patterns. Unlike cloud seeders, however, Reich's device was not really artificial but worked by drawing air masses to an area in a simple way. Experience has shown that there is definitely an art to the effective use of cloud busters. Reich was careful to inform the appropriate authorities of his weather-modifying efforts and to point out that when this technology becomes effective, it will necessarily call for some form of international control. In the meantime, the U.S. government is attempting to bring order and regulation into this whole area, although it already seems that tampering with the weather, by the U.S. military in Vietnam and by farmers elsewhere, may be producing new and unusual weather patterns with serious long-term effects.

On the basis of his reflections on DOR clouds and their effects, Reich finally concluded that chronic DOR cloud conditions contribute to the creation of deserts. He pointed out in various articles that throughout the world deserts are growing at an alarming rate. Thinking about artificial deserts where organic life has dried up, in a leap of intuition Reich declared that the desert-making process corresponded to the making of deserts in human lives. His earlier insights into human irrationality, impotence, neurosis, armor, and bodily shrinking he now integrated with this phrase "the emotional desert." As Boadella has so lucidly pointed out, "The ecological wakening-up, . . . since Reich focused on the desert problem, has shown in a thousand ways how man threatens to destroy the apparently inexhaustible riches of the biosphere . . . by reckless pollution of the atmosphere, the soil, the rivers, and oceans."[18]

We don't have enough information yet to know whether Reich's DOR concept is but a crude explanation for the mixture of atmospheric pollutants harmful to growing plants or constitutes another quite different phenomenon, perhaps related to fallout from nuclear testing. What we do know is that as early as 1953 Reich called attention to the worsening condition of our atmosphere and its inevitable effect on plant life, and vainly urged the U.S. government to take appropriate action.

In his last attempt to make a difference, Reich transported a cloud buster all the way from Maine to Arizona in 1954 and tried experimentally to bring rain to the Tucson desert area. He also wanted to test his theory that DOR contamination slowly leads to the disintegration of rocks and contributes to desert formations. As he and his coworkers drove to the Southwest from Maine, they frequently observed extensive DOR clouds. In Arizona, with a cloud buster powered by a milligram of radium, which he called *orur*—nuclear matter treated by concentrated orgone—they claimed to have achieved a significant increase in humidity in a few weeks, resulting in a one-foot-high grass cover in a large area that had been barren for generations. Also, after about two months of sustained cloud busting, there was plentiful rainfall. "On one morning there was so much rain that planes were unable to land, a rare event in Tucson."[19]

It is fascinating to note that by this time Reich had achieved an amazing empathy with natural atmospheric conditions, something akin to his unusual skill in clinical diagnosis. The trip by car to Arizona is described in Reich's *Contact with Space* and includes a section on his daily observations, In it, Boadella notes:

Reich's account of the 3,200-mile journey is a masterpiece of reportage on subtle nuances that he noticed in the atmosphere, in vegetation, and in the soil on the journey. To read it is to learn how much we all walk about with our eyes shut and how insensitive we tend to be toward the emotional feel of the environment. "Looking back," wrote Ilse Ollendorff, "I think one had to be either a genius or an artist trained in visual observations to distinguish the nuances and variations in the color of rocks, in the shape of the clouds. They were mostly subjective impressions, and although there were objective factors involved, Reich often saw these phenomena first on a subjective basis, and expected others to see the same things."[20]

Reich had developed an uncanny ability to "read" the natural landscape that was quite similar to that demonstrated by North American Indians and other "primitive" peoples such as Australian aborigines. Reich attributed this keen awareness to the characteristic sensitivity of the unarmored organism. To the degree that we have loosened up or shed our armoring, we become sensitized to the subtle messages broadcast by all living organisms, animals, clouds, trees, plants and so on. Those who experience a sense of unity with the natural world often move toward a philosophy of natural, as opposed to supernatural, mysticism, as did Reich.

Reich's feeling for the slightest variation in natural phenomena, and his ability to make rain with the cloud buster, might suggest to an anthropologist that he had developed shamanistic powers. He would deny this, and assert that he was simply an enthusiastic, hardworking natural scientist, observing and reading nature and picking up its laws and regularities. There was a lot of trial and error involved in his successes. He was quick to admit and learn from his mistakes, to report important findings to the government, and to seek confirmation from other scientists. Unfortunately, except for a handful, scientists have thus far ignored his weather-control successes, just as the U.S. government ignored his early warnings of atmospheric pollution. Since his death, thouh, countless environmentalists have emerged to urge loving care and preservation of our air and water resources; their efforts are crucial. Those groups now campaigning vigorously against the proliferation of nuclear power plants are also taking up Reich's work, although they are largely unaware of his early leadership in this struggle.

Because of increased sulfuric dioxide concentrations and the depletion of the ozone layer, we are likely to experience worsening climatic conditions in the days ahead and may be forced into elaborate weather-control projects just to survive. But if these efforts are to be effective, they must be based on working with nature, rather than trying to dominate it. The scientists involved must appreciate and learn from Reich's intuitive approach, which leads us to our next theme: Reich's critique of contemporary, mainstream science—what he called mechanistic science.

A SCIENCE FOR THE FUTURE: ORGONOTIC FUNCTIONALISM

In the late 1940s, Reich evolved a new approach to the scientific process, based on his reflections on how he "did science" and how it differed from and often aroused the opposition of conventional scientists. He claimed that all the great scientists had made their discoveries by functionally perceiving relationships between things or processes, whereas the dull plodders, with their tight, armored character structure, handled their experiments and conceptions mechanistically. By this he meant that they tended to express a rigid and mechanical rather than a free and adventurous approach to their subject matter.

The mechanistic scientist, by Reich's definition, is timid and cautious in experimenting and theorizing, dogmatic about what is known and can be known, lives within tight disciplinary boundaries, is suspicious of those who do innovative interdisciplinary work, and accepts an authoritarian approach to knowledge, quoting accepted experts and entrenched knowledge if faced with new facts or theories. Such scientists refused to look into Galileo's telescope, for they *knew* they would learn nothing (or were afraid they might), and they ridiculed the Wright brothers' attempt to fly heavier-than-air machines. In our day, they are certain that the orgone accumulator could never concentrate any life energy, but never do they look at the evidence —or try sitting in an orgone accumulator.

By contrast, the scientist following what Reich termed *orgonotic functionalism* has the inner freedom to roam among different disciplines, takes an adventurous approach, has a capacity for vivid imagination, is curious about investigating new theories and phenomena, is open to new versions of truth, and accepts as authorities only those who have done careful work within a given field. In this unarmored approach to the world, the functionalist scientist is more likely to happen upon a startling discovery and to savor the excitement of the scientific process itself.

Another distinction lies in the approach to living material. The mechanistic biologist examines, for example, only stained —that is, dead—blood cells, thereby gaining information relative only to the blood's dead structural components and missing its living qualities or essence. Reich claimed that an armored character structure prevents such a scientist from sensing that dead blood is not the same as that which courses through the living body. So he or she is incapable, constitutionally, of realizing that aliveness must be examined by studying living samples: blood cells that are unstained.

Typically, mechanistic scientists are content to work from secondhand or indirect contact with phenomena, whereas functionalist scientists demand direct, immediate contact with nature, for they know that this is the only way at arriving at living truths. A functionalist biologist would seek to observe and record the phenomenon being studied, always within the context of all its interrelationships. He would list the evidence of his own senses, regardless of textbook conclusions, and would be ready to revise preconceived ideas in the light of fresh evidence. The advantage of this approach is that it opens the researcher to broader areas of insight, correlation, and truth.

Thus when Darwin wanted to study evolution, he traveled to the Galapagos Islands and immersed himself in the phenomena there instead of just reading books or working in a lab. His biographer, G. Himmelfarb, has explained that although Darwin's colleagues, the systematizers, knew more than Darwin did about particular species, comparative anatomy, and so on, they failed to ask the big question on the pattern of creation, "on the grounds that these were not the proper subjects of science. Darwin, uninhibited by these restrictions, could range more widely and deeply into the mysteries of nature."[21] There are many other examples of this different kind of approach to scientific inquiry.

Reich's discoveries exemplify a genius for grasping the underlying functioning principles of various phenomena. Behind many forms of sexual dysfunction he found a common condition of orgastic disturbance. Uniting a great variety of characterological and neurotic maladies was the common binding and immobilization of libidinal energy, or what he called sexual stasis. When he likened the cancer cell to a protozoa or the convulsive movements in orgasm to the movements of a jellyfish, he was not noting details of structure but functional identities. When he discovered the similarity between SAPA (bion) radiation from sand and the energy accumulated in the metal orgone box, he postulated a common energy, the orgone.

While in recent years there has been some sharp criticism of science—in terms of its size, its impersonality, and its tendency to be dogmatic and elitist—little of it is as penetrating as Reich's critique. Most of his comments were included in *Ether, God and Devil* (1949). In this book, he argued that mainstream science, because of the armored character of its practitioners, is inevitably committed to arid analysis and myopic classification and is inclined to persecute any major innovator. Reich further insisted that armoring affects the eyes and other sense organs, and that heavy armoring actually hampers the perceptual process. The mechanistic scientist may feel apprehension at the sight of little wiggly bions in his microscope, fail to note their purposive clustering, and label the process mechanistically as Brownian movements, a random motion of particles, thus slavishly following past definitions of the phenomenon.

Reich argued, in effect, that there is a significant subjective element in all research. Political, scientific, or even emotional biases intrude. Any scientist is able to either carry out or report experiments as an entirely neutral observer. In recent years, certain notables in physics and other sciences have come close to Reich's position that the experimenter is not fully detached from any given experiment and that allowance must always be made for the "experimenter effect."

Thus, Reich leveled a radical critique at today's science and urged his new approach: orgonotic functionalism—that is, looking for the fundamental processes in nature. He maintained that all great scientific breakthroughs had been made by innovators unconsciously using this method. In essence, its aim is to find the "common functioning (or functional) principle" (CFP) that underlies and unites natural processes that are usually seen as separate and distinct. Reich declared that motion and energy were the guidelines of his conceptual approach, and gave numerous examples of how the great thinkers and doers had used this principle: Newton pointed to the common unity governing the movement of the planets and the behavior of falling objects; Darwin "discovered" similarities among species in their struggle for existence; Marx came up with the fundamental principle of intergroup conflict epitomized in the class struggle. The secret is that the functionalist scientist, as Marshall McLuhan has urged, seeks out the fundamental or dominating patterns in life and in society.

It is very interesting to see how Reich utilized the common functioning principle in his discoveries in the realm of sex. He begins by noting that in sexuality and religion the CFP is sensing nature in the human body. As patriarchy developed, it repressed sexual expression and feelings. The result was a severe contradiction, which set sinful sexuality against religion, which claimed to be liberating. In primitive religions, religion and sexual sensations had not been antithetical but unified in feelings of deep excitement. Both sexual and religious activities were seen as liberating.

From a functionalist standpoint, it is clear that the same emotions are aroused by sex and religion, but that patriarchal religion has created a huge division and mutual estrangement. So religious people fear sexuality and those who abandon religion give way, often, to pornography or degenerate sexual acts. This contradiction creates a trap in which the mechanistic scientist and the mystic remain trapped, unable to accept the unity of sex and religion. They, too, perpetuate the dichotomy by their actions and beliefs, whereas the functionalist thinker breaks through it by finding the common features in the emotions experienced—the oceanic experience—in the nature and origin of sex and religion.

Each new CFP, Reich argued, can be used as a springboard to a new field of inquiry. This is done by pursuing the connections in an opposite direction. DeBono, in *The Use of Lateral Thinking*, describes it as looking for suggestive connections in other disciplines instead of simply conducting the conventional search within one's given discipline or specialization. For example, Reich pursued the concept of orgastic impotence into the realm of sociology, noting the parallels between character structure and social structure. Later, he conceptualized clouds and weather systems as energetic phenomena and extended the orgone theory, previously tied to biological organisms, to account for basic meteorological processes. Finally, seeing a similar pattern in the structure of galaxies and the superimposition of organisms in the sexual embrace, he further extended his orgone hypothesis to "explain" the interfacing of arc-shaped galaxies and the formation of mass particles. These latter speculations demonstrate the same bold thinking that has brought wide recognition to astronomer Fred Hoyle.

In Reich's view, it is the person who can readily cross traditional realms of knowledge and whose character structure is daring and flexible who sees significant new connections. This person is usually a scientific rebel, someone who can ask unthinkable questions and suddenly perceive fundamental patterns and unexpected likenesses. Reich argues that it is precisely the protester against mechanistic scientific thinking who leaps over disciplinary borders and makes the big breakthroughs. The rebel does this by relying on direct observation of nature, which helps him or her see the common functioning principles. These protesters are also rebels in their style of thinking, stepping over fixed barriers, staying alive in their methodology. They are the ones who ask the big questions about such things as the connections between energy and mass and between humankind and the larger world.

This innovating rebel is directly in touch with life processes. He is relatively unarmored, rigid in neither body nor mind. Because he is in touch with life, he is hostile to rigidities of any kind. He trusts his own senses and thinking processes. Reich adds that the rebel scientist is aware of his realm of uncertainty and monitors it experimentally. Unlike the mechanist, who narrows down the search, he trains himself to observe everything that is going on. His viewpoint is that nothing is impossible; by comprehending the basic connections between the sciences, he can leap over the disciplinary barriers and continue his search for common functioning patterns.

In essence, then, functionalist scientists are alive and vital, in touch with all their capacities, both rational and intuitive. They go with the flow of discovery, move across specializations and disciplines, and exemplify interdisciplinary and lateral thinking. For an inspiring journey into this process, one needs only to read, in *The Double Helix*, how James Watson discovered the DNA. Besides getting a firsthand, exciting account of the discovery, we see how Watson and his colleague, Frances Crick, both young, questing scientists, felt free to disregard conventional research norms and boundaries, how they used their imagination creatively to produce preliminary hypotheses, and how dramatic success finally crowned their efforts. It would seem from this revealing book as if Reich's theory of orgonotic functionalism is pertinent, especially in the process of such major scientific breakthroughs. It represents another spinoff of his fundamental vision that free, untrammeled thinking is the path to the kind of scientific productivity needed in today's confusing world.

In this chapter we have presented a broad picture of the far-ranging vision and revolutionary outlook of Wilhelm Reich. Space prevents us from adequately discussing some of these unusual conceptions, let alone critically examining the evidence pro and con. In hundreds of articles and twenty books, Reich sketched out his ever-expanding insights and hypotheses. That large portion of them that arose from the orgone theory he brought together after 1948 under the heading of orgonomy, the scientific study of the orgone. In the years left to him, he increasingly saw himself as a natural scientist and gave much less direct attention to social and political concerns. But we can readily see that what he had to say about social liberation was remarkably original—and that it will both inspire and challenge social thinkers and social scientists for decades to come. For, among other things, Reich was a social prophet, a fitting colleague of the Old Testament prophets Hosea, Micah, and Isaiah, who have inspired Judeo-Christian thinking for so long.

CHAPTER 9

Harnessing
the Reichian Legacy

Don't try to improve nature. Try, instead, to understand and protect it.

The streaming of love and life in the body will be finally known and understood.
—WILHELM REICH

I n his widely read book, *Future Shock,* Alvin Toffler makes it clear that from now on we must be prepared for tremendous and very rapid change. One great danger many of us face is an inability to adjust to the speed and ferocity of these changes. This certainly would not have presented unusual difficulty for Wilhelm Reich, for the broad sweep of his extraordinary career showed that he was always ready, as he said, "to move ahead." He was prepared to re-evaluate earlier formulations, theories, or conclusions. He was willing to give up his early communism and his early identification with Freudian thought, and in his later days he even lost faith in the ultimate value of therapy. He was looking ahead, constantly, to identify *new* threats and to determine what we must do in order to cope with them effectively. This is perhaps most evident in his concern, in his later years, for changes in the weather and his vision of the importance to humanity of making the deserts arable, which led to his rain-making trip to Arizona in 1954. By all accounts, Reich was a man for the future, a man who was prepared to make changes, adjust, and fashion his thinking and activities to meet our emerging crises and difficulties.

Another distinguishing characteristic of Reich's life was an underlying pattern of uniting theory to social action. He was the opposite of the conventional armchair theorist who spins great notions and weaves fascinating new hypotheses but never tries them out. Reich had some inner compulsion to go straight from hypothesis and theory to demonstration. Think of his going from theories on the sexual revolution to the opening of sex-hygiene clinics in Germany; from discovering the orgone to making orgone accumulators and renting them out to the medical personnel; from perceiving the threat of nuclear radiation to trying to control it in the Oranur experiment; from developing cloud busting to becoming concerned about desert formation and visiting the Arizona desert to bring rain. In short, like Karl Marx, Reich believed that theory is good only if tested in action. It seems clear that, in his concepts, Reich was much more revolutionary—in the truest sense of that word—than the founder of communism.

Indeed, Reich's thinking about science and his demonstration of the role of intuition and feeling in action fit him to appeal to the new-age thinking of young people throughout the Western world. Decades before physical science began to grudgingly accept the idea that the experimenter plays a role in the final result of the experiment, Reich pointed out in the 1940s and 1950s that there is no physically objective science; he echoed Marx in saying that all science has a subjective, ideological component. It may well be that his biophysical theories and his orgonotic functionalism will come to provide a basis for an entirely new kind of science, one in which feeling, intuition, and subjectivity will play as great a role as objective experimentation and logical analysis.

A DARING VISIONARY

During his lifetime, Reich dared to dream of a time when we would not just survive together in peace but would live supremely happy, productive lives, guided by reason and intuition and experiencing in our bodies a unity with nature. He disavowed original sin and believed that if infants and children could regulate themselves naturally they would grow up to be happy, productive, and able to achieve profound sexual satisfaction while still retaining a child's spontaneous wonder and delight in all of nature's creations. Reich always carried within him the effects of his farm upbringing and his early love for rocks, trees, birds, insects, and everything that crawls and creeps, and he intellectually expressed these feelings and experiences in an ever-expanding prolife philosophy.

In formulating this philosophical outlook, Reich stood on the shoulders of Marx, Freud, the French philosopher Henri Bergson, and many lesser-known innovators. From Freud he took seriously the existence of libido, developed it into an elaborate cosmic orgone theory, and explored more deeply the significance of sexuality, illuminating the somatic effects of its involuntary repression. From Marx he gained a sociological appreciation of social conflict, oppression, and social change, and then added a social psychology to Marx's insights in his theory of sexual repression and character formation. From Bergson he received a vision of a universal living force—an *élan vital*—that he expanded into a theory of cosmic orgone animating all of space.

The final result was Reich's daring, prophetic vision of the human potential. This vision is now embodied institutionally in the human potential movement, but it was Reich who first dreamed of a free human existence guaranteed by the elimination of character armoring and supported by an egalitarian, nonauthoritarian society. Science and philosophy in that society would respect our intuitive capacities, our need to grow and change, and our capacity to create by working with one another and with natural processes.

In this vision Reich identified the basic characteristic of life as pulsation or vibration, energy, and motion. Einstein had shown that matter is but frozen energy. Reich claimed that to freeze human life into rigid molds or ideas is to wage a losing fight against the basic urge of nature—to move, change, expand, develop, and modify everything around itself. It is the very nature of life to change. But superficial, external change, or change imposed too rapidly, will produce pathological reactions;

it must be slow, gradual, organic, from within. Reich was thus the supreme prophet of life's positive qualities.

A sociological interpretation of Reich's life and thinking shows that they represented a reaction against certain mainstream cultural trends of the time. This is clearly the case with his deep interest in Freud and then Marx. His concern about sexual freedom, too, reflected the widespread revolt against Victorianism, which had begun in the early years of the twentieth century.

On the other hand, much of his approach to life and religion reflected eighteenth-century Enlightenment influences in its tremendous faith in reason and rational solutions to life's existential issues. He was also heir to the romantic interests and values of that period; one might even call him a lineal descendent of Jean Jacques Rousseau, whose works on political philosophy, education, and morality must have influenced him. For it was Rousseau who spoke admiringly of the "noble savage" and who saw in the directness, simplicity, and freedom of the life of savage tribes values that civilized people lost and must recover. Rousseau also took a romantic and very sympathetic view of human potential, as did Reich.

After Reich arrived in America around 1940, and especially after he settled in the remote rural town of Rangeley, Maine— moving one step closer to Rousseau's "noble savage"—we can see an early expression of the alienation from urban, metropolitan forces that was later to become widespread, especially among the young in America. Out of this experience of living close to the natural world, Reich's views blossomed into a kind of natural religion, and this too was later echoed by our youth in the 1960s. His attack on mechanized mainstream science, which came to a head in *Ether, God and Devil,* also foreshadows the criticism of science's great power, irresponsibility, and bureaucratization that has emerged strongly in recent years.

Overall, we can see that Reich was affected by a variety of influences. What is distinctive is that he frequently perceived and reacted to these influences ten to thirty—sometimes fifty— years ahead of the general intellectual community. Reich was our century's early-warning indicator of things to come, of fears and trends and dangers that were and are about to erupt.

THE OPPOSITION FIGHTS BACK

It is small wonder that entrenched leaders and institutions—
Hitler, Stalin, the Communist Party, the International Psychoanalytic Association, leading psychiatrists in Norway and the
United States, and, of course, the Food and Drug Administration—were disturbed by both Reich's practices and their underlying theories, and that they tried to defame the man and his
vision. They resorted to lies, smears, and persecution, the full
story of which would fill several chapters. His was one of the
most challenging and revolutionary dreams; if implemented, it
would completely destroy much of contemporary medicine, religion, and science, three of our most powerful establishments.
As indicated earlier, young followers of his ideas led the 1968
student demonstrations in Germany and France that almost
overturned the structure of first the universities and then the
national governments.

Governments, powerful professions, and other entrenched
establishment institutions sought, and still seek, to confine or
kill Reich's ideas. For example, a late as 1974, U.S. law apparently forbade the manufacture of orgone accumulators. Fearing
legal reprisals, the *Journal of Orgonomy,* the official organ of orthodox Reichians in the United States, decided against reprint-
ing a chapter on orgone blankets from Dr. Mann's book even
though it had originally been their own proposal. In fact, even
today, Reich's ideas continue to be viciously distorted in American academic circles. For example, a textbook in the sociology of
medicine published in 1980 by a very large New York house
has, in a two-page treatment of Reich's ideas, a total of sixteen
factual errors. Some of them are minor, but most of them
vicious distortions, such as the following two:

> Patients could gather in groups during the summer months in
> Maine and experience collective orgasms after proper exposure
> to concentrated orgone.

> Reich proceeded informally . . . to try to cure cancerous patients
> by attempting to work on their bion material.[1]

Such distortions, while perhaps laughable to those who know
better, will be read by thousands of students and professionals,
feeding the notion that Reich was either a quack or a nut.

Each time we consider the breadth of Reich's thinking and insights, we cannot help but be stunned by the tragedy of his final years, which featured a large-scale book burning and a prison sentence during which he died. He was the only intellectual in American history to meet such a fate.

One can see, right away, a number of fairly obvious considerations. Reich's orgone theory and its ramifications were too far ahead not just of the masses but of most avant-garde intellectuals. After a brief exposure to Reich's ideas, even such advanced thinkers as H. G. Wells and Einstein dismissed Reich dogmatically. H. G. Wells (then an old man) called the *Function of the Orgasm*, which had been sent to him by A. S. Neill, an "awful gabble," lacking "any fresh understanding"; he concluded the letter containing these comments with "Please don't send me any more of this stuff."[2] Einstein, who had initially been impressed with Reich after a personal meeting with him, later dismissed the orgone theory after a most inconclusive testing of an accumulator. But by then he was deeply involved in the Manhattan atomic bomb project.

Unfortunately, in many books and articles, Reich's ideas were not expressed in conventional scientific-writing style: the claims made were not supported by evidence that would be convincing to skeptics and, often, the supporting evidence was available only in journals that were difficult to obtain (especially after the FDA book burnings destroyed Reich's unsold journals). Altogether, Reich wrote over a hundred articles in hard-to-find journals, many of them published by his own organization and available in few libraries or bookstores. Until the 1970s, most big universities carried few of his books and none of the journals. Moreover, in the 1940s he often wrote in a great hurry and failed to present his ideas persuasively, prompting critics to dismiss his claims as superficial. Some of Reich's supporters felt that he published most of his data too soon, and pointed out to him that he should have waited until he had amassed a more convincing body of material.

In short, Reich failed to take into account the resistance of the public and of professionals to dramatic new social concepts. Also, toward the end, he tended to put forward hypotheses and novel ideas as if they were proven facts or generalizations, giving the impression of not being a thorough, conscientious researcher. This is not to say that his basic approach to such topics as character armoring, health and disease, orgone theory, weather control, and ecology was not characterized by an essentially sound scientific procedure, but only that the expression of these concepts failed to convince many readers.

Part of the difficulty is that Reich was an inspired innovator, and an unruly one at that. His extremism—typical of those whose intuition knows no bounds—tended to put off potential supporters. A central procedural characteristic of the scientist who is formulating new theories is to narrow the focus on his or her main concern or theory and carry it over to explain diverse phenomena and puzzles of life. Reich took an unusual idea—the orgone energy concept—and in his later years found it to be the illuminating answer to problems and other unresolved observations in ever-expanding areas of thought: cancer, meteorology, astronomy, and even gravity. Thus, it seemed to explain how cancerous cells developed; it explained the nature not only of clouds, tornadoes, and hurricanes but of weather conditions (DOR) that dampened life in plants and humans; it threw light on the nature of the aurora borealis and on the basic form of many galactic systems (developed in his book *Cosmic Superimposition*); and it may have provided a clue to the nature of gravity.

Like any great pioneer, Reich pushed ahead, dogmatically demanding to be heard even though some of the important connections between data were often clear only to him and a few others. At the end he grew impatient with those who could not follow his ideas and intolerant of making sound compromise on practical issues.

In explanation, let us recall that Reich had experienced a lot of rejection. He was thrown out of both the International Psychoanalytic Association and the Communist Party; he was forced to flee Germany and then had to leave Norway. By the time he arrived in New York, then, he had experienced four major rejections and was only marginally active in medicine and mainstream politics. As a result, he became increasingly isolated and lonely. In reaction to all these heartrending blows, he rejected many who could have followed him and antagonized more than a few potential supporters. Toward the end, he became neurotically suspicious, and at times found fault even with his closest associates.

Dr. Myron Sharaf, a colleague of Reich's in the 1940s who is now completing the definitive biography of Reich, has clarified the consequence of these developments. Noting first that the highly revolutionary character of Reich's work was bound to upset many, Sharaf says:

> Take this work, add to it the fact that people generally avoided or opposed it, add to that, active hate on the part of some, add to that the fact that the world is in extremis and that Reich's work could help considerably, add to that a proud man who loved to be with human beings, who liked to help, who had the normal need for reward, appreciation, and honor for work well done, and you have a situation conducive to driving a person into extreme reactions, even before you add to it all the neurotic elements in Reich.[3]

REICH'S FIGHT AGAINST ORTHODOX MEDICINE

In America, the rejection of Reich both before and after his eventual public persecution was tied to his opposition to the medical establishment. It is only in the last few years that widespread public distrust of Big Medicine has really emerged. As never before, this vast army of technicians with their fancy equipment, arrays of pills and injections, and preposterous medical bills, is being challenged. But for decades the assumption had been that the more money and staff thrown at our diseases, the better would be the health of our society. Few believe this anymore.

Ironically, Big Medicine was probably enjoying its heyday of admiration during the years that Reich leveled his most trenchant criticism against it. It is no wonder that he was viewed as an isolated malcontent or as a crank. Newspapers from the 1940s and 1950s almost daily featured glowing, optimistic reports of some new "wonder drug" to eliminate illness, and the latest "cure for cancer" was always just around the corner. Doctors still made house calls, and the rise of the impersonal "medical centers" with which we are all too familiar was still some years away. The public was enamored of the medical profession as it then existed. As late as the early 1960s, in fact, doctors were portrayed as stars of prime-time television shows. They were wise, glamorous, and sexy.

When Reich raised his farsighted objections to modern medicine, almost no one had heard of the dangerous side effects of drugs. Almost no one was critical of collusion between the drug companies and the medical establishment. Today, however, millions of consumers are making the same criticisms of Big Medicine and its often misguided approach to human suffering and health that Reich first articulated. It has taken long years for this turnaround in attitude to occur. Undoubtedly, it was necessary for people to experience firsthand some of the shortcomings of modern medicine and technology in order to arrive at Reich's conclusions.

We must never forget that Reich's ideas did—and still do—carry a powerful political message. As we have seen, he was not interested in earning easy money by treating a wealthy elite of neurotic patients or simply training a small cadre of like-minded followers. In contrast to myriad lesser therapists today, he insisted on battling the full forces of Big Medicine and its allies in government and industry. Throughout his life, he argued loudly and forcefully for fundamental social change.

It is hardly surprising that Reich was quick to point out the injustices in our society's treatment of illness. As is now all too clear, there is a close relationship among governmental agencies and private business in many sectors of public life, particularly those relating to health care. As recent exposes have shown, this collusion has for decades effectively dampened innovation in the fields of cancer research, nutrition, and psychosomatic medicine, among others. No matter how cleverly Reich might have labored to gain official support for his views, his fundamentally antiestablishment perspective would inevitably have aroused powerful groups to act to suppress his ideas. For example, the basis for his approach to health and disease was that our major noninfectious illnesses relate powerfully to our society's deepest values and way of life. This was not a view that would sit well with the FDA.

Moreover, Reich's latter-day excursions into the philosophy

of religion—what we like to call natural mysticism—made him a ready target for disparagement from the scientific establishment of the day. He often spoke of a science of the future that would embrace both subjective and objective elements. He decried the dry impersonality of the modern technological approach to knowledge and insisted that "we must literally love the object of our investigations." Reich correctly traced our current obsession with objectivity to the persecution of early scientists in the Middle Ages by Church dogmatists. And he maintained that, today, modern science had become a de facto religion in its own right, denying the importance of compassion, tenderness, or wonder in its one-dimensional quest for knowledge.

Prophetically, Reich warned that this denial would have serious consequences, not only for our understanding of the natural world but also for the very protection of that world against the forces of technology. Because he insisted upon the legitimacy of the poet or dreamer in the steady march of science and medicine, Reich was attacked as a foolish romantic. And by mixing spiritual and moral values with scientific findings in his writings, he committed an unpardonable sin in the eyes of the orthodox scientific community.

Another reason for Reich's isolation from mainstream scientists can be seen in the way in which research has come to be carried out in current science and medicine. By the time Reich came to the United States on the eve of World War II, and certainly soon after the war, the emphasis was primarily on big teams of scientists working in large, expensive labs, funded by the government or a university, and engaged in almost endless quantitative duplication of experiments. Reich repeatedly called himself a "natural" scientist and placed himself in the tradition of such thinkers as Bruno, Newton, and Freud. He worked apart from large institutions with a tiny group of colleagues, moving from experiment to experiment, duplicating little and always following hunches. He preferred to strike out on his own, mapping new continents of knowledge that others would later study in fine detail.

Reich's professional training was grounded in his ten-year association with the Freudian circle in Vienna, whose members drew conclusions from the intensive examination of a few cases of pathology followed by day-to-day observation and discussions with colleagues. In the post-World War II era, however, even in psychiatry and related disciplines, researchers were expected to carry out large-scale studies involving thousands of cases, using precise statistical tools. The intuitive approach favored by Reich was viewed with suspicion by most scientists, especially in such fields as biology and physics. Top scientists were expected to apply for huge grants and work with secretaries, administrative assistants, and a host of technological instruments and procedures to verify results. Emerging out of the European intellectual tradition of Marx, Freud, and Einstein, Reich was not personally equipped to fit into this new mold— any more than Einstein could have been a slick administrator of a large midwestern technological institute. Thus, his rather old-fashioned approach to science helped keep Reich isolated.

And yet, had he worked more diligently to build an organizational structure to back his ideas—as Freud had done some decades earlier—he might have been more influential in heading at least a strong movement or becoming a rallying point for other visionaries in the healing and scientific professions. As a solitary iconoclastic thinker, he was not the person to head up such an organization, but, like Freud, he might have served as its moral or spiritual leader.

Perhaps if Reich had addressed himself more energetically to gaining acceptance among his peers, he might have won greater consensus for his ideas. But he consistently refused to participate in mainstream professional conference or symposia and refused to submit his work for review in the orthodox journals of the day. Typically, he arrived at his brilliant insights quickly, after rapid-fire review of the work of earlier investigators and a few basic experiments. His attitude was: let others come after to complete the investigation.

Indeed, one cannot imagine Reich laboriously working out statistical validation for his hypotheses in small-scale, step-by-step studies. He was a bold and intuitive thinker rather than a cautious experimenter. He was a visionary, not an organization man. When he declared that there is an important link between cancer and stress or that breast-fed babies are healthier than bottle-fed, he had a minimum of objective proof to support his contention. And yet, history has again and again proven him right.

PERSONALITY PROBLEMS

Undoubtedly, as we briefly mentioned in Chapter 1, part of Reich's isolation must be directly attributed to his personality. He had no time for small talk or polite evasions. From reports of his family and friends, it seems that he was domineering and that he almost deliberately sought confrontations. Those who disagreed with him ran the risk of his wrath. A. S. Neill has said, "Any attack on his work was met with rage. He had a quick temper and did not try to disguise or restrain it. With it went a wonderful capacity for softness and tenderness."[4] In his later years, he appears to have driven away many psychiatrists and psychotherapists—two of the most notable being Nic Waal, a Norwegian, and Theodore Wolfe, an American—including some who might have had the ability to organize support for him. Psychoanalyst Nic Waal, who knew him for years, has pointed out that Reich "lacked the faculty to understand his counterparts. They had to be totally loyal and trusting in him or else get criticized as cowards."[5]

Something in his emotional makeup—perhaps the childhood tragedies of his mother's suicide and his father's unhappy death—compelled him to cherish independence of spirit and action. Possibly his own early upbringing in the country also fed this rugged independence. Certainly he was a man of great pride, a pride that contributed to his downfall. Some observers believe that if his own analysis in the 1920s had been completed instead of having been broken off accidentally at critical junctures, he might possibly have transcended some of his basic emotional flaws.

Reich was always sure that he possessed the truth, and did not hesitate to proclaim his genius. In his last years he often railed at the world for not heeding him more closely. Despite his confidence that his ideas would eventually be accepted, he was bitter about the popular acclaim that seemed to constantly elude him. Clearly, after all the naked hostility he had met, first in Europe and then in the United States—from both the medical profession and the FDA—he had every reason to believe that he was being unjustly persecuted. Even so, it may well be that his powers of scientific judgment weakened toward the end, and that his sense of self-importance had become unduly expanded.

TO EVERY THING A SEASON

Today, innovators in nearly every scientific discipline have begun to articulate ideas that closely parallel Reich's. From psychiatry and allied fields to quantum physics, the way of the mystic and the way of the laboratory researcher are merging. Reich's speculations on the existence of a life energy once seemed only a fanciful attempt to make concrete Freud's libido concept, but, as we have seen, research all over the world has dramatized the accuracy of his intuitive hunches. His long legal battle, trial, and imprisonment in a very real way hindered his ability to continue his discoveries in this groundbreaking field.

The fact is that in spite of opposition from governments and powerful establishments, Reich's visions are now attracting a worldwide following. For instance, two successful conferences on his life and work were held in 1974, one at York University in Toronto and the other in San Francisco, under the auspices of the famed Esalen Institute. The former drew almost two hundred and the latter close to a thousand persons, mostly from the fields of psychology, psychotherapy, and academia. Interest and research were further sparked by these two conferences, so that by 1980 a gradual recognition of Reich's innovative stature was emerging in the United States.

A number of neo-Reichian therapies are gaining a wide following. Students are doing graduate and doctoral theses on his work in Australia and Canada as well as in America. Professors are teaching accredited courses concentrating on Reich at universities in Maine, New York State, California, and Toronto, Canada. A museum devoted to Reich's life and work in Rangeley, Maine, draws thousands of visitors every summer. There are now intellectually respectable journals of Reichian studies published in the United States (see Appendix C), Canada, France, Britain, Italy, and Germany. Reich's books in English are selling annually in the tens of thousands. One documentary film on Reich *(Mysteries of the Organism)* has been circulating for years after winning a prize at Cannes, and two more are known to be in the works.

In addition to those in the United States, groups are studying Reich's theories and engaging in Reichian therapy in Mexico, Canada, Britain, Italy, Germany, Austria, Holland, Norway, France, Spain, and Australia. The number continues to grow as a result of the lectures on his ideas and demonstrations of his therapy given by his older daughter, Eva Reich, M.D., in many parts of the world.

It seems evident, then, that Reich's genius as a man ahead of his time—and, in many ways, ahead of ours—is slowly but surely going to be recognized, first by some of our more unconventional and courageous thinkers, later by more cautious figures from the worlds of science and letters. Since he did not record his major ideas in a totally systematic way but rather expressed them in varying styles as they developed over the years, sometimes giving the impression that he shot "from the hip," it could be that full recognition of Reich's contribution awaits someone who will both systematize and popularize his ideas, as Marshall McLuhan did for the arcane ideas of Canadian economic historian Harold Innis.

On the other hand, it could happen that Reich will become a hero to new-age youth or the focus for a new twentieth-century religion. In *The Murder of Christ,* he identified himself with Jesus, and this, combined with his persecution and tragic death, could possibly be the basis for the emergence of a cultlike religion. For our part, we see Reich's work as groundbreaking and brilliant, but not as a finished form of ultimate truth. Rather, we regard it as a most important stepping stone on the path to ever-deeper understanding and insights. And we feel this is how he would want to be regarded.

Certainly if Reich had lived twenty more years, he would have kept on moving intellectually and would inevitably have changed certain aspects or emphases of his overall vision. To create a personality cult around him or freeze his vision into a dogmatic ideology would be to betray his essential mission. History demonstrates that the truly innovative ideas of the great have often been killed or fearfully distorted by zealous if well-meaning followers. And Reich was all too aware that this could easily happen to his ideas.

We believe that Reich will open the eyes of many in this generation to the energetic character of the universe, to the bioenergetic basis of human existence, and to the quite possible equivalents of energy in consciousness. His exploration of the bioenergy spectrum and his ability to make crucial connections between character armoring, healing ability, and psychic phenomena have paved the way for many to look sympathetically both at parapsychology and at Oriental and mystical theories or religions. In fact, Reich's conception of a cosmic life-supporting orgone energy, which is responsible for our very existence on this planet and embodies creative and learning capacities, may provide the basic elements for a myth that this age needs in order to regroup itself. For with the near collapse of the traditional Christian myth and the virtual death of Marxist "faith," people everywhere are looking for a new, firm basis on which to work out the meaning of life. Many will discover that Reich has provided some brilliant observations in this area.

In any case, it is clear that, for years to come, Reich will be the center of heated controversy. Scientists will range themselves for and against, and we can expect sexual and other smears to keep surfacing as the frightened try to kill his influence.

His visions await realization. In a conversation with A. S. Neill, Reich projected a thousand-year march to enlightenment. But, in *The Murder of Christ,* he was even less confident and suggested that it might be a million years before humankind would completely throw off its damaging armoring. However long it takes—and we claim no clairvoyance—it seems fair to say that history will eventually vindicate Reich's vision, because our progress toward inner and outer freedom, toward the union of reason and intuition, and toward a truly integrated society seems historically inevitable.

A Chronology of Reich's Life and Works

1897 March 24	Wilhelm Reich is born in Dobryzcynica, German-Ukranian part of Austria (Galicia)
1900	Robert, Reich's brother, is born.
1903–1907	Reich is instructed privately at home by tutors.
1911	Mother commits suicide.
1914	Father dies of self-induced pneumonia.
1915	Reich graduates from *gymnasium*.
1916–1918	Reich serves as lieutenant in Austrian Army.
1918	Reich enrolls in University of Vienna School of Law, then switches to its medical school.
1919	Reich organizes and leads Viennese medical students' seminar on sexology. First meeting with Freud.
1920	Reich attains membership in Vienna Psychoanalytic Society.
1921	Reich marries Annie Pink, a fellow medical-analyst student. Reads his first paper to Vienna Psychoanalytic Society.
1922	Reich is appointed clinical assistant to Freud's Psychoanalytic Clinic in Vienna upon completion of medical school.
1923–1924	Reich in post-graduate training.
1924	Eva, first child, is born. Reich becomes director of the Seminar for Psychoanalytic Therapy at the Psychoanalytic Clinic.

1926	Reich's brother, Robert, dies of tuberculosis at age twenty-six.
1927	Reich contracts TB, recuperates in a Swiss sanitarium. Witnesses the July Vienna Socialist uprising, becomes politically involved in the Socialist Party. *The Function of the Orgasm* is published.
1928	Lore, second child, is born. Reich joins the Communist Party, leaving the Socialists. Becomes vice-director of the Psychoanalytic Clinic. Becomes involved in "Worker's Help," a leftist medical organization.
1929	Reich heads several clinics, including the Socialist Society for Sex Consultation and Sexological Research. Presents public lectures on such topics as sex education and masturbation. Travels to Moscow, presents two lectures there, returns somewhat disappointed.
1930	Reich's last meeting with Freud. Moves to Berlin with Annie and children.
1931	Reich presents sex platform at World League for Sexual Reform; platform is rejected by League as "communistic." Heads German Association for Proletarian Sexual Politics.
1931–1932	Communist Party publishes several leaflets and pamphlets by Reich and his wife Annie.
1932	Reich meets Elsa Lindenberg, a ballet dancer, in his Party cell. German Communist Party condemns his writings as "ideologically incorrect."
1933	Reich expelled from the Communist Party.

	He and Annie separate. He escapes to Denmark, then goes to Sweden. *Character Analysis* is published. *The Mass Psychology of Fascism* is published.
1934	Reich arrives in Oslo, Norway, and is invited to join staff at Institute of Psychology at University of Oslo. Elsa moves to Oslo with Reich; Eva and Lore stay with Annie. He is expelled from the International Psychoanalytic Society.
1935	Reich presents lectures on character formation and its biological basis. Begins seminar for psychiatrists and psychotherapists.
1936	Reich conducts time-lapse photography of protozoa.
1937	Norwegian "press campaign" vilifies Reich. A. S. Neill becomes Reich's patient, joins the Institute. Reich publishes experiments on bioelectricity and sexuality; produces films on protozoa.
1938	*The Bion* is published. Dr. Theodore Wolfe visits Reich from the United States.
1939	Reich separates from Elsa, who "goes underground" to Sweden. Invited to teach at New School for Social Research in New York City. Experiments with bions in Norway. Emigrates to New York City in August. Meets and marries Ilse Ollendorff in New York.
1940	Reich discovers orgone energy in atmosphere, constructs first orgone accumulator, and tests its use with human beings.

	Lectures on "biological aspects of character formation" at New School for Social Research.
	Goes camping in Maine, buys cabin near Rangeley.
1941	Reich meets with Albert Einstein.
	Treats cancer patients with orgone accumulator.
	He and Theodore Wolfe set up their own publishing house.
	Summer in Maine; buys a house in New York City.
	Imprisoned in New York for three weeks as a "suspicious alien"; released in January 1942.
1942	*Discovery of the Orgone* is published.
	Reich purchases 280 acres of land at Rangeley.
1944	Peter, third child, is born.
1945	Reich teaches seminar on the newborn child.
	Develops energy-field meter.
1946	Revised English edition of *The Mass Psychology of Fascism* is published.
1947	FDA inspectors appear at Reich's property, Orgonon, after defamatory articles are published about him.
1948	Reich moves entire laboratory to Rangeley from New York City.
	The Cancer Biopathy and *Listen, Little Man!* are published.
1949	Reich has several blackouts due to coughing spasms, excessive smoking habit.
	The Wilhelm Reich Foundation is legally incorporated in Maine.
	Ether, God and Devil is published.
1950	Reich's family moves permanently to Maine.
	Oranur experiment with atomic energy.

1951	Reich suffers severe heart attack, attempts self-cure with orgone therapy, quits smoking entirely.
1952	FDA agents visit Orgonon; Reich orders them to leave.
	Experiments with weather control.
	He and Ilse decide to separate.
1953	*The Murder of Christ* is published.
	Reich continues experiments on weather and pollution control.
1954	FDA injunction against Reich's work.
	Theodore Wolfe dies.
	Reich travels to Arizona on rain-making expedition.
1956 April-May	Contempt-of-court trial.
May 25	Reich sentenced.
June-August	Reich's books burned and laboratory partly destroyed by United States government.
1957 March 12	Reich taken in custody to Danbury prison.
March 22	Reich transferred to Lewisburg prison
November 3	Reich dies two days before parole hearing.

A Selection of Wilhelm Reich's Books Available in English

The Cancer Biopathy. New York: Orgone Institute Press, 1948.

Character Analysis. Translated by Theodore P. Wolfe. New York: Farrar, Straus & Giroux, 1949.

Conspiracy: An Emotional Chain Reaction, Vols. I and II. New York: Orgone Institute Press, 1955.

Contact with Space: The Second Oranur Report. New York: Core Pilot Press, 1957.

Cosmic Superimposition. New York: Orgone Institute Press, 1951.

"Dialectical Materialism and Psychoanalysis." Translated by Anna Bostock. **Studies on the Left** 6 (1966).

The Discovery of the Orgone, Vol. 1: The Function of the Orgasm. 1st edition—New York: Orgone Institute Press, 1942. 2nd edition—New York: Farrar, Straus & Giroux, 1948, 1961.

The Discovery of the Orgone, Vol. 2: The Cancer Biopathy. Translated by Theodore P. Wolfe. New York: Orgone Institute Press, 1948.

Ether, God and Devil. Chapters 1–4 translated by Myron Sharaf. New York: Orgone Institute Press, 1949. New York: Farrar, Straus & Giroux, 1973.

The Function of the Orgasm. Translated by Theodore P. Wolfe. New York: Farrar, Straus & Giroux, 1961. Translated by Vincent R. Carfargo. New York: Farrar, Straus & Giroux, 1973.

Genitality in the Theory and Therapy of the Neuroses. New York: Farrar, Straus & Giroux, 1973.

History of the Discovery of Life Energy—The Einstein Affair. New York: Orgone Institute Press, 1953.

"The Impulsive Character." Translated by Barbara Koopman. **Journal of Orgonomy,** 1970–72.

Legal Writings. New York: Orgone Institute Press, 1957.

Listen, Little Man! New York: Orgone Institute Press, 1948. New York: Farrar, Straus & Giroux, 1967.

The Mass Psychology of Fascism. Translated by Theodore P. Wolfe. New York: Orgone Institute Press, 1946.

The Murder of Christ. New York: Orgone Institute Press, 1953. New York: Farrar, Straus & Giroux, 1972.

The Oranur Experiment: First Report. New York: Orgone Institute Press, 1951.

The Orgone Energy Accumulator: Its Scientific and Medical Use. New York: Orgone Institute Press, 1951.

People in Trouble. New York: Orgone Institute Press, 1953. New York: Farrar, Straus & Giroux, 1976.

Sex-Pol. Lee Baxandall, ed. New York: Vintage, 1972.

The Sexual Revolution. Translated by Theodore P. Wolfe. New York: Farrar, Straus & Giroux, 1962.

Wilhelm Reich: Selected Writings. New York: Farrar, Straus & Giroux, 1960.

Contemporary
Reichian Journals

Communications sur l'energie vitale emotionnelle. LOG,
22 rue Franklin, 34500 Beziers, France.

Energy and Character. Abbotsbury Publications, Abbotsbury,
Dorset, England.

International Journal of Life Energy. P.O. Box 8900, Station B,
Willowdale M2K 2R6, Ontario, Canada.

Journal of Biodynamic Psychology. Copy Centre, 50 George
Street, London W.1., England.

Journal of Orgonomy. Orgonomic Publications, Inc.,
P.O. Box 565, Ansonia Station, New York, NY 10023.

Quaderni del Movimento Reichiano di Napoli. Edited by
Umberto Rostain, Naples, Italy.

Radix. P.O. Box 97, Ojai, CA 93023.

Sexpol. 42 rue du Rousseau, Paris-18e; or BP 265, 75866 Paris
Cedex 18, France.

Wilhelm Reich Blatter. Bernd A. Laska, Postfach 3002, D 8500,
Nürnberg 1, West Germany.

The Orgone Theory: A Ten-Point Summary*

1. Being mass-free, orgone energy itself has no inertia or weight. This, it is noted, is one of the main reasons why it is difficult to measure with conventional techniques.

2. Present everywhere, it fills all space, although in differing degrees or concentrations. It is even present in vacuums.

3. It is the medium for electromagnetic and gravitational activity. It is held to be the substratum of the most fundamental natural phenomena, the medium in which light moves and electromagnetic and gravitational fields exert force.

4. Orgone energy is in constant motion, and this can be observed under appropriate conditions. For instance, the bluish heat waves seen shimmering above wooded areas and mountains are said to be orgone energy movements. Its motion has at least two characteristics, a pulsation form—that is, alternating expansion and contraction—and a flow normally along a curving path.

5. It "contradicts" the law of entropy. Orgone energy is attracted to concentrations of itself. Unlike heat or electricity, which manifests a direction of flow from higher to lower potential, orgone flows from low orgonotic potentials to higher. Thus, high concentrations of orgone energy attract orgone from their less orgone-concentrated surroundings. (An analogy is found in gravitation, where the larger bodies attract, or "pull," the smaller.) Nonentropic orgonotic processes, moreover, do not run their course mechanically, but are qualitatively entirely different from entropic processes.

6. It forms units or entities which are the foci of creative activity. These orgone energy units may be living or nonliving. The living ones include bions, cells, plants, and animals, and the nonliving include clouds, storms, planets, stars, and galaxies. All

---

*This list of properties of the orgone was first summarized in C. R. Kelley, "What Is Orgone Energy," *The Creative Process*, Vol. II, No. 1, pp. 58–80. It is presented here with slight changes, with permission.

of these orgone energy units have *certain* features in common. For instance, all are "negatively entropic" in the sense mentioned above, so that they acquire energy from their environment, and all have a "life cycle" passing through birth, growth, maturity, and decline.

7. Matter is created from orgone energy. Under appropriate conditions, matter arises from mass-free orgone. These conditions are held to be neither rare nor unusual.

8. It is responsible for life. Orgone energy is the *life* energy and as such is responsible for the special characteristics which differentiate the living from the nonliving.

9. Separate streams of orgone energy may be attracted to each other and then superimpose. The superimposition function is held to be the fundamental form of the creative process. Thus, in free space, superimposing orgone-energy streams typically show the form of two streams of energy converging in a spiral. This is seen in spiral galaxies and also in the structure of hurricanes and other cyclonic storms. Celestial functions such as sunspot cycles, aurora borealis, hurricanes, tides, and major weather phenomena are considered expressions of the interplay of two or more cosmic energy systems and also involve spiral forms of superimposition. In living nature, mating is a principal expression of superimposition: two separate streams of energy flow together and superimpose during the coital act.

10. It can be manipulated and controlled by orgone energy devices, the best-known being the accumulator. ... Certain experiments indicate that the air temperature within the accumulator, and the body temperature of anyone sitting in it, rises up to one degree centigrade, with variations depending upon the outside weather, the time of day, and the sitter's character structure. Other evidence includes an increase in the impulse rate of the Geiger-Müller counter when exposed to orgone concentrations in an accumulator.

How to Build and Use an Orgone Energy Accumulator

The Orgone Energy Accumulator was invented by Reich in 1940. The accumulator is intended to concentrate, for practical use, the orgone energy that pervades space. The accumulator charges the organism with the bioenergy.

General Use of an Orgone Energy Accumulator

The cabinet accumulator can be used for any undercharged condition (Anorgonia), including but not limited to the following: at the first suspicion of the onset of colds or other illness; in acute states of fatigue or exhaustion; after operations or child-birth; for chronic low, weak, or tired states; for shock; for food poisoning; for fainting attacks; for low resistance to infection.

Local Use of an Orgone Energy Accumulator

The local accumulator (cone, funnel, blanket, shooter, etc.) is applied promptly within a few minutes to wounds, burns, contusions, lacerations, sprains, and other injuries as soon as possible after an accident. It is placed over affected areas, metal side inward, close to but not touching the body.

INSTRUCTIONS

Length and Frequency of Irradiation to Luminate

For general charging, one daily half-hour session is recommended. The initial local application is half an hour; application can be repeated several times a day for shorter periods of time, as needed. Irradiation with the cabinet accumulator is continued for either thirty minutes or to the point of lumination.

Lumination is accompanied by the subjective feeling of heat, expansion, fullness—a soft, glowing sensation. Lumination time varies, depending on weather, time of day, and personal energy levels. The accumulator is most effective under 50 percent humidity, around noon, in a fresh atmosphere.

Overcharged people may not tolerate sitting inside the accumulator for more than five to ten minutes, while an undercharged individual may need weeks of daily charging to luminate.

Overcharge

Overcharge can be discharged by immersing affected body parts in liquids (water, alcohol, witch hazel, epsom salts) or by prolonged soaking of the whole body in a tub bath.

Storage

The accumulator should be stored in a *dry* and *airy* place, such as a garage, balcony, or outbuilding. Local devices can be stored inside plastic bags, away from living areas.

Warning: Never use the accumulator near television, fluorescent lights, radium-dialed watches, microwave ovens, X-ray machines, or nuclear power plants. Do not use it during periods of nuclear fallout or during thunderstorms. Do not apply electric currents to the metallic parts.

CONSTRUCTION OF A THREE-FOLD ORGONE ENERGY ACCUMULATOR

1. General Information
   a. The accumulator is made in six panels which are to be screwed together. All panels, except the bottom, are constructed in the same manner; they differ only in dimension. Each panel consists of an inner surface of iron and an outer nonmetallic surface that encloses a braced wood frame and alternating layers of glass wool and steel wool.
   b. Materials specified may be replaced by other materials: plastic or wallboard may be used instead of upson board;

cotton or rock wool may be used instead of glass wool. If substitutions are made, however, some adjustments in the dimensions of the frames may be necessary.

   c. Consult the accompanying drawings and tables for dimensions, construction details, and so on.

2. Constructing the Frames
   a. Rabbet the 1¼-inch-by-1¼-inch pine stock and cut to specified lengths. Miter the corners and join with corrugated fasteners. Brace each frame with a 3-inch piece of pine placed in the center of the frame. Join with corrugated fasteners.
   b. Construct the bottom frame with ¾-inch-by-1¼-inch pine. No bracing is necessary.

3. Attaching the Outer Surface
   a. Cut upson board to fit inside the rabbets of each frame. Fasten in place with 1-inch finishing nails.
   b. Cut two pieces of ¼-inch plywood the same size as the bottom frame. Screw one piece of plywood onto frame using flat-head wood screws.

4. Placing Glass Wool and Steel Wool in the Panels
   a. Place 1¼-inch layer of glass wool inside the frames on the inner surface of the upson board. Do not compress the glass wool and avoid lumps and holes.
   b. Place a layer of steel wool on the glass wool. Steel-wool pads, when unrolled, are the correct thickness. Make the layer as uniform as possible, but leave the steel wool "fluffy."
   c. In a similar manner, place the remaining alternate layers of glass wool and steel wool in position.
   d. The bottom panel has a different number of layers.

5. Attaching the Inner Surface
   a. Cut the sheet iron slightly smaller than the frames. Round the corners and file the edges where exposed. Punch holes through the iron and nail to the frames with small nails.
   b. For the bottom panel, screw the remaining ¼-inch plywood to the frame. Then attach sheet iron over this.

6. Attaching the Side Supports to the Bottom Panel
   a. Cut 1-inch-by-3-inch cedar or redwood stock to width of door and top.

    b. Screw them onto the bottom of the bottom panel a few inches from the front and back.

    c. Supports should project 1¼ inches from each side of the bottom panel to support the side panels.

    d. Attach sliders to underside of supports.

7. Assembling the Accumulator

    a. Place one side in position on the projections from the bottom panel. Drill two screw holes through frame of side panel into bottom frame. Screw through side panel using 2½-inch wood screws.

    b. Place back in position. Drill and screw through side panel into back, and through back panel into bottom.

    c. Place the other side in position. Drill and screw through side panel into back and bottom.

    d. Place top in position (it will project over front of side panels). Drill and screw through top into both sides and back.

    e. Screw hinges onto the door frame. Place the door in position and screw through hinges into side frame.

    f. Screw the hooks into the door and the eyes into side frame, one set on the outside, one set inside. The inside hook will screw into the brace of the door frame.

8. Finishing the Exterior

Finish the outside of the accumulator with varnish, polyurethane, etc.

ORGONE BLANKET
(THREE LAYERS)

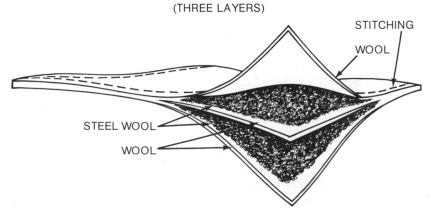

ORGONE ACCUMULATOR

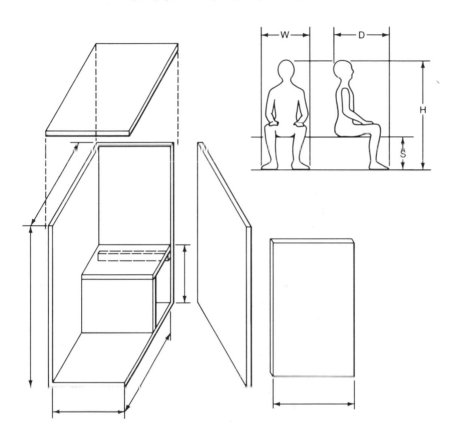

PANEL	WIDTH	LENGTH
Top	W+8.5″	D+6.5″
Back	W+6″	H+4.25″
Sides	D+5.25″	H+4.25″
Bottom	W+6″	D+4″
Door	W+8.5″	H+4.25″
Seat Top	W+6″	16″
Seat Front	W+6″	S–1.25″
Chestboard	W	14″

Notes

The unnumbered notes at the beginning of each chapter are the references for the opening quotes of that chapter.

Chapter 1   A Passionate and Persecuted Thinker

Wilhelm Reich, *Listen, Little Man!* (New York: Farrar, Straus & Giroux, 1967), p. 52.

1. Mary Higgins and Chester M. Raphael, *Reich Speaks of Freud* (New York: Farrar, Straus & Giroux, 1972), p. 5.

2. Ibid., p. 78.

3. Ibid., p. 57.

4. Ibid., p. 80.

5. Wilhelm Reich, *The Mass Psychology of Fascism,* trans. Theodore P. Wolfe (New York: Orgone Institute Press, 1946), p. xix.

6. Wilhelm Reich, *The Cancer Biopathy* (New York: Orgone Institute Press, 1948), p. 183.

7. Reich, *Listen, Little Man!* p. 16.

8. Wilhelm Reich, *Ether, God and Devil* (New York: Farrar, Straus & Giroux, 1973), p. 83.

9. Reich, *Listen, Little Man!* pp. 50, 54–55.

10. Rick Fields, "A Visit to Orgonon," *New Age Journal,* August 1979, p. 46.

11. Ibid.

Chapter 2   The Quest for Full Sexual Union

Reich, *Listen, Little Man!* p. 58.
Higgins and Raphael, *Reich Speaks of Freud,* p. 24.

1. Reich, *Listen, Little Man!* p. 115.

2. Wilhelm Reich, *The Murder of Christ* (New York: Farrar, Straus & Giroux, 1972), p. 30.

3. Wilhelm Reich, *The Function of the Orgasm,* trans. Theodore P. Wolfe (New York: Farrar, Straus & Giroux, 1961), p. 79.

4. David Boadella, "Genital Contact and Sexual Hang-Ups," *Energy and Character* 10, no. 1 (1979), p. 23.

5. Reich, *The Function of the Orgasm,* p. 85.

6. Shere Hite, *The Hite Report* (New York: Dell, 1976), p. 201.

7. Marie Robinson, *The Power of Sexual Surrender* (New York: New American Library, 1959), p. 36.

8. Ibid., pp. 37–38.

9. Ibid., pp. 38–39.

10. Ibid., p. 39.

11. Ibid., pp. 216–217.

12. Stella Resnick, "The Erotic Lifestyle," *New Age Journal,* August 1978, p. 28.

13. Ibid., p. 37.

14. Hite, *The Hite Report,* pp. 152–153.

15. Wilhelm Reich, *La Lutte des Sexuelle Jeunes* (Paris: pirated edition, 1966), p. 107.

16. Ibid., p. 119.

17. Bertell Ollman, *Social and Sexual Revolution, Essays on Marx and Reich* (Boston: South End Press, 1979), p. 173.

18. Wilhelm Reich, *The Sexual Revolution* (New York: Farrar, Straus & Giroux, 1962), p. 83.

19. Reich, *Listen, Little Man!* p. 62.

20. Ibid., p. 61.

21. Reich, *The Sexual Revolution,* trans. Therese Pol (New York: Farrar, Straus & Giroux, 1974), p. 126.

22. Ibid., pp. 125–126.

23. *AA News* 1, no. 1 (1977), pp. 25–26.

24. *Alternative Lifestyles,* August 1978, p. 194.

25. "The Bore of Sex," *Fanfare, Toronto Globe & Mail,* 6 October 1979, p. 10.

26. David Boadella, "Genital Contact and Sexual Hang-ups," *Energy and Character* 10, no. 1 (1979), p. 27.

Chapter 3   The Surrender of the Body

Higgins and Raphael, p. 5.

Reich, *The Murder of Christ,* pp. 28–29.

1. Reich, *The Function of the Orgasm,* p. 267.

2. Ibid., p. 145.

3. Ibid., p. 273.

4. Peter Davis, "Energetic Psychology: The Healing and Transformation of the Whole Human Being" (Ph.D. diss., Columbia Pacific University), p. 58.

5. Reich, *The Function of the Orgasm,* p. 273.

6. Ibid., p. 272.

7. Ibid., p. 268.

8. Ray L. Birdwhistell, cited in Ashley Montagu, *Touching* (New York: Harper & Row, 1971), p. 105.

9. Reich, *The Function of the Orgasm,* p. 272.

10. Ibid., p. 271.

11. Ibid., p. 299.

12. Wilhelm Reich, *The Function of the Orgasm,* trans. Vincent R. Carfagno (New York: Farrar, Straus & Giroux, 1971), p. 340.

13. Wilhelm Reich, cited in David Boadella, *Wilhelm Reich* (Chicago: Regnery, 1974), p. 119.

14. Reich, *The Function of the Orgasm* (Wolfe trans.), p. 269.

15. Alexander Lowen, *The Betrayal of the Body* (London: Collier, 1967), p. 55.

16. Reich, *The Function of the Orgasm* (Wolfe trans.), p. 122.

17. Ibid., p. 241.

18. Ibid., p. 241.

19. Ibid., p. 289.

20. Reich, *The Murder of Christ*, p. 209.

21. Reich, *The Function of the Orgasm* (Carfagno trans.), p. 356.

22. Reich, *The Cancer Biopathy*, p. 334.

23. Ibid.

24. Ibid., p. 339.

25. Reich, *The Function of the Orgasm* (Wolfe trans.), p. 196.

26. Reich, *The Cancer Biopathy*, p. 328.

27. Reich, *Listen, Little Man!* p. 121.

28. Reich, *Ether, God and Devil*, p. 134.

29. Ibid., pp. 134–135.

Chapter 4 Pioneer in Holistic Health

Higgins and Raphael, p. 86.

Reich, *Listen, Little Man!* p. 94.

1. Reich, *The Cancer Biopathy*, p. xvi.

2. Ibid., p. 86.

3. Ibid., p. 168.

4. Reich, *Ether, God and Devil*, p. 68.

5. Reich, *The Cancer Biopathy*, pp. 69–70.

6. Ibid., pp. 348–349.

7. Ibid., p. 234–235.

8. Ibid., p. xviii.

9. Ibid., p. xvi.

10. Ibid., p. 345.

11. Ibid., p. 1331.

12. Reich, *Ether, God and Devil*, p. 125.

13. Reich, *The Cancer Biopathy*, p. 234.

14. Reich, *The Murder of Christ*, pp. 188–189.

15. Reich, *Listen, Little Man!* p. 74.

16. Reich, *The Cancer Biopathy*, pp. 269–270.

17. Ibid., p. 254.

18. Reich, *Listen, Little Man!* p. 36.

19. Reich, *The Function of the Orgasm* (Wolfe trans.), pp. 110–111.

20. Ibid., p. 111.

21. Reich, *The Cancer Biopathy*, p. 177.

22. Reich, *The Function of the Orgasm* (Wolfe trans.), p. 321.

23. Ibid., p. 323.

24. Reich, *The Cancer Biopathy*, p. 177.

25. Ibid., pp. 177–178.

26. Ibid., pp. 180–181.

27. Ibid., p. 187.

28. Ibid., p. 183.

29. Ibid., pp. 345, 349, 354.

30. Dan Hertz and Milton Rosenbaum in *Psychosomatic Medicine*, ed. Eric Wittkower and Hector Warnes (New York: Harper & Row, 1977), p. 250.

31. Harold R. Lewis and Martha E. Lewis, *Psychosomatics* (New York: Pinnacle, 1975), p. 237.

32. Ibid., p. 178.

33. Constance Holden, "Cancer and the Mind: How Are They Connected?" *Science*, 23 June 1978, p. 1363.

34. George Leonard, "The Holistic Health Revolution," *The Journal of Holistic Health* 1 (1977), pp. 80–83.

35. Judith G. Rabkin and Elmer L. Struening, "Life Events, Stress, and Illness," *Science*, 3 December 1976, p. 1014.

Chapter 5   Psychotherapies for Healing Wholeness

Reich, *Listen, Little Man!* p. 16.
Higgins and Raphael, pp. 43–44.

1. Reich, *The Function of the Orgasm* (Wolfe trans.), p. 64.

2. Ibid.

3. Ibid., p. 96.

4. Ibid., p. 97.

5. Ibid., p. 101.

6. Wilhelm Reich, *Character Analysis*, trans. Wolfe (New York: Farrar, Straus & Cudahy, 1949), pp. 361–362.

7. Ibid., p. 363.

8. Ibid.

9. Reich, *The Function of the Orgasm* (Wolfe trans.), p. 280.

10. Ibid., p. 304.

11. Orson Bean, *Me and the Orgone* (New York: Fawcett, 1971), p. 46.

12. Reich, *The Function of the Orgasm* (Wolfe trans.), pp. 305–306.

13. Bean, *Me and the Orgone*, pp. 32–34.

14. Ibid., pp. 65–66.

15. Reich, *Character Analysis*, p. 454.

16. Reich, *Listen, Little Man!* p. 100.

17. Elsworth F. Baker, *Man in the Trap* (New York: Avon, 1974), p. 16.

18. Ibid., pp. 42–43.

19. Ibid., p. 12.

20. Lowen, *The Betrayal of the Body*, p. 209.

21. "A Conversation with Alexander Lowen," *Somatics*, Autumn 1979, p. 58.

22. Ibid., p. 58.

23. Lowen, *The Betrayal of the Body*, p. 2.

24. "A Conversation with Alexander Lowen," p. 61.

25. Charles Kelley, *Orgonomy, Bioenergetics, and Radix: The Reichian Movement Today* (Ojai, Calif: The Radix Institute, 1978), p. 13.

26. Ibid., p. 14.

27. *The Teachings of Michio Kushi* (Boston: East West Foundation, 1971), vol. 2, p. 41.

28. Ray Rosenman, "Role of Type A Behavior Pattern in the Pathogenesis of Ischemic Heart Disease, and Modification for Prevention," *Advanced Cardiology* 25 (1978), p. 41.

29. Reich, *The Cancer Biopathy*, p. 136.

30. Fritz Perls, *Gestalt Therapy Verbatim* (New York: Bantam, 1972), p. 38.

31. Ilse Ollendorff Reich, *Wilhelm Reich* (London: Elek 1969) p 70

32. Reich, *The Sexual Revolution* (Wolfe trans.), p. 263.

Chapter 6 Orgone: The All-Embracing Life Energy

Reich, *Ether, God and Devil*, p. 115.
Ibid., p. 94.

1. Reich, *The Cancer Biopathy*, p. xvii.

2. Ibid., p. 211.

3. Ibid., p. 211.

4. Swami Rama, Rudolph Ballentine, and Swami Ajaya, *Yoga and Psychotherapy* (Glenview, Ill.: Himalayan Institute, 1976), p. 50.

5. Dennis Milner and Edward Smart, *The Loom of Creation* (New York: Harper & Row, 1976), p. 203.

6. Ibid., p. 13.

7. Theodore Roszak, *The Unfinished Animal* (New York: Harper & Row, 1975).

8. *Family Circle*, July 1973, p. 110.

9. Sheila Ostrander and Lynn Schroeder, *Psychic Discoveries Behind the Iron Curtain* (New York: Bantam, 1971), pp. 209–210.

10. J. G. Marinho, "Kirlian Photography and Evidence on Energy Transfer from Person to Person" (Monte Carlo, Monaco: Proceedings of the Second International Congress on Psychotronic Research, 1974), p. 492.

11. Thelma Moss, John Hubacher, Jack Gray, and Frances Saba, "Laboratory Study of Unorthodox Healing" (Monte Carlo, Monaco: Proceedings of the Second International Congress on Psychotronic Research, 1974), p. 442.

12. Ibid., p. 443.

13. Hiroshi Motoyama (Monte Carlo, Monaco: Proceedings of the Second International Congress on Psychotronic Research, 1974), p. 377.

14. Ibid.

15. Victor Inyushin, "Bioplasma: A Fifth State of Matter?" in *Future Science*, ed. Krippner, Stanley, and White (New York: Doubleday, 1978), p. 120.

16. Reich, *Ether, God and Devil*, p. 14.

Chapter 7   Spiritual Reawakening

Reich, *Listen, Little Man!* p. 25.
Reich, *The Murder of Christ,* p. 175.

1. Reich, *The Mass Psychology of Fascism,* trans. Vincent R. Carfagno (New York: Farrar, Straus & Giroux, 1971), p. 126.
2. Ibid., p. 129.
3. Sigmund Freud *(Moses and Monotheism),* cited in Robert Ornstein, *The Mind Field* (New York: Viking, 1976), p. 137.
4. Reich, *The Mass Psychology of Fascism* (Carfagno trans.), p. 54.
5. Ibid., p. 55.
6. Ibid., p. 63.
7. Reich, *Ether, God and Devil,* p. 11.
8. Ibid., p. 107.
9. Ibid.
10. Merlin Stone, *When God Was a Woman* (New York: Harcourt Brace Jovanovich, 1976), p. 61.
11. Reich, *Ether, God and Devil,* p. 89.
12. Reich, *The Murder of Christ,* p. 22.
13. Ibid., p. 92.
14. Reich, *Ether, God and Devil,* p. 179.
15. Ibid., p. 9.
16. *Zohar,* trans. Harry Sperling and Maurice Simon (London: Soncino Press, 1931-1934), vol. 4, p. 194.
17. Ibid., vol. 5, p. 93.
18. Higgins and Raphael, p. 24.
19. Bhagwan Shree Rajneesh, *The Psychology of the Esoteric* (New York: Harper & Row, 1978), pp. 16-17.
20. Ibid., p. 49.
21. Reich, *The Function of the Orgasm* (Carfagno trans.), pp. 358-359.
22. Reich, *The Mass Psychology of Fascism* (Carfagno trans.), pp. 144-145.

Chapter 8   The Liberation of Humanity

Riggins and Raphael, p. 109.
Reich, *Listen, Little Man!* p. 100.

1. Wilhelm Reich, cited in David Boadella, *Wilhelm Reich,* p. 213.
2. Wilhelm Reich, *People in Trouble* (New York: Farrar, Straus & Giroux, 1976), p. 121.
3. Boadella, *Wilhelm Reich,* p. 220.
4. Ibid., p. 221.
5. Ibid., p. 222.
6. A. S. Neill, *Neill! Neill! Orange Peel! An Autobiography* (New York: Hart Publishing, 1972), p. 194.
7. Ray Hemmings, *Children's Freedom* (New York: Shocken Books, 1973), p. 132.
8. Ibid.

9. Jean Liedloff, *The Continuum Concept* (London: Duckworth, 1975), p. 72.

10. Neill, *An Autobiography*, p. 247.

11. Reich, *The Mass Psychology of Fascism* (Carfagno trans.), p. 291.

12. Boadella, *Wilhelm Reich*, pp. 212–213.

13. Reich, *Ether, God and Devil*, p. 117.

14. Ibid.

15. Paul Goodman, *Compulsory Mis-Education and the Community of Scholars* (New York: Vintage, 1962), p. 33.

16. Paul Ritter, ed., *Wilhelm Reich* (Nottingham: Ritter Press, 1958), p. 14.

17. James DeMeo, "Preliminary Analysis of Kansas Weather Coincidental to Experimental Operation with a Reich Cloudbuster" (M.A. thesis, University of Kansas, Dept. of Geology and Meteorology, 1977), p. 1.

18. Boadella, *Wilhelm Reich*, p. 308.

19. Ibid., p. 307.

20. Ibid., p. 305.

21. G. Himmelfarb, *Darwin and the Darwinian Revolution* (New York: Anchor, 1959).

Chapter 9   Harnessing the Reichian Legacy

Reich, *Listen, Little Man!* p. 76.
Reich, *The Murder of Christ*, p. 75.

1. William Rosengren, *Sociology of Medicine: Diversity, Conflict and Change* (New York: Harper & Row, 1980), p. 221.

2. Boadella, *Wilhelm Reich*, p. 377.

3. Ritter, *Wilhelm Reich*, p. 50.

4. Boadella, *Wilhelm Reich*, p. 377.

5. Ritter, *Wilhelm Reich*, p. 45.

Glossary

Armor. The physical and/or emotional defenses shown by an individual. Armor has a dual purpose: to keep potentially explosive emotions bottled within and to ward off the emotions of others.

Bioenergetics. The therapeutic approach developed by Dr. Alexander Lowen, who studied under Reich for several years. It emphasizes the release of emotion through work on the body, but differs from Reich's method in several aspects.

Bions. Energy vesicles, intermediate in aspect between living and nonliving substances. Reich believed that bions constantly form in nature by a process of disintegration of organic and inorganic matter and are charged with *orgone energy*.

Biopathies. The modern noninfectious diseases, such as heart disease, high blood pressure, and cancer, that Reich viewed as being closely related to one's emotional makeup and attitude toward life.

Body armor. The blocking of emotional release through chronic muscular tension. Body armor is resistant to change and also serves to inhibit the experience of physical pleasure.

Bodywork. Contemporary term to describe the school of psychotherapy that relies upon direct physical contact between the therapist and patient. The goal of such therapy typically is to release chronic tension in the musculature and its accompanying suppressed emotions.

Character. An individual's overall personality, including his or her typical ways of experiencing and reacting to situations. One's character is formed early in life.

Character analysis. Reich's technique of therapy in the 1920s. It was based on psychoanalysis and emphasized the patient's body language as a key indicator to his or her character.

Character armor. A person's attitudes, particularly toward pleasure, that inhibit his or her physical and emotional aliveness. Character armor and body armor are intertwined within each individual.

Characterological resignation. The quality of self-defeat and inner emptiness that Reich viewed as an important component in the development of cancer.

Emotional plague. The destructive and antilife forces within society.

Free association. The psychoanalytic technique in which the patient is encouraged to verbalize whatever thoughts or feelings surface to consciousness. Reich found this method too slow and inefficient, and therefore developed his own approach to psychotherapy.

Freedom giddiness. The tendency of persons to become irresponsible when restrictive laws and mores are lifted too suddenly.

Freedom peddlers. Those individuals who promise instant gratification without recognizing the responsibility necessary to handle freedoms.

Functional illness. Disease that is induced by emotional causes, such as chronic tension or stress. The functional illness is to be differentiated from disease caused by external forces such as infection.

Genital character. The ideally functioning person, one who is able to give and receive love fully.

Life energy. A fundamental bioenergy postulated to exist by diverse spiritual traditions throughout history. It has been called *chi* or *ki* in the Orient, *prana* in yogic systems, and *ruah* in the Hebraic tradition. Reich's name for it was *orgone.*

Medical orgone therapy. Reich's term to describe his therapeutic approach as it was finally evolved. It emphasizes the changing of a person's character by directly freeing the flow of biological energy.

Natural mysticism. A spiritual approach that extols the wonder of the natural world rather than developing abstract ideas or cosmologies. Reich came to favor a natural mysticism in his own religious beliefs.

Neo-Reichian therapies. Those forms of psychotherapy or healing that derive from Reich's emphasis on body language and direct physical release of pent-up emotions.

Bioenergetics, Orgonomy, and *Radix* may be included in this category.

Neurosis. The term used by Reich to describe an individual's inability to give and receive love fully. The neurotic person, Reich believed, is in touch with reality but is not truly aware of his or her deeply held emotions.

Orgasm reflex. Reich's term for the involuntary body movements of contraction and expansion experienced during complete sexual surrender. He viewed the presence of the orgasm reflex as a key indicator of emotional-physical health. See *Orgastic potency.*

Orgastic potency. The capacity to experience the *orgasm reflex.* Reich differentiated orgastic potency from mechanical sexual prowess, and instead emphasized the ability to surrender one's need to "conquer" or "achieve" during sex.

Orgone accumulator. Reich's device for concentrating orgone energy, thereby accentuating its flow in the human body. Reich was fined and imprisoned for distributing the accumulator in violation of a court order.

Orgone energy. Reich's term for a fundamental bioenergy that comprises all living things and indeed permeates the entire universe. See *Life energy.*

Orgonomic functionalism. The holistic approach to science, and Reich's term for his work in which all aspects of the universe are viewed as completely interrelated.

Orgonomy. The field of science that Reich termed his explorations from sociology to biology and physics. Its central theme is the study of the *orgone energy.* Orgonomy today is the name that Dr. Elsworth Baker has given to his therapeutic approach derived from Reich's.

Pleasure anxiety. An individual's fear of fully releasing all long-suppressed emotions and of experiencing intense physical pleasure. Reich believed that pleasure anxiety is engendered by modern society.

Polarity therapy. The therapeutic approach developed by Dr. Randolph Stone. It represents a parallel to Reichian therapy in certain respects, emphasizing the flow of life energy through the body. By direct work on the body, this method seeks to harmonize and regularize the course of this energy current.

Psychoanalysis. The theory and therapeutic system developed by Freud. Traditionally, it has relied upon *free association* and verbal analysis as the key features of psychotherapy.

Psychosomatic. The term used by Reich and others to describe illness that is strongly affected by a person's emotions, such as unexpressed anger or sexuality.

Radix. The therapeutic approach developed by Dr. Charles Kelley. Like *Orgonomy* and *Bioenergetics*, it stresses the release of emotion through techniques designed to loosen the *body armor.*

Self-regulation. The principle of trusting in the innate wisdom of the body during both childhood and adulthood.

Sex economy. The study of sexuality and economics within one discipline. Reich developed this approach in the early 1930s in order to understand the nature of sexuality in modern industrial society.

Somatic. Referring to a person's body or physical aspect, distinguished from such mental characteristics as thoughts or feelings.

Streamings. Intense, currentlike waves of pleasure experienced during full orgasm or in the dissolving of basic armoring.

Transference. The phenomenon in psychotherapy in which the patient displaces emotions held toward important figures from his or her past, unconsciously refocusing them onto the therapist. By making the patient aware of this development, the therapist elicits insight into problems in the patient.

Vegetotherapy. Reich's term for his therapeutic approach during the 1930s and 1940s. It marked a transition between his *character analysis* and *medical orgone therapy* and consists of both psychological techniques and direct bodywork.

Work democracy. The carrying out of all work responsibilities through shared decision making. Reich contrasted his concept of work democracy with that of the typical hierarchical model in contemporary society.

Selected Bibliography

AA News 1 (1977): 1.

Alternative Lifestyles. August 1978.

Atkins, Thomas R. **Sexuality in the Movies.** Bloomington: Indiana University Press, 1975.

Baker, Elsworth F. **Man in the Trap.** New York: Avon, 1974.

Barbara, Hannah. **Jung, His Life and Work.** New York: Putnam, 1976.

Baxandall, Lee. **Sex-Pol Writings 1929–34.** New York: Random House, 1972.

Bean, Orson. **Me and the Orgone.** New York: Fawcett, 1971.

Bentov, Itzhak. **Stalking the Wild Pendulum.** New York: Bantam, 1979.

Birdwhistell, Ray. **Kinesics and Context.** Philadelphia: University of Pennsylvania Press, 1970.

Boadella, David. "Genital Contact and Sexual Hangups." **Energy and Character** 10, (1979).

———. **In the Wake of Reich.** London: Coventure, 1976.

———. **Wilhelm Reich.** Chicago: Regnery, 1974.

Bortner, R. W.; Rosenman, R. H.; and Friedman, M. "Familial Similarity in Pattern A Behavior: Fathers and Sons." **Journal of Chronic Disease,** 23 (1970): 39.

Boston Women's Health Book Collective. **Our Bodies, Ourselves.** New York: Simon and Schuster, 1976.

Brownmiller, Susan. **Against Our Will: Men, Women and Rape.** New York: Simon and Schuster, 1975.

Bulletin of Structural Integration 4 (1975): 4.

Burr, Harold Saxton. **The Fields of Life.** New York: Ballantine, 1973.

Butensky, A.; Faralli, V.; Heebner, D.; and Waldron, I. "Elements of the Coronary-Prone Behavior Pattern in Children and Teenagers." **Journal of Psychosomatic Research** 20: 439–444.

Capra, Fritjof. **The Tao of Physics.** New York: Bantam, 1977.

Castaneda, Carlos. **Journey to Ixtlan.** New York: Simon and Schuster, 1972.

Constable, Trevor. **The Cosmic Pulse of Life.** Steinerbooks, 1977.

"A Conversation with Alexander Lowen." **Somatics** 3 (Autumn 1979): 57–61.

Daly, Mary. **Beyond God the Father.** Boston: Beacon, 1973.

Davis, Peter. **Energetic Psychology: The Healing and Transformation of the Whole Human Being.** Mill Valley, Calif.: Columbia Pacific University, unpublished doctoral dissertation, 1979.

DeBono, Edward. **New Think.** New York: Avon, 1971.

DeLangre, Jacques. **The First Book of Do-In.** Magalia, Calif.: Happiness Press, 1971.

DeLeuze, J. P. F. **Animal Magnetism.** New York: S. R. Wells, 1880.

DeMeo, James. **Preliminary Analysis of Kansas Weather Coincidental to Experimental Operation with a Reich Cloudbuster.** Lawrence: University of Kansas, Department of Geology and Meteorology, unpublished masters thesis, 1979.

Dodge, D. L., and Martin, W. T. **Social Stress and Chronic Illness.** Notre Dame, Ind.: University of Notre Dame Press, 1970.

Dunbar, F. **Mind and Body: Psychosomatic Medicine.** New York: Random House, 1955.

East West Foundation. **A Nutritional Approach to Cancer.** Boston: East West Foundation, 1977.

———. **The Teachings of Michio Kushi,** Vol. II. Boston: East West Foundation, 1971.

Espinosa, Juan E., and Zimbalist, Andrew. **Economic Democracy.** New York: Academic Press, 1978.

Fields, Rick. "A Visit to Orgonon." **New Age Journal,** August 1975.

Fisher, Seymour. **Body Consciousness: You Are What You Feel.** Englewood Cliffs, N.J.: Prentice-Hall, 1973.

———. **Body Experience in Fantasy and Behavior.** New York: Appleton-Century-Crofts, 1970.

Freud, Sigmund. **Civilization and Its Discontents.** New York: Norton, 1963.

———. **The Future of an Illusion.** New York: Norton, 1975.

———. **Moses and Monotheism.** New York: Random House, 1955.

Friedman, Meyer, and Rosenman, Ray H. "Association of Specific Overt Behavior Pattern with Blood and Cardiovascular Findings." **Journal of the American Medical Association** 169 (1959): 1286–1296.

———. **Type A Behavior and Your Heart.** New York: Fawcett, 1978.

Fromm, Erich. **Escape from Freedom.** New York: Holt, Rinehart & Winston, 1963.

———. **The Sane Society.** New York: Holt, Rinehart & Winston, 1955.

Gerard, Alice. **Please Breastfeed Your Baby.** New York: Signet, 1971.

Glass, D. C. "Stress, Behavior Pattern, and Coronary Disease." **American Scientist** 65 (1977): 177–187.

Goldman, Sherman. "Sketches for an Ark." **East West Journal,** January 1980, pp. 50–58.

Goodman, Paul. **Compulsory Mis-Education and the Community of Scholars.** New York: Vintage, 1962.

———. **Growing Up Absurd.** New York: Vintage, 1960.

Gordon, Richard. "Polarity Energy Balancing." **Alternatives,** January 1979, pp. 30–37.

Graves, Robert. **The White Goddess: A Historical Grammar of Poetic Myth.** New York: Farrar, Straus & Giroux, 1966.

Greenfield, Jerome. **Wilhelm Reich vs. the U.S.A.** New York: Norton, 1974.

Gurdjieff, G. I. **Views from the Real World.** New York: Dutton, 1975.

Haire, Doris. "The Cultural Warping of Childbirth." **Environmental Child Health** 19 (1973): 171–191.

Hall, Edward T. **Beyond Culture.** New York: Anchor, 1977.

———. **The Hidden Dimension.** New York: Doubleday, 1969.

Hemmings, Ray. **Children's Freedom.** New York: Schocken, 1973.

Herskowitz, Morton. "The Body Therapies." **Journal of Orgonomy** 13 (1979).

Hertz, Dan G., and Rosenbaum, Milton. "Gastrointestinal Disorders." In **Psychosomatic Medicine,** Eric D. Wittkower and Hector Warnes, eds. New York: Harper & Row, 1977.

Higgins, Mary, and Raphael, Chester M. (eds.). **Reich Speaks of Freud.** New York: Farrar, Straus & Giroux, 1972.

Hite, Shere. **The Hite Report.** New York: Dell, 1977.

Hoffman, Edward. "The Kabbalah: Its Implications for Humanistic Psychology." **Journal of Humanistic Psychology** 20 (1980): 33–47.

Holden, C. "Cancer and the Mind: How Are They Connected?" **Science** 200 (1978): 1363–1369.

Holt, John. **Freedom and Beyond.** New York: Dutton, 1972.

Horney, Karen. **New Ways in Psychoanalysis.** New York: Norton, 1966.

Hull, D. "Life Circumstances and Physical Illness: A Cross Disciplinary Survey of Research Content and Method for the Decade 1965–1975." **Journal of Psychosomatic Research** 21 (1977): 115–139.

Illich, Ivan. **Medical Nemesis.** New York: Random House, 1976.

Inyushin, V. M. "The Study of Acupuncture Points' Electro-Bio Luminescence With and Without the Action of Laser Radiation." First International Conference on Psychotronics Prague, 1973.

Johnson, Kendall. **The Living Aura.** New York: Hawthorne, 1975.

Kelley, Charles. **Orgonomy, Bioenergetics, and Radix: The Reichian Movement Today.** Ojai, Calif.: The Radix Institute, 1978.

Kempe, Ruth S., and Kempe, C. Henry. **Child Abuse.** Cambridge, Mass.: Harvard University Press, 1978.

Khan, A. V. "Effectiveness of Biofeedback and Counterconditioning in the Treatment of Bronchial Asthma." **Journal of Psychosomatic Research** 21 (1977): 97–104.

Kinsey, Alfred C. **Sexual Behavior in the Human Female.** Philadelphia: Saunders, 1953.

———; Pomeroy, Wardell B.; and Martin, Clyde E. **Sexual Behavior in the Human Male.** Philadelphia: Saunders, 1948.

Kleck, R. E.; Richardson, S. A.; and Ronald, L. "Physical Appearance, Cues, and Interpersonal Attraction in Children." **Child Development** 45 (1974): 305–310.

Koestler, Arthur. **Darkness at Noon.** New York: Bantam, 1970.

——. **The Roots of Coincidence.** New York: Random House, 1972.

Koopman, Barbara, G. "Mysticism, Or, and DOR." **Journal of Orgonomy** 12 (1978).

Kotelchuck, David. **Prognosis Negative: Crisis in the Health Care System.** New York: Vintage, 1976.

Krippner, Stanley, and Rubin, Daniel. **The Energies of Consciousness.** New York: Gordon and Breach, 1975.

Krishnamurti, J. **Think on These Things.** New York: Harper & Row, 1970.

Kuhn, Thomas. **The Structure of Scientific Revolutions.** Chicago: University of Chicago Press, 1970.

Kurtz, Ron, and Prestera, Hector. **The Body Reveals.** New York: Harper & Row, 1976.

Laing, Ronald. **The Politics of Experience.** New York: Ballantine, 1967.

Lancaster, David, and Toerien, Dawn. "Ether, Chi, and Orgone." **Energy and Character** 7 (1976): 41–45.

Lander, Louise. **Defective Medicine.** New York: Farrar, Straus & Giroux, 1978.

LeBoyer, Frederick. **Birth Without Violence.** New York: Knopf, 1975.

Leonard, George. "The Holistic Health Revolution." **Journal of Holistic Health** 1 (1977): 80–86.

Lewis, Martha E., and Howard, R. **Psychosomatics.** New York: Pinnacle, 1975.

Liedloff, Jean. **The Continuum Concept.** London: Duckworth, 1975.

Lowen, Alexander. **The Betrayal of the Body.** London: Collier, 1967.

——. **Bioenergetics.** New York: Penguin, 1976.

Mann, W. Edward. **Orgone, Reich, and Eros.** New York: Simon and Schuster, 1973.

Marinho, J. G. "Kirlian Photography and Evidence on Energy Transfer from Person to Person." Proceedings of the Second

International Congress on Psychotronic Research, Monte Carlo, 1974.

Maslow, Abraham. **Toward a Psychology of Being.** New York: Van Nostrand, 1968.

Masters, William H., and Johnson, Virginia E. **Human Sexual Inadequacy.** Boston: Little, Brown, 1970.

————; and Kolodny, Robert C. **Ethical Issues in Sex Therapy and Research.** Boston: Little, Brown, 1977.

Meek, George. **From Enigma to Science.** New York: Weiser, 1973.

Milner, Dennis, and Smart, Edward. **The Loom of Creation.** New York: Harper & Row, 1976.

Montagu, Ashley. **The Natural Superiority of Women.** New York: Macmillan, 1952.

————. **Touching.** New York: Harper & Row, 1971.

Moss, Thelma; Hubacher, John; Gray, Jack; and Saba, Frances. "Laboratory Study of Unorthodox Healing." Proceedings of the Second International Congress on Psychotronic Research, Monte Carlo, 1974.

Mosse, George L. **The Crisis of German Ideology.** New York: Grosset & Dunlap, 1964.

Motoyama, Hiroshi, and Brown, Rande. **Science and the Evolution of Consciousness.** Brookline, Mass.: Autumn Press, 1978.

Neill, A. S. **Neill! Neill! Orange Peel! An Autobiography.** New York: Hart, 1972.

————. **Summerhill.** New York: Hart, 1960.

Obradovic, Josip, and Dunn, William N. **Workers' Self-Management and Organizational Power in Yugoslavia.** Pittsburgh: University of Pittsburgh, University Center for International Studies, 1978.

Ollman, Bertell. **Social and Sexual Revolution: Essays on Marx and Reich.** Boston: South End Press, 1979.

Ornstein, Robert. **The Mind Field.** New York: Viking, 1976.

Ostrander, Sheila, and Schroeder, Lynn. **Psychic Discoveries Behind the Iron Curtain.** New York: Bantam, 1971.

Patai, Raphael. **The Hebrew Goddess.** New York: Avon, 1978.

Pelletier, Kenneth R. **Mind as Healer, Mind as Slayer.** New York: Dell, 1977.

Perls, Frederick. **Gestalt Therapy Verbatim.** New York: Bantam, 1972.

———; Hefferline, Ralph; and Goodman, Paul. **Gestalt Therapy.** New York: Delta, 1951.

Perls, Fritz. **The Gestalt Approach and Eyewitness to Therapy.** Palo Alto: Science and Behavior Books, 1973.

Playfair, Guy L., and Hill, Scott. **The Cycles of Heaven.** New York: St. Martin's Press, 1978.

Rabkin, J. G., and Struening, E. L. "Life Events, Stress, and Illness." **Science** 194 (1976): 1013–1020.

Rajneesh, Bhagwan Shree. **Meditation: The Art of Ecstasy.** New York: Harper & Row, 1978.

———. **The Psychology of the Esoteric.** New York: Harper & Row, 1978.

Raknes, Ola. **Wilhelm Reich and Orgonomy.** New York: Penguin, 1971.

Rama, Swami; Ballantine, Rudolph; and Ajaya, Swami. **Yoga and Psychotherapy.** Glenview, Ill.: Himalayan Institute, 1976.

Ravenscroft, Trevor. **The Spear of Destiny.** New York: Putnam, 1973.

Regush, Nicholas M. (ed.). **The Human Aura.** New York: Berkley, 1974.

Reich, Ilse Ollendorff. **Wilhelm Reich.** London: Elek, 1969.

Reich, Peter. **A Book of Dreams.** New York: Fawcett, 1973.

Reich, Wilhelm. **The Cancer Biopathy.** New York: Orgone Institute Press, 1948.

———. **Character Analysis.** Translated by Theodore P. Wolfe. New York: Farrar, Straus & Giroux, 1949.

———. **Ether, God and Devil.** New York: Farrar, Straus & Giroux, 1973.

———. **The Function of the Orgasm.** Translated by Theodore P. Wolfe. New York: Farrar, Straus & Giroux, 1961.

———. **The Function of the Orgasm.** Translated by Vincent R. Carfagno. New York: Farrar, Straus & Giroux, 1973.

———. **Genitality in the Theory and Therapy of the Neuroses.** New York: Farrar, Straus & Giroux, 1980.

———. **History of the Discovery of Life Energy—The Einstein Affair.** New York: Orgone Institute Press, 1953.

————. **Listen, Little Man!** New York: Farrar, Straus & Giroux, 1967.

————. **The Mass Psychology of Fascism.** Translated by Theodore P. Wolfe. New York: Orgone Institute Press, 1946.

————. **The Mass Psychology of Fascism.** Translated by Vincent R. Carfagno. New York: Farrar, Straus & Giroux, 1971.

————. **The Murder of Christ.** New York: Farrar, Straus & Giroux, 1972.

————. **People in Trouble.** New York: Farrar, Straus & Giroux, 1976.

————. **Selected Writings.** New York: Farrar, Straus & Giroux, 1960.

————. **Sex-Pol.** Lee Baxandall, ed. New York: Vintage, 1972.

————. **The Sexual Revolution.** Translated by Theodore P. Wolfe. New York: Farrar, Straus & Giroux, 1962.

————. **The Sexual Revolution.** Translated by Therese Pol. New York: Farrar, Straus and Giroux, 1974.

Resnick, Stella. "The Erotic Lifestyle." **New Age Journal,** August 1978.

Richardson, S. A., and Friedman, M. J. "Social Factors Relating to Children's Accuracy in Learning Peer Group Values Toward Handicaps." **Human Relations** 26 (1973): 77–87.

Ritter, Paul (ed.). **Wilhelm Reich.** Nottingham, Eng.: Ritter Press, 1958.

Ritter, Paul, and Ritter, Jean. **The Free Family.** London: Gollancz, 1959.

Robinson, Margot. "Visual Imagery, Bioenergetics, and the Treatment of Cancer." **Energy and Character** 9 (1978): 2–13.

Robinson, Marie. **The Power of Sexual Surrender.** New York: New American Library, 1959.

Rosengren, William R. **Sociology of Medicine: Diversity, Conflict, and Change.** New York: Harper & Row, 1980.

Rosenman, Ray H. "Role of Type A Behavior in the Pathogenesis of Ischemic Heart Disease and Modification for Prevention." **Advanced Cardiology** 25 (1978): 35–46.

————, and Friedman, Meyer. "Association of Specific Behavior Patterns in Women with Blood and Cardiovascular Findings." **Circulation** 24 (1961): 1173–1184.

————. "Modifying Type A Behavior Pattern." **Journal of Psychosomatic Research** 21 (1977): 323–331.

Roszak, Theodore. **The Unfinished Animal.** New York: Harper & Row, 1975.

Russell, Edward W. "The Fields of Life." In **Future Science,** John White and Stanley Krippner, eds. New York: Anchor, 1977.

Schatzman, Morton. **Soul Murder: Persecution in the Family.** New York: Mentor, 1976.

Scholem, Gershom G. **Major Trends in Jewish Mysticism.** New York: Schocken, 1954.

Schumacher, E. F. **Small Is Beautiful.** New York: Harper & Row, 1976.

Selye, Hans. **The Stress of Life.** New York: McGraw-Hill, 1976.

Serizawa, Katsusuke. **Massage, the Oriental Method.** San Francisco: Japan Publications, 1972.

Simonton, O. Carl; Matthews-Simonton, Stephanie; and Creighton, James. **Getting Well Again.** Los Angeles: Tarcher, 1978.

Spring, Joel. **A Primer of Libertarian Education.** New York: Free Life Editions, 1975.

Staffieri, J. R. "Body Build and Behavioral Expectancies in Young Females." **Developmental Psychology** 6 (1972): 125–127.

————. "A Study of Social Stereotypes of Body Image in Children." **Journal of Personality and Social Psychology** 7 (1967): 101–104.

Starz, Kenneth. "The Researches of Karl von Reichenbach." **The Creative Process** 3 (1963): 25–33.

Stellman, Jeanne M., and Daum, Susan M. **Work Is Hazardous to Your Health.** New York: Vintage, 1973.

Stone, Merlin. **When God Was a Woman.** New York: Dial Press, 1976.

Stone, Randolph. **Easy Stretching Postures.** Orange, Calif.: Pierre Pannetier, 1978.

————. **Health-Building.** Orange, Calif.: Pierre Pannetier, 1978.

Swan, Jim. "'Energies': Beginnings of a Western Paradigm." **Somatics** 2 (1978).

Toffler, Alvin. **Future Shock.** New York: Random House, 1970.

Wachsmuth, Guenther. **The Etheric Formative Forces in Cosmos, Earth, and Man.** London: Anthroposophical Publishing, 1932.

White, John, and Krippner, Stanley (eds.). **Future Science.** New York: Anchor, 1977.

Wittkower, E. D., and Warnes, H. **Psychosomatic Medicine.** New York: Harper & Row, 1977.

Zohar. Translated by Harry Sperling and Maurice Simon. London: Soncinco Press, 1931–1934.

Zucconi, Alberto, and De Marchi, Luigi. "Life Energy and Kirlian Photography." **Energy and Character** 6 (1975): 48–60.

Index